DATE DUE

JAN 0 5 2009		
MAR 0 6 2009		
APR 2 9 2009		
DEC 1 5 2009		
MAY 2 4 2010		
JAN 0 3 2011		
NOV 3 0 2011		
MAR 2 1 2013		
MAR 3 1 2015		
GAYLORD		PRINTED IN U.S.A.

had visited Aden, in order to study how the Arabs grew and processed their coffee. And two years later a plant was exported to Holland.

For several decades following, horticultural experts (tulip growing was already being conducted on a mass scale) applied themselves to the breeding of coffee shoots in their various garden nurseries around the country, particularly in the vicinity of Amsterdam, in order then to transplant them in their colonies, of which they now had quite a number.

After 1626, with the establishing of the West Indies Company, the Dutch stepped up their activities considerably on the American continent. They had already been established in northern Brazil since 1624, openly impinging on Portuguese interests in the process. In 1661 they sold all their Brazilian possessions to the Portuguese for eight million guilders, and in 1667 they exchanged their North American territories with the British for Dutch Guiana (Surinam).

Coffee plantations developed on a large scale in Sri Lanka from 1658. The young plants came from Amsterdam. In 1699 the Dutchman Henricus Zwaardecroon succeeded in transplanting coffee trees from the Malabar Coast to Java. The further spread of coffee cultivation by the Dutch on their islands took place systematically in quick succession: Sumatra, Bali, Timor and later Celebes. From 1718 Dutch coffee was also being grown on the American continent in Dutch Guiana.

The French, who after much endeavour had also managed to establish colonies outside the Spanish and Portuguese spheres of influence, were not quite so successful in coming into possession of the coffee plant. In the early 1700s, while the Dutch were already harvesting coffee on their islands, the French could not even lay claim to a single healthy coffee plant in one of the flower pots of the Jardin des Plants in Paris. All experiments to breed a plant there from the Amsterdam Botanical Garden had failed. The plants had barely arrived in Paris when they began to wither and sooner or later die. The suspicion gradually gained currency that the Dutch in their own way were proving as successful as the Arabs had once been in jealously guarding their valuable plants. Only in 1714 did Paris receive a serviceable plant from Amsterdam. The sturdy and healthy tree grew to a height of five feet. It was a personal gift from the Mayor of Amsterdam to the Sun King Louis XIV himself, and the diplomatic activity surrounding this one tree gives some idea of the value which the Dutch put on their plants. No obstacle had been put in the way of the successful growth of this particular tree. It flourished and blossomed and duly supplied the berries whose seeds, in the same manner as those from Amsterdam, found their way to the French colonies over the years, and contributed not inconsiderably to facilitating the expansion of French coffee cultivation.

Of course, several years were to pass before "seaworthy" successors could be bred from the Paris tree. In the meantime the French made do by "obtaining" healthy seeds or plants from Mocha and elsewhere where coffee growing was already established. Thus French coffee was being grown on Haiti (Santo Domingo) from 1715, and on the island of Bourbon (Réunion) east of Madagascar from 1716, where rapid progress was soon being made in the cultivation of the plant.

For those concerned with the cultivation of coffee, of whom by now there were not a few, the transport of the seedlings of young plants by sea continued to present the biggest problem. A fair number of sea captains and colonial officers have gone down in the history of coffee, or rather in the history of their respective countries, in performing a major service by successfully transporting plants by sea. The best-known must be the

Leipzig, circa 1720

"Leipzig, which possesses many singular garden enthusiasts, much devoted to exotic plants, who obtain such examples at great expense from Holland, has also in the meantime had the good fortune to see and to own one of these (coffee) trees which, however, did not last for long, soon withering and dying."

Johann Heinrich Zedler (Editor), Grosses vollständiges Universal Lexicon . . ., Halle/Leipzig, 1733, Vol. IV, column 535.

young French Captain Gabriel Mathieu de Clieu, who in 1720 (or 1723) successfully shipped undamaged one of the descendants of the original tree presented to Louis XIV across the Atlantic Ocean to Martinique. The stirring tale of the eventful four-week voyage beset by pirates and storms, in which De Clieu risked his life by using his own precious supply of drinking water for the plant stored on deck, is so popular that in addition to his exploits finding their way into numerous works of literature, he has been given a hero's place in French history books. The plant which De Clieu brought to Martinique flourished on the island, and within three years was already bearing fruit of sufficient quality for further propagation. The climatic and soil conditions on the Caribbean islands were ideal in every respect for coffee cultivation. By 1777, a period of fifty years, there were nearly nineteen million coffee trees on Martinique.

A pre-condition for the spread of the plants was the transport of germinable seeds or young shoots, and not infrequently such transport was associated with risky smuggling adventures, for anyone possessing coffee took great pains to ensure that his possession was exclusive. As already mentioned above, it is thought that the Arabs were the first to put a ban on the export of seedlings or young bushes, but in any event there is plenty of evidence to show that this was certainly the practice of the colonial powers. By 1725 both the Dutch and the French were growing coffee in their respective parts of divided Guayana. Competition was extremely fierce, and the export of seeds or shoots strictly forbidden. In fact it carried the death penalty in both countries. The French, however, had already succeeded in "removing" a quantity from the neighbouring Dutch colony in 1720. The interest of the Portuguese, who had bought the territory of Brazil from Holland in 1661, was particularly intense, for it was quite evident that the soil and altitude of Brazil were as equally suitable for coffee cultivation as the Guianas. The only question remaining was how to obtain possession of some seedlings.

An opportunity came on the occasion of a diplomatic mission undertaken in 1727 to Guayana by the officer Francisco de Melo Palheta from the State of Pará. He was to act as an intermediary between the Dutch and the French who had become embroiled in a boundary dispute. The charming lieutenant discharged his diplomatic mission to the complete satisfaction of both parties. But what the two governors did not know was that the young man had a quite different mission to carry out, namely to bring out with him some coffee saplings. The ambitious officer succeeded in bringing them out, concealed in an enormous bouquet of flowers with which he had been presented on the eve of his departure by the wife of the French governor. On the next day he boarded his ship in full view of the assembled dignitaries holding in his arms the bouquet in which the shoots were concealed. The deed, carried out at risk of death, succeeded. However, it was to take many more years before Brazil was to become the de facto coffee supplier to the world, leaving all competitors far behind—for initially the main emphasis continued to lie with the cultivation of sugar cane.

It was not until 1752 that coffee growing was carried on to any significant degree in Brazil, with plants and seeds coming from a number of different regions. For example a quantity were brought from Portuguese Goa in 1760. In 1770 the first shoots reached Rio de Janeiro, to be planted in the Paraíba region and in southern Minas Gerais. In 1800 Brazil commenced its coffee exporting.

The English, who in the meantime had also been striving to obtain the plant, brought it to Jamaica in 1730. In 1740, true to the strategy of their Order to involve themselves in political and economic affairs, Spanish Jesuits brought the coffee plant to the Philip-

pag. 86

5   Coffee branch with fruits and seeds. Copperplate engraving by Johann Hainzelmann in: Nicolas de Blegny, *Le bon usage*. . ., Paris, 1687.

6   Coffee tree "drawn from life". Copperplate engraving after Simon Thomassin in: La Roque, *Gründliche und sichere Nachricht. . .*, Leipzig, 1717 (taken from the French edition published in Paris in 1716). Leipzig, Universitätsbibliothek.

7   Branch of a coffee tree showing blossom, fruit and seeds. Copperplate engraving in: John Coackley Lettsom/John Ellis, *Geschichte des Thees and Kofees*, Leipzig, 1776. Leipzig, Universitätsbibliothek.
"Elucidation of the copperplate: A branch of the coffee tree with blossom and fruit.
A   A blossom, opened up and showing the filaments and anthers. B   The calyx with its four serrations which contains the seed vessels. . . C   A complete fruit showing the depressed point at the top. D   Fruit in longitudinal section showing that it consists of two seeds surrounded by a pulp. E   A fruit cut through in horizontal section in order to demonstrate how the beans are arranged so that they face each other along their planar side.
F   A bean which is surrounded by a thin parchment-like skin. G   A bean with this parchment opened to provide an exact picture of the bean. H   A bean without this parchment."

Der Cafe Baum in Arabien   nach dem Leben gezeichnet.

Eine zeitige Café Frucht.

Eine dürre Frucht.

Ein angeschnittenes Stück von gedachter Frucht.

Der Kern oder die so genannte Café-Bohne.

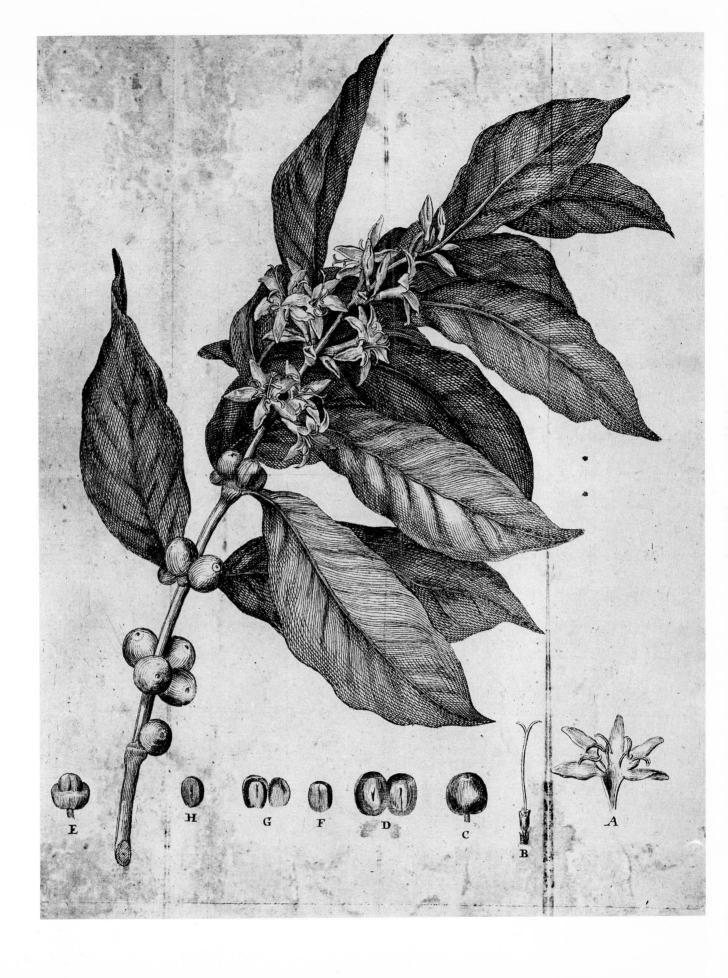

8   Flowering branch of *Coffea arabica*.

9   Branch of *Coffea arabica* fully-laden with ripe fruit (coffee-cherries).

10 Plucking coffee-cherries. On many plantations banana trees are planted between the coffee bushes to provide a natural protection from the sun.

11   The wet or wash process. Coffee-cherries in the washing tanks.

12   Sorting the beans by hand on drying trays.

In the countryside among the peasantry there were few such coffee parties. Social intercourse took place in the village inn or at evening time at the farmyard gate. Apart from these, social gatherings were restricted to festivals and family celebrations. They were a family affair, with whole families reciprocating visits to one another. *Kaffeekränzchen* were restricted to the learned members of the community, the teacher, the priest, the doctor, who had interests in common, and even more so to their wives, the men preferring as a rule the company of the village inn.

However, gatherings of this kind by no means have to be private affairs. Less than thirty years ago the "Association of German Kaffeekränzchen" was set up, holding its constituent meeting in Hamburg in 1958. Some two thousand female enthusiasts flocked to the "First Federal Kaffeekränzchen" from all over the Federal Republic of Germany and heard the President of the Association deliver an address on the "Kaffeekränzchen in our time".

Apart from the more formal and ritualized morning coffee and coffee parties, the taking of tea and coffee, to which guests were invited, the serving of coffee (or alternatively tea or chocolate) as an adjunct to other kinds of social visits, became increasingly prevalent. The ritual of paying one's respects, of holding a small or larger gathering were essential elements of social exchange among the middle classes in the 18th and 19th centuries. The serving of coffee to guests, both invited and uninvited, became a widespread custom during this period. The sumptuous hospitality formerly lavished on guests in pre-industrial times gradually led to the practice of serving coffee by way of welcome, prior to departure or as a means to pass the time as a feature of modern industrial society. All this was connected with a variety of ceremonial.

This change in habits is clearly reflected in one of Theodor Storm's characters, when she says: "No, Aunt Friede; this is not 1747 when it was still the habit not to offer any coffee, and upon departure not to offer any stimulating drink other than wine. . ."[32].

Any young man making his "grand tour" of Europe, any travelling student, poet or aesthete, painter or musician, teacher or cleric, anyone indeed from among the cultured middle classes to which some sections of the gentry also now belonged, would be received by his peers while on his travels, and welcomed at least with coffee or tea. In the correspondence, travel literature and memoirs of the 18th and 19th centuries there is a whole number of accounts of individuals being invited to coffee or tea, or served with the same when paying their respects to someone else. In Germany for some decades in the early 1800s, it was tea which became the fashionable drink among the upper classes. The somewhat sudden elevation of the drink to its exclusive status in Germany was part of the *mode à l'anglaise* prevailing throughout Europe at the time. After 1806, of course, the continental blockade became a further contributory factor, but in the first instance the reason lay with coffee's "decline" in status consequent on its universal consumption, and its rather "common" reputation. After 1800 coffee was no longer what it had formerly been! The all-pervading presence of the prestigious and once fashionable drink might have pleased the fancies of the middle and lower middle classes, but this development in turn was greeted with a certain contempt on the part of the more wealthy and elevated strata. They followed instead the fashion for drinking tea cultivated in the French salons. In so doing they were also adhering to one of the chief bourgeois virtues, for tea was often cheaper than coffee.

For our purposes, the bourgeois virtue of thrift, by now elevated to ideology, finds remarkable expression in the German term "visitor's coffee". For the purposes of receiving visitors, another coffee would be prepared to that normally drunk in private. Visitor's coffee would differ both in terms of composition and mode of preparation from the coffee used daily by the family, which, until well into the 20th century, was nearly always mixed with additives. Out would come the good china, the amount of chicory included would be reduced, possibly the coffee would be filtered when on other occasions it would not be. Visitor's coffee had to be "good"—whatever was understood by this designation. It was expected to be of higher quality than coffee for other occasions.

Although nowadays coffee is a commonplace drink, and the concept of visitor's coffee no longer exists, nevertheless the invitation to a "cup of coffee" is among all the coffee-drinking nations, still attended by a certain prestige-laden protocol. It almost appears as though with the evolution of such ceremony surrounding coffee within the context of bourgeois manners and customs, an essential element of the life-style of previous centuries has been preserved albeit in greatly reduced form in the modern age. That of all drinks it is coffee which was assimilated into the European diet partly for reasons of pressures of time, that has become occasion for a time-consuming, congenial, relaxing, recuperative and enjoyable ritual, represents one of the many apparent paradoxes which emerge repeatedly in social history.

Despite the fact that there are no binding norms for this ceremonial generally, both in the past and today, certain minimum standards have been set for entertaining visitors to coffee whose non-adherence on the part of the host will require a comment. "The company must drink unfiltered coffee from our commonest crockery and outside in the open. Father forbids special ceremony and the good wife must obey"[33], was the plea for understanding expressed by a housewife in the year 1795. And the Americans invite their guests to "come for coffee" in the afternoon or in the evening after supper, and apologize when only instant coffee is offered.

Coffee— the everyday drink of the 20th century

Since 1900 there has been a discernible growth of coffee consumption among all the industrialized countries and more recently among the countries of the Third World. However, there can also be times of regression, as for example was the case during and after the two world wars. In those countries where traditionally tea has been drunk, the consumption of coffee has also slowly but steadily risen.

In addition to the generally applicable and most important factor in ensuring coffee's universality, namely that in an increasingly performance-oriented world, its properties contribute to raising performance, and that furthermore it is suitable for every social context (family, leisure time, work) and for every situation (the everyday and the festive), there are in every country particular factors which have also encouraged this increase in consumption. In the United States, for example, the prohibition laws prompted a dramatic increase in coffee-drinking, aided and abetted by cheap imports from Brazil which had been unable to unload its coffee on European markets during the First World War.

The continuing high taxes on alcoholic drinks and by comparison relatively low duties on coffee explains why, at the moment, the Scandinavian countries with Finland in the lead have the highest per capita consumption of coffee. As once was the case in 18th-century Italy, in Finland and Sweden today coffee is drunk ten times and more during the course of a day. This figure is surpassed only by the coffee fanatics of Latin America who drink more than twenty cups per day. There, coffee is on the boil the whole day long, from the most opulent Victorian villas to the poorest peasant shanties. Devotion to coffee and the *macho* image go hand in hand in Brazil and Colombia, with the coffee produced in one's own country being naturally the best, and the highest prices being paid for so-called pearl coffee—where the fruit contains one seed instead of the two plano-convex—which in these countries are regarded as "manly" and bear a correspondingly virile name of *café macho*, representing the very highest-class coffee.

Among the many factors which have promoted the rise in coffee consumption are the complete transformation of working conditions since 1900 in the greatly expanded business and office sector, the evolution of the culture of the office world with its coffee breaks (Ill. 20), the ban on drinking alcohol at work and at the steering wheel, and not least the regular appearance on the market of the very latest coffee products (instant coffee, de-caffeinated coffee, etc.) and even the placing of coffee machines in canteens, self-service establishments or simply on the nearest street corner. And the readiness to consume even greater quantities of coffee is aided by a variegated and consumer-oriented advertising campaign on the part of manufacturers, or even the habit initiated in the first place, as the example of Japan shows, where for several decades concerted efforts have been made to awaken an interest in coffee: all this true to the motto of a Brazilian president, "There is no such thing as overproduction, only under-consumption".

The spread of coffee during the 18th and 19th centuries was fundamentally bound up with the availability of suitable additives and substitutes. And similar phenomena in the 20th century are continuing to encourage this development. De-caffeinated coffees (Ill. 31) and instantly soluble coffee powders have come onto the market as alternatives to quality coffee—though not acknowledged as such by every coffee drinker. Together with genuine bean coffee they have made coffee into the true number one, everyday drink.

In France, Italy, Austria, Hungary and Switzerland, coffee is all but obligatory after the midday meal, and the same is true in Portugal, where the *xicara* (cup of mocha) rounds off every major meal. By contrast, in the two German States, though there is a trend in the same direction, this is by no means the general habit, even in those parts of the Federal Republic of Germany lying nearest to France. The Germans drink their coffee in the morning and in the afternoon. According to statistics published in the Federal Republic of Germany a few years ago (Nestle-info), eighty-seven percent of the population drank coffee for breakfast, nineteen percent after the midday meal, fifty-five percent during the afternoon and six percent after the evening meal. In the German Democratic Republic, the situation is similar, although in all far less coffee is consumed. The Germans tend to have the habit of drinking their breakfast coffee outside of the home, as has long been the tradition in the case of certain occupational and social groups in many countries (e.g. Austria, Spain, France).

The all-pervading character of coffee as an everyday drink has led in many spheres to direct forms of communication. Thus, for example, a similar ceremonial to that found in private circles has now evolved at the workplace, in the form of the coffee break (Ill. 19, 20). Particularly in the business world, the communal coffee break plays an important if frequently underestimated role. Its significance is similar to that found in social drinking in terms of the need for social contact. "Something within me dies" is the first line of a song from the Broadway musical *How to Succeed in Business without Really Trying*, which describes the feelings of an office worker who is not allowed to take a coffee break. According to the rather euphemistic simile of an American journalist, the coffee break is to

Latin America today

"The dedicated coffee drinker in Colombia or Brazil fortifies himself with a cup of tinto first thing upon getting up in the morning, and proceeds to drink tintos non-stop until he is once more in bed—at meals, at work, in the coffee-house, in the street at the coffee stall. In Latin American offices there are no coffee breaks, for with such a thirst for the drink, such breaks would occupy the whole working day. In their place a woman bustles from desk to desk, constantly serving up cups of tinto as she goes. Twenty cups per day is regarded as a moderate consumption of the drink."
Jonathan Norton Leonard, Die Küche in Lateinamerika, Hamburg, 1979, p. 147.

20   "Hurry, you'll miss the coffee break!", title page of the anthology of coffee break cartoons from the *Wall Street Journal*, New York, 1955.

the daily routine of the office worker what the bubbles are to champagne. To the same extent, from another angle, it is the last and only opportunity in the alienating modern-day work environment for mutual communication of any kind.

Coffee-making utensils, serving and drinking vessels

Four stages have to be gone through before a cup of coffee is ready for drinking: roasting the beans, grinding, infusion/boiling/filtering and serving. For all these stages utensils, serving and drinking vessels are necessary.

Whereas in the countries of Europe or America on account of the wide-ranging selection of the most varied roasted or pre-ground coffees, few people today actually make the effort to roast their coffee beans themselves, in the Arab world and in the countries of Africa it is still very much a commonplace procedure, not merely as a formality or because of a shortage of roasted coffee. The marvellous scent which fills the air during the roasting of coffee is indeed the first step in its enjoyment. People who have time—and in the East they continue to make sure that they do—are not prepared to forego the pleasure. The true freshness of roasted coffee, and the real meaning of "aroma", which the advertising managers of the major coffee firms like to attribute to their products, are things which can only be appreciated by those who have once roasted coffee for themselves.

ROASTING Until a few decades ago, roasting pans and drums were to be found in every large household. Despite the fact that in the 17th and 18th centuries coffee-roasting was carried on as a trade in the towns, because it had been proved that it is more advantageous to roast large rather than small quantities at one time, a new household appliance gradually made its appearance everywhere and in a multitude of different makes, its use becoming increasingly widespread by the second half of the 19th century. The traditional roasting pans of the East were modified further into drums, which gained such rapid acceptance that revolving drums and pots (with a stirrer inside) were soon available in every conceivable shape and size. It is even thought that in some rural areas roasting machines were to be found in use before a single coffee bean had been seen, the knowledge of roasted substitutes—barley, chicory, beet—having spread faster than the coffee trade.

Initially it was the normal practice for the early roasting drums to be placed over an open stove fire, over charcoal embers or directly in the fireplace. Drums which were held by a long stick turned slowly over a fire were already known by the middle of the 17th century. The large quantities of smoke thus engendered and the not infrequent acrid smell (when the beans really were "roasted"), meant that the apparatus would often be placed out on the street, in the courtyard or on the side of the garden. In all European cities in the 18th and 19th centuries, the coffee and chicory smoke hung over the narrow lanes giving off its characteristic smell (Ill. 21).

The difficulties involved in ensuring uniformity of roasting and colour led to ever new inventions, with major improvements being achieved with the ability to regulate the supply of heat—spirit, oil or gas (Ill. 22). Uniform heat for example was guaranteed by a spherical coffee burner invented by the Austrian Max Bode, which on account of its compactness and practicality attracted much attention when it was put on show at the World Exhibition of 1851, and was subsequently much imitated. It received its heat from a certain quantity of spirit specified in the instructions, which burned for precisely

Caspar David Friedrich writing to relatives on 28 January, 1818

"In short, since 'I' has been turned into 'we', there have been a few changes . . . Coffee drum, coffee grinder, coffee siphon, coffee sack, coffee pot, coffee cup have become necessaries; everything, everything has become necessary."

Caspar David Friedrich in Briefen und Bekenntnissen, *edited by Sigrid Hinz, Berlin,* [2]*1974, p.35.*

as long as was necessary for roasting. The smallest version of the spherical burner, a mini model designed for 60 grams of coffee, is one of the most sought-after objects for collectors of old household articles.

In the 1880s the English firm of Parnall & Sons of Bristol patented a "national, atmospheric gas coffee roaster", which represented another step forwards in the development of coffee roasting, because the supply of gas guaranteed an even steadier application of heat than that of the spirit flame. The apparatus, named to appeal to national sentiments, had a capacity of between 500 grams and 50 kilos. According to the specifications, cocoa, chicory, malt, beet and all cereals could also be roasted in this versatile appliance.

The range and variety of household roasting machines seems to be almost limitless, extending from more traditional forms to an American patent by which the coffee would be roasted in a bath of hot oil. Today all of these implements have disappeared apart from individual examples to be found at antique markets and on second-hand stalls, and more recently in some cases as valuable antique pieces.

Anyone wishing to take the trouble to roast their own coffee must for better or worse resort to the time-honoured methods of the East, namely by constantly stirring the raw product in an open pan over the stove, or better still heating it in a firmly covered pot, or roasting in a medium-heated oven until it "crackles", i.e., the beans burst, swell by one third of their size and assume a brown colour. One very soon discovers the length of time required for the roasting (a few abortive attempts will have to be met with patience). This can range from two minutes if the coffee is warmed-up first, or up to an

Complaint against coffee roasting, London, 1656
"Disorders and annoys. Item we present James Farr, barber, for making and selling of a drink called coffee, whereby in making the same, he annoyeth his neighbours, by evil smells and for the keeping of ffire for the most pt. night and day, whereby his chimney and chambr. hath been sett on ffire, to the great danger and affrightment of his neighbours."
Edward Forbes Robinson, The Early History of Coffee-Houses in England, *London, 1893, p. 222.*

21 Coffee-roasting in front of the coffee-house. Mid-18th century copperplate engraving in: *Spectacle de la nature et des arts. . .,* Vienna, 1775, No. 17.

22 Mechanical household coffee-roasting machine, an American patent from the firm Mills & Thompson, Hazel Green, Wisconsin, 1874. Wood engraving in: *Illustrirte Zeitung*, Leipzig, 30 January, 1864.
A Wheels with clockwork key, B Spring, C Axle, D Driving-wheel, E Coffee drum, F Holding fixture, G Rotating crusher (turner), H Tinplate sliding cover.

hour when a slower heat is used. What is important is that the pot is often moved from side to side so that the beans are evenly roasted on all sides. Once the beans have attained a uniform colouring, which can range from light to dark brown, and the characteristic aroma fills the room, they must be cooled as quickly as possible. In order to minimize the loss of aroma various quick-cooling methods are employed. The Arabs and the Turks use special hardwood board, but any marble or wooden tray will do. It is also possible to briefly immerse the beans in water. This latter has the advantage that the remains of the silver skin which have been loosened by roasting will be washed away. Anyone attempting to employ a table fan for cooling the beans must reckon with finding such remains scattered about the room!

GRINDING   Although a locksmith produced the first coffee mill in London in the year 1665, initially until well into the 18th century grinding was done in the same mortars which existed in every kitchen for the pulverizing of drugs and spices. It rapidly became apparent that it was best to use a special mortar. The most suitable material for ensuring neutrality of taste and aroma was stone or metal—brass, iron, copper. Even today in Ethiopia, in the Arab countries (particularly among the nomads), and here and there in Turkey as well, the beans are pulverized in a mortar. In the Balkans the traditional mortar was made from hollowed-out linden or cherry wood. The cherry-wood mortar is supposed to enhance the aroma, and is still found today in parts of Bosnia-Herzegovina.

The tremendous physical effort and noise which the first professional coffee-makers of Marseilles, London or Vienna had to put up with, can be readily imagined by anyone who has ever tried to grind even a quarter pound of coffee in a mortar! For large amounts had to be pulverized every day in order to satisfy the demand. Some of the mortars which were used in the coffee shops were not much smaller than those to be found in the back-rooms of the apothecaries. People of a more sensitive disposition were even known to move house when a new coffee parlour was opened up in their neighbourhood.

Not a few coffee connoisseurs have claimed that coffee tastes better when pulverized in a mortar rather than when ground. The French gastronomist Anthelme Brillat-Savarin (1755–1826) who clearly from his "physiologie du gout" did indeed understand matters of taste, took two quantities of coffee from the same sample, and ground one in a hand mill and the other he pulverized in a mortar. Having poured an equal amount of water onto both, he found a clear difference in taste between the two, to the advantage of the crushed sample.[34] A similar experiment was undertaken by Carl G. Maassen, which produced equally noteworthy results for this coffee connoisseur.[35] But despite the greater quality of taste provided by the crushed coffee, the days of the coffee mortar were numbered in Europe. It was gradually replaced after 1700 by the most varying sorts of coffee mills. They were first produced on a large scale in England and France. In Germany, by 1700 Nuremberg and Leipzig had become the centres of coffee-mill production, manufacturing smaller models for household use and the larger versions for the grocers' shops, and the largest for the specialist coffee traders. Despite the many differences in outward appearance, in the material of which they were made—wood, metal, ceramic—and the drive mechanism—crank or flywheel—, the actual milling mechanism itself has not changed at all over the centuries. All hand-driven mills, be it the mocha mill from the 17th century, grandmother's porcelain mill fixed to the wall with its glass drawer from the year 1910 or the sophisticated special designs with several milling grades from fine to coarse, all are based upon the same mechanical principles. It was only a few decades ago with the appearance on the scene of the electric circular blade that one can talk of a new development, for even the electric mills which had previously existed were still fitted with a milling mechanism (Ill. 40–45). Since 1950, electric mills have established themselves so firmly that the production of hand mills in comparison to overall production has declined to less than one percent in Europe.

The slim brass mill (mocha, travelling or field mills), on account of its long grinding wheels produce a very fine coffee powder which makes a correspondingly powerful brew. The name mocha mill derives from the fact that the mocha (or Mocca) is used to denote generally stronger sorts of coffee—but not the Arab coffee of the same name, a rarity today.

The so-called Arab mocha mills to be found offered for sale in antique shops today, do not in any way date from the 17th century. They were manufactured by the thousand in England and France as compact travelling mills, and frequently embellished with some sort of oriental decoration (Ill. 40).

Designed to be held between the knees, or firmly fixed to some flat surface like a table-top or the arm of a chair, the milling mechanism of the cuboid, octa- and hectahedrally-shaped mills were initially hand-wrought and later mass-produced, and set in sheet-iron, wood, and in rarer cases cast iron. The beans are inserted into a metal bowl, either open or with a sliding panel, and the ground coffee collects at the base of the milling wheels in a container which can then be pulled out. Produced by the million, such coffee mills were commonplace household gadgets in daily use in nearly all countries where coffee was drunk. It is thought that about three hundred different kinds of mill were produced. In the United States alone, one hundred and eighty-five coffee-mill patents were registered between 1789 and 1921.

The world-renowned Turkish coffee
"When I think how I have been swindled by books of Oriental travel I want a tourist for breakfast. For years and years I have dreamed of the wonders of the Turkish bath . . .

Then he brought the world-renowned Turkish coffee that poets have sung so rapturously for many generations, and I seized upon it as the last hope that was left of my old dreams of Eastern luxury. It was another fraud. Of all the unchristian beverages that ever passed my lips, Turkish coffee is the worst. The cup is small, it is smeared with grounds; the coffee is black, thick, unsavoury of smell, and execrable in taste. The bottom of the cup has a muddy sediment in it half an inch deep. This goes down your throat, and portions of it lodge by the way, and produce a tickling aggravation that keeps you coughing and barking for an hour."
Mark Twain, The Innocents Abroad,
New York, London, 1870.

The first English producer of coffee mills, 1660
That Nicholaas Brock, living at the Sign of the Frying-pan in St. Tulies-street against the Church, is the only known man for making of Mills for grinding of Coffee powder. Which Mills are by him sold from 40. to 45. shillings the Mill.
Advertisement on a London leaflet dating 1660.
Facsimile taken from William H. Ukers, All about Tea,
New York, 1935, Vol. 2, p. 294.

57

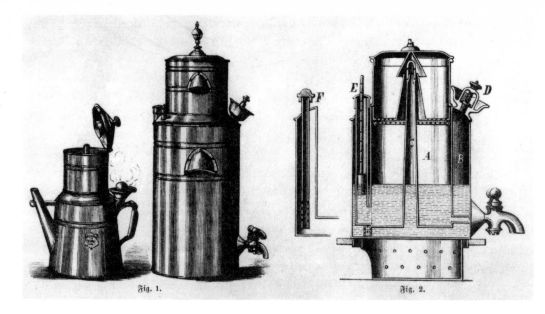

23 Automatic tea and coffee cooker. American patent from the firm of Sherwood of New York, 1877. Wood engraving in: *Illustrirte Zeitung*, Leipzig, 29 December, 1877.
Fig.1 Family size; Fig.2 Commercial size.
A Container for finished brew, B Water container, C Vertical tube, D Valve, E Float, F Heating pipe.

Fig. 1.   *Fig. 2.*

Apart from the occasional luxury model, the coffee mill was supremely simple and functional. Decoration was restricted to the addition of line, painting was rare.

That the spirit of invention and constant improvement was no less diminished when it came to the coffee mill can be demonstrated by an example which can serve for many: A German patent from the 1880s shows a coffee mill which at the same time contains a coffee tin and a coffee measure. The upper section contains exactly 250 grammes of coffee. A variety of grades of powder can be achieved by the turn of a screw. A patent stopper prevents more than 8 grammes at a time being milled. The stop effect can be released with the touch of a finger, and the next 8 grammes inserted for grinding.

By 1850 at the latest, the coffee mill was one of the most indispensable household gadgets in the kitchens of all social strata, being found both in upper-class households and in the midst of proletarian deprivation (Ill. 56), and more often than not the very same model.[36] Although the number of mills which were produced in the course of three hundred years was enormous, and hundreds of firms were engaged in their manufacture, today there are hardly any examples to be found of mills from the 17th and 18th centuries. The fact that even today hand mills can still be found in many homes—partly out of the conviction that the aroma is stronger and partly out of nostalgia—cannot conceal the fact that the old, mostly iron, hand mills have indeed become scrap, and things are not much different in the case of the less coveted wooden models. Nowadays enthusiasts and collectors will indeed have to look far and wide in order to find any older model at all.

BOILING/INFUSION/FILTERING   Between 1600 and 1700, travellers reported two basic kinds of methods used to boil coffee in the East. Either the drink bubbled for hours on end in an earthenware pot or the coffee powder was mixed with water and repeatedly brought to the boil in specially formed long-handled metal jugs, and drunk only then. These jugs come in various sizes, with a capacity of up to between one or one and a half liters and are to be found throughout the East. Their form has remained the same up to the present day, a conical vessel, tapering towards the top with a relatively short spout or one incorporated in the rim. The width varies, generally about one half or a third of

Beethoven's coffee machine

"*For breakfast he partook of coffee, which for the most part he had prepared himself in a glass machine. Coffee appears to have been his most indispensable form of nourishment, which he consumed to the same excessive degree as was known to be the case with Orientals. Sixty beans would go into one cup of coffee, often counted out exactly, particularly if guests were present.*"
Anton Schindler, Biographie von Ludwig van Beethoven, *Leipzig, 1970, p.436.*

the diameter of the base (Ill. 39, 40). They are for the most part made of galvanized copper. The long handle is made out of wood or metal, but anyone using this method to prepare coffee will readily appreciate the value of a wooden handle, even when the jug is not being placed on the charcoal fire of the Bedouins or in the red-hot sand of the coffee-makers of the Black Sea but on a hot-plate in the comfort of a modern kitchen. Connoisseurs claim that the truncated cone shape is the best because it ensures the least loss of aroma during boiling.

A special container for preparing coffee of the Turkish type with the simple method of pouring over the hot water, has not evolved in Europe. The shorter Turkish process is conducted both in jugs and cups.

All coffee which is transferred from the container in which it is brewed up to one in which it is served via a strainer, can be regarded as filtered coffee, which brings us to the equipment with the help of which the European variation, filter coffee, was born. In early times the consistency of the boiled or brewed coffee was far from palatable to the Europeans, particularly to the women. And while in Venice after 1650 people still sat with crossed legs on soft cushions in the coffee tents, and drank of the strong, bitter liquid from minute cups with even smaller sips, in England and France the "improvers" were already at work. The filtering of coffee was invented and the first "coffee machines", the filter apparatuses, were being successfully tried out by about 1670. The designs ranged from filter bags hung in the jug, or funnels placed on top lined with filter paper, to filter cups and jugs with built-in filters. They all served the one purpose of providing larger or smaller quantities of filtered coffee.

Depending on how practical they were and how easy to operate, certain filter methods have become commonplace throughout the world, even when this has jeopardized to some extent the strength of the aroma of the coffee. One form of filter frequently to be found is the porcelain, metal or plastic filter which is lined with filter paper. Linen sacks which were initially used have not proved so successful because they absorb the granules, and even after limited use have a decidedly negative effect on the taste. Before filter paper was produced on a mass-scale, horsehair filter bags were used, but today these have been completely replaced by synthetic bags.

The description coffee machine is given to those appliances in which separate compartments are filled with cold water and ground coffee powder and designed in such a way that, after the application of heat, filtered coffee is ready for drinking. From the first "machines" of the 17th century with a capacity of two cups to the ultra-modern designs controlled by micro-processors, with an hourly capacity of between two hundred and seven hundred and fifty cups, was indeed a long way, in the course of which a whole multitude of versions were developed or designed. Even to attempt to take stock of all the improvements and modifications of boiling, brewing, percolating, and lixiviation methods registered as patents would appear to be a near endless task, let alone to compile a record of all the manufacturing firms in Europe and the USA which, over the course of the past two hundred years, have engaged in the production of coffee machines (Ill. 23, 24, 49). Despite the tremendous variety of design, here too there are basically only two systems by which coffee machines operate. According to the pressure system, water vapour is passed only once through the powder, e. g. the percolator principle. In the case of the circulation system, the coffee powder is repeatedly leached in the filter compartment. The percolator system operates on the principle of the expansion and contraction of water. Many machines made in the 18th and 19th centuries—for instance the cele-

24 Coffee machine in the shape of a locomotive. Austrian patent from Wagenmann and Böttger, 1840. Lithograph and quotation from: H. Gauss, *Der wohlservierte und elegante Kaffeetisch . . .*, Weimar, 1847, plate VI. A contemporary advertisement for the machines draws attention to the fact that they have "an attractive appearance, in that they have the form of locomotives of every kind, steam ships and other similar items, thereby permitting the most varied forms, making them all the more suitable as elegant pieces of furniture . . ."
A Siphon, B Plugs, C Water container, D Receptacle for coffee powder, E Fine strainer, F Coarse strainer, G Lid, H Milk warmer with handle, K Cover for milk warmer, L Slide valve, M Warming planes, N Container for matches, O Spirit flame placed under C, P Baseplate, R Container for finished drink with faucet.
Figs. 25/26 are parts of other coffee machines.

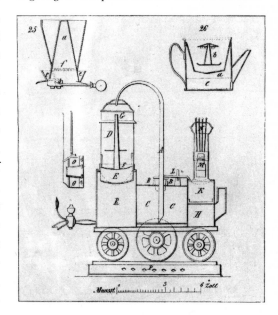

25 Coffee pots, France, 17th century. Copperplate engraving by Johann Hainzelmann in: Nicolas de Blegny, *Le bon usage . . .*, Paris, 1687.

brated glass-sphere coffee machines, the machine *à la balance* etc.—were based on this system. Normally they consisted of two containers—e.g. glass balloons—which are secured to a stand. In the lower section is put the hot water, and in the upper, the ground coffee. With the application of heat (petroleum flame, electric current) the water is heated further and then expands, that is to say it rises from the lower balloon to the upper, passing through the coffee powder. If the supply of heat is cut off, a vacuum is created and the coffee, which is now ready for drinking, "contracts", that is to say is sucked under pressure into the lower container from which it is served. Coffee machines of this type are still to be found today in nearly all households in Portugal and Scandinavia, they are also used in France and more recently in Japan.

With quite a few ultra-modern micro-electronically controlled household coffee machines, which might almost be said to have become over-perfected, coffee can be both ground and then prepared. The selection of functions in such machines is greater than will probably be used in practice. Four, five or even six different grades of coffee grounds produce minimal variations of flavour, which the normal consumer is barely able to detect. Furthermore anyone training their palate to such a level of refinement as to be able to appreciate these nuances, would have no need of this level of grade selection anyway, for the last thing he or she would do would be to use an electric coffee mill.

SERVING   During the course of the 18th and 19th centuries, a certain canon evolved for the obligatory elements of the coffee set, which despite many changes permits a basic pattern to be discerned. In the early days, that is to say in the second half of the 17th century, coffee was drunk from pre-existing large or small beakers, *koppchen*, cups or bowls, which were made of silver, pewter, traditional pottery or fayence (Ill. 27). In 1683 in Vienna, coffee was being served in pewter soup bowls and large brass cups. It would appear that coffee was drunk from equally simple vessels in most coffee shops in England and France. Among the upper classes and at Court fayence bowls were used, or if one possessed such finery and was prepared to take the risk, one drank from expensive oriental porcelain bowls (Ill. 55). Of course this did not apply in equal measure everywhere. For example in the Netherlands cheap imported Chinese household porcelain had been available since the beginning of the 17th century, and, thanks to the supremacy of Dutch maritime trade, porcelain bowls could be bought without rival in terms of price and quality. The domestic fayence manufacturers who unabashedly called themselves porcelain manufacturers, in the beginning did not even make the effort to produce drinking vessels. Hence it is well within the bounds of possibility that, by around 1700, Chinese porcelain bowls were by no means unusual in Dutch coffee-houses as well as doubtlessly in some English establishments too.

A wealth of literature exists surrounding the history of the multitude of forms of utility and luxury tableware, and we must confine ourselves here to some characteristic details of coffee service types.

The wide drinking bowls of Chinese type and the small hemispherical bowls of oriental type began to be placed on saucers between 1650 and 1700, and after 1700 were increasingly embellished with a handle. If the drinking vessel had no handle, it was customary to drink out of the saucer. This custom persisted even after cups were given handles, and it was not until the end of the 18th century that the practice of drinking from the saucer was generally treated with disdain. The variety of shapes of coffee cups is immense—more than one thousand have been counted. Sometimes they were tall, sometimes squat, sometimes large, sometimes small. Sometimes they stood on feet or had a cover. Espresso coffee is served from covered cups in the Café Gerbeaud in Budapest. Sometimes they were similar in appearance to bowls or beakers and as such virtually indistinguishable from tea or chocolate cups. As a rule coffee cups are—and always have been—rounded. Square mocha cups or the octagonal cups of the *nouvelle cuisine* are exceptions, as are other extravagant designs or curiosities. Among these latter can be included the coffee bowls in the Petit Trianon in Versailles, which are discreetly modelled on the bust of Marie Antoinette.

One feature which is very much common to all coffee cups is that, as a general rule, they are narrower and taller than tea bowls, and this is as true of individual pieces as it is of parts of sets, lavish or modest, expensive or cheap. Individual pieces include the collector's cups—an invention of the 19th century. The less well-to-do who were unable to buy a complete coffee set, could in this way enjoy a share of the prestige of owning genuine porcelain.

A highly original special shape is the moustache cup, which today as an individual piece attracts more amusement than admiration for its form. A shelf fitted into the body of the cup ensured that a bearded person did not have to soak his moustache in coffee before reaching the liquid to drink.

Ceramic has become the material used world-wide for the making of coffee cups (e. g. pottery, porcelain). By way of exception, coffee glasses have been used in Austria and France since the 19th century, and since 1950 have become almost exclusively established also in Hungary and Czechoslovakia.

Coffee bowls made out of metal, mostly copper, of the kind still used today by the nomadic herdsmen of the Arab world, have their origins in the need for ease of portability. They need to be more robust than the vessels of more sedentary peoples. Nowadays cylindrical holders out of leather or brass in which the cups are stacked can be found in every bazar in the East. An exception to the fact that such portable sets are rarely to be found among the less mobile population of the countries of northern and western Europe, is provided by the coffee cups of figures such as Napoleon or Frederick the Great (Ill. 53), which these distinguished men carried with them on their campaigns, protected in leather holders.

Today, the coffee pot is as universal a part of the table setting as was originally the case with the tea pot for the English, the samovar for the Russians or the cocoa jug for the Spanish. In Germany in the 18th and early 19th century, affectionate nicknames were even coined for the large coffee pots which stood in the middle of the table and contained a sufficient quantity of coffee for a whole family.

In the same way as the tea pot, the coffee pot is unable to conceal its oriental, or more precisely Turkish or Egyptian origins. The Arabs poured their coffee out of tall metal pots, which usually had an upward-pointing spout incorporated into the lower end, or they used an equally high, but rather rotund pot, without exception also made of metal (brass, copper) with a spout incorporated in the rim. These two basic forms were gradually assimilated into the European tradition, the transition facilitated by the existence of certain European precedents such as pewter pots with spouts or the jug form. Even if the material changed, the basic form persisted and has continued to do so down to the present day. That tea pots possess a squat apple-like form and coffee pots are more elongated and pear-shaped has nothing to do with the properties of the two drinks but is accounted for by their origins.

26 Portable warming stove with coffee jugs, France, 17th century. Engraving by Johann Hainzelmann in: Nicolas de Blegny, *Le bon usage . . .*, Paris, 1687.

27 Coffee serving trays (*cabarets*), France, 17th century. Copperplate engraving by Johann Hainzelmann in: Nicolas de Blegny, *Le bon usage . . .*, Paris, 1687.

The smallest, complete coffee service is the breakfast service, also known as *déjeuner* or *tête-à-tête* for two persons. It consists of a coffee pot (and/or) a tea pot, a sugar bowl, a cream jug, and two cups with saucers. The most extensive complete coffee services are thought to be a part of the largest tableware collections of all, namely the Meissen Swan service, manufactured in 1739. It was designed for one hundred persons and consists of two thousand pieces; further there is the Flora-Danica service made in Copenhagen in 1800 and consisting of more than one thousand eight hundred pieces. Between these two extremes lie the normal-sized services for the bourgeois household (stoneware or porcelain). Services for six, twelve and twenty-four persons were and still are standard.

With the eventual consolidation of coffee as the morning drink of the middle classes, after 1800 the four-piece silver breakfast service, which originated in England, became increasingly widespread. It consisted of a coffee pot, a tea pot, a cream jug, and of a sugar bowl.

The tremendous range of forms of the coffee service can be seen in all its variety in the sample books or later in the sales catalogues of all the manufacturing firms of Europe and farther afield. This wealth of variety was surpassed only by the tremendous diversity of artistic decoration and embellishment. Décor and trim are the main elements of the respective styles which distinguish one make of porcelain from another. The flourishing exchange of décors between the manufacturers in the 18th century, the influence of the person commissioning the work (monogram, names, dedications, etc.), the emergent preference for particular designs (flowers and ornamental motifs are by far the most common for coffee porcelain) in course of time led to this tremendous variety. Industrial methods of production have facilitated the mass-production of decoration and the possibilities are now virtually limitless. Everything is now possible in design, from large and small floral motifs to scenes from everyday life, to didactic admonitions not to drink coffee to excess. Appeals to patriotic sentiments are found on coffee cups and pots as are erotic scenes. At the latest by the time of the *Biedermeier* period in the first half of the 19th century the display character of decoration had started to play a major role. The desire for ostentation on the part of the bourgeoisie came to the fore, and porcelain began to be designed more for the sideboard, for display than for daily use. With its more widespread availability, the initially expensive porcelain used as a sign of prosperity which the upper strata placed in cabinets and on display plinths gradually filtered further down the social ladder, moving as it did so from the magnificently mirrored wall into the cabinets or the dressers of the late 19th century. In doing so, room was made for the four-piece coffee and tea sets, which originally were made of silver but subsequently of cheaper alloys, sterling and plate. Thus, like porcelain before it, now the once aristocratic representative silver was also transported down the social ladder, stripped of its former class allegiance and placed on every bourgeois breakfast table from the prosperous middle classes upwards. For at least fifty years, from 1850 onwards, domestic silver, a unique creation, both stylish and durable, dominated the table settings of the bourgeoisie of the coffee and tea-drinking countries around the world, a status symbol of both the prosperous middle classes and petit bourgeois alike. In Germany the desire to display one's treasures was particularly strong at the end of the 19th century. The neo-Gothic glass cases and the Renaissance sideboard offered plenty of room for showing off one's coffee set to its best advantage.

The reform in taste which took place between 1896 and 1908, which pervaded many fields of culture and life, also had an influence on the shape and decoration of everyday tableware, which took on a more modest form. The historicist imitations were replaced by *Art Nouveau* and *Art Déco*, although these innovations were not produced on a mass-scale (Ill. 57).

Since the mid-1970s there has been a marked return to the forms and designs of earlier generations as well as a trend towards the revival of older kinds of household gadget such as coffee mills. Contemporary design would appear to incorporate the whole range of designs which have evolved up to this time. The Baroque forms of the luxury porcelain of the 18th century are available in the large department stores, albeit not so expensive and produced on a mass-scale, and so too are coffee sets in Rococo, *Biedermeier* or *Art Nouveau* styles. Octagonal cups are to be found as well as the most outlandish creations.

Even the porcelain tableware, produced on a mass-scale for the catering trade has not escaped a variety of Baroque "styling". The desire to return to the forms of times gone by as part of the generally prevalent nostalgia, has now taken precedence over what was once regarded as the great design break-through of such heavily used tableware, namely that it should be durable and designed for stacking in large quantities.

Finally, it must be borne in mind that it is still the case today that coffee making utensils and coffee sets assume a special place among household objects in daily use, a place which largely derives from their position as status symbols and the function of serving the need for display and elegance. The "good" china is still kept out of the kitchen today, being stored in the living room, or exhibited in glass cabinets.

Coffee mills from grandmother's time, which even fifteen years ago would have been unceremoniously consigned to the dustbin, have experienced a miraculous revival and a correspondingly fantastic increase in price. The recent trend has been for the electric grinder to be discreetly concealed within an elegant wooden casing complete with shining brass parts and the addition of traditionally styled milling components.

The habit of coffee drinking reflected in painting and the graphic arts

The first notice taken by art of the new drink took the form of woodcuts and copperplate engravings used to illustrate the many books and tracts which duly appeared in the wake of coffee's first appearing, both in those publications spreading the word about the new drink, and generally advocating its beneficial properties as well as those devoted to its denigration.

In the period before and after 1700, both supporters and opponents of the new fashion spared no efforts in augmenting and perfecting their fund of arguments, complete with appropriate illustrations, in order to demonstrate that coffee is either highly injurious to health or, on the contrary, that it is a most salubrious drink. In accordance with the practice of the day, the opposing parties assiduously copied out or translated the tracts of their foreign precursors, who had it seems already put their near obligatory controversy behind them. And this in turn explains why the accompanying illustrations, with some degree of embellishment, are the old pictures in new guise rather than new creations. Initially it was the "botanical" engravings of the coffee plant, in all their incompleteness, which were repeatedly used. In 1666 a small tract appeared (Franciscus Peters, *De Potu Coffi*, Francofurti, 1666), which contains an illustration depicting three coffee beans, a branch of the coffee tree and a roasting drum. This ensemble was to be repeatedly copied for the next thirty years—it is to be found in all the editions of the *Drey Neuen Curieusen Tractätgen* ... by Spon or Dufour, once with an additional inscription in Latin (e.g. in the Budissin edition of 1686) or in French (e.g. the Lyons edition of 1685)

(Ill. 4). In some cases a coffee pot and drinking bowl is also shown. The branch of the coffee tree, showing three to five beans, is to be found faithfully copied in many botanical textbooks or dietary works, for instance that of Elsholtz of 1682 or in a household manual by Franciscus Philippus Florinus of 1705.

The same is true with illustrations depicting coffee drinkers or coffee-drinking scenes. In fact it can be seen that the proponents of the new drink were more successful in finding artistic means to add weight to their arguments than their adversaries. How magnificent appear the Orientals in all their finery with their coffee pots, in the copperplates included in Spon's tract (which went into at least twelve editions in four languages), and how ineffectual and unconvincing appear—by comparison—the illustrations which gravely warn the coffee drinkers of their rapid demise, or highlight the alleged dangers of excessive coffee drinking. The titles of such works are overpowering enough: "Of the abuse of hot and stimulating foods and drinks . . ." (1707); "Thoughts on the three notorious seducers of the people" (1738); "Scene showing the misfortune brought down on Germany by the coffee bean" (1781); or the unceremoniously laconic "Suicide. A tale" (c. 1770). But the accompanying illustrations fail completely to live up to these portentous warnings. Indeed it is tempting to think that the engravers involved in their production had little desire to lend their skills to the campaign being waged by coffee's opponents. It is difficult to believe for instance that the group of coffee drinkers to be seen in Duncan's engraving which bears the significant inscription "To die of drink" are facing imminent death (Ill. 15). On the contrary—they appear to be in the very best of health and spirits!

Great originality was shown by those illustrators whose works bordered on caricature. Fortune-tellers reading coffee-grounds, coffee parties and family scenes are popular themes which on occasion spill over into biting satire (Ill. 47). There is an immense profusion of caricatures on such themes from all coffee-drinking nations. They are surpassed only by the ludicrous possibilities presented to the artist by the attempts of the Germans to "extend" their coffee supply.

By the early 1700s, from time to time members of the aristocracy and upper classes were already having portraits made of themselves surrounded by the standard attributes of the fashionable pursuit of coffee drinking (drinking bowl, coffee pot and, on frequent occasions, smoking materials, set in an oriental interior with ottomans, cushions and Turkish robes). The real danger from the Turks had by now receded, to be replaced by a mania for things Turkish, including their drink! Baroque sensuality is represented by one Johann Samuel Mock's "At Coffee Drinking", as is by the more subtle portraiture of a "Turk with Coffee Cup", painted by Rosalba Carriera in 1739 (Ill. 55). Mention too should be made of the portraits of the celebrated and notorious Mesdames de Pompadour and Dubarry, by Carl van Loo and Dechreuse. The imposingly dressed women hold delicate coffee cups in the hand. The presence of a Moorish boy and a coloured maid-servant in the pictures lends emphasis to the exotic atmosphere to which the ruling classes of Europe with their oriental fashion and chinoiseries were so attracted in the 18th century.

Although there are well-known examples, such as the portrait of the merchant Schmidins of Nuremberg by Johann Kupetzky (1730) or the "Le Déjeuner" (1744) by François Boucher, representative scenes of coffee drinking among the bourgeoisie in their private circle are relatively rare before 1800, and astonishingly so in England and the Netherlands where one would expect to find pictures from this early on (Ill. 28–30). The

28–30 Probably the first depiction of a private gathering of coffee drinkers in northern Europe. Vase with lid by Jakob Wemmersz Hoppensteyn. Faience, Delft, c. 1661. Halle, Staatliche Galerie Moritzburg.
The encircling scene shows six gentlemen (one of them is shown boiling water), four ladies and a maid. The ladies are wearing their hair in the highly-fashionable Fontange style, created by a mistress of Louis XIV.
Significantly the maid serving the coffee does not wear the hair in this style. That this is a noble gathering is evidenced by the decorative pomegranates, grapes and laurels, as well as the Pan figure holding up the table.

31 Advertisement for de-caffeinated coffee.
Poster by Lucien Bernhard, 1909. Berlin,
Museum für Deutsche Geschichte.

32 Advertisement for Quieta blended coffee.
Poster, 1910. Private collection.

33 Morning coffee for the upper classes of Paris, *c*.1840.

34 Morning coffee in the servants' quarters of Paris, *c*. 1840.

35 Morning coffee among the poor of Paris, *c*. 1840.

36 Morning coffee in a Parisian coffee-house, *c*. 1840. Caricatures from lithographs by Abel Damourette in: *Illustrirte Zeitung*, Leipzig, 1 May, 1847.

37 Johann Kaspar Lavater and Gotthold
Ephraim Lessing being entertained by Moses
Mendelssohn in Berlin, *c.* 1762. Lithograph
by Moritz Daniel Oppenheim, mid-19th
century. Berlin, Märkisches Museum.

38 Coffee circle. Pen and ink drawing by
Guthknecht in: *Illustrirte Zeitung*, Leipzig, 16
December, 1876.

41   Table coffee mill with wooden holder ready for attaching to the table as required. France, early 18th century. Dombasle, Bloch Collection.
A mill similar to this was owned by George Washington (today Washington, United States National Museum, Peter Collection).

42   Turned handmill, in a particularly elegant finish, mahogany and ivory. France, *c.* 1800. Dombasle, Bloch Collection.

43   Decorated lap-mill, wood and brass. Alsace-Lorraine, 1880. Dombasle, Bloch Collection.

44/45   Four hand-mills (field mills), contained in soldiers' field packs, iron and aluminium. France and Italy, 1870–1940. Dombasle, Bloch Collection.

Eine beÿ denen Marquetenern
gebräuchliche Coffee Machine, womit
sie in der Stadt und Lager herumgien
gen, davon die eine Helffte mit Coffee
die andere mit Milch angefüllt war.

Eine Fränckische Marquetenerin beÿ der Reichs Armee.

46 Large coffee machine from the 18th century of the kind carried by the female sutlers of the European armies. Water colour from the illustrated journal of Johann Christian Becher, *True report of the events . . . of the mighty war of Frederick II, King of Prussia, with the Queen of Hungary Maria Theresa . . .*, Vinaria, no date.

47 English breakfast scene with coffee urn, coffee and tea pots and cups. Copperplate engraving by James Gillray, 1805, in: Georg Hirth, *Kulturgeschichtliches Bilderbuch aus vier Jahrhunderten*, Munich, 1925.

MATRIMONIAL-HARMONICS.

48   Pewter coffee pot, Philadelphia, 1780–1798. Winterthur, Delaware, The Henry Francis du Pont Wintherthur Museum.

49   Electric coffee machine in the form of an American coffee urn made of silver. Manufactured by the Württembergische Metallwarenfabrik Geislingen, *c.* 1925. Dresden, Staatliche Kunstsammlungen, Museum für Kunsthandwerk.

50   Coffee pot made of red stoneware, Plaue (Havel), *c.* 1715. Dresden, Staatliche Kunstsammlungen, Porzellansammlung.

51   Embossed silver coffee pot, Paris, 1735. Leipzig, Museum des Kunsthandwerks.

52   Individual pieces of the golden coffee service commissioned by the Elector Augustus II from the Court goldsmith Dinglinger in 1697. Of particular interest is the skilfully deceptive imitation of porcelain, as well as the fact that they reveal the transition phase between handleless bowls (*koppchen*) and cups with handles. Dresden, Staatliche Kunstsammlungen, Grünes Gewölbe.

55   Coffee drinker in Turkish costume.
Pastel by Rosalba Carriera, 1739.
Dresden, Staatliche Kunstsammlungen,
Gemäldegalerie Alte Meister.

56   Woman with coffee mill.
Oil painting by Fritz Junghans, 1931.
Berlin, Staatliche Museen,
Nationalgalerie.

Tasse
Henkel – grün = Rand

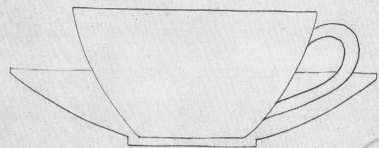

Die Form für alle Tassen

Boden innen
(Tasse)

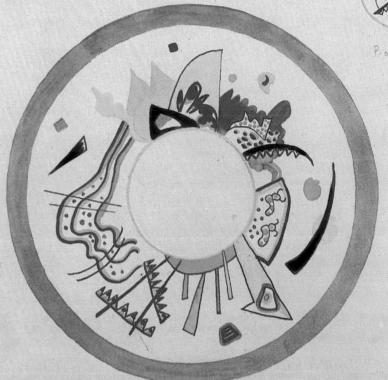

Untertasse

Kandinsky

incorporation of coffee—and tea—into the evolving diet of the bourgeoisie becomes first markedly apparent in artistic terms during that most bourgeois of all epochs, the *Biedermeier*. The number of aristocrats or members of society who had had themselves painted in settings which gave prominence to coffee drinking was minimal compared to the profusion of coffee ensembles forming the background to portraits of the *Biedermeier* period, where they are a constant feature.

Paintings of families seated at the coffee table or depictions of visits have a documentary character as family portraits in the first half of the 19th century, or else are designed to embody to a certain degree the solid bourgeois ideals. The harmonious family idyll, one of the most fundamental of bourgeois virtues can be presented most "naturally" with the whole family assembled around the table. Hence it is not surprising that breakfast scenes and families partaking of coffee and tea appear more frequently than others, for it is here that the good bourgeois finds confirmation of his true or desired way of life.

Even where there is no specific table scene as such (where the obligatory presence of coffeeware is readily explained) but rather interiors, group and individual portraits, nevertheless the artists must have felt themselves compelled to include utensils for the preparation of coffee or tea or porcelain as incidental to the picture. Their frequent appearance is more than mere chance.

Coffee and tea machines and the corresponding porcelain rank among the status symbols of the *Biedermeier* period. This becomes apparent when considering paintings which date at the latest from the years immediately preceding 1848 in Germany and Austria. In line with the sociological assumption that living-room furniture can be treated as a general indicator of the overall status of a family,[37] there is ample evidence of the prestige borne by such items in the pictures of the *Biedermeier* period. When taking together all the factors indicative of status in the *Biedermeier*, then the habit of taking morning coffee and the Sunday coffee ritual, together with the requisite utensils and drinking vessels, must have assumed an important place as yardsticks of status.

A very different attitude is evident in the critical and realist art of the 19th century which is devoted to picturing the life of the lower classes. In these paintings the presence of the coffee mill, of simple pewter or ceramic pots for drinking or a pewter jug for transporting the drink do not denote status in the proletarian or rural milieu, they represent objects which are indispensable for the preservation of one's existence. The coffee mill accompanied the extreme forms of social deprivation, eviction or emigration, as the last household effect.

In the paintings, drawings and newspaper illustrations of the 19th century, particularly those of the second half, there are to be found depictions of the working classes from all over the world which reflect in a multitude of ways the integration and commonplace character of coffee in the private and working worlds of the lower strata: sentimental, picturesque illustrations of coffee drinking beggars, petit bourgeois contemplation or mordant satire on such themes as the mobile coffee stall (Ill. 144), the serving of coffee at the factory, crusts of bread and the coffee bottle brought by the worker himself or later by children. The various attempts of the middle classes to resolve social problems, as for example with the instance in 1868 of miners being presented with one-third of a liter of good coffee upon coming to the surface, or the representatives of welfare or temperance associations distributing free soup and chicory, are also depicted, either in a glowing light or subjected to caustic criticism depending on the standpoint of the artist.

°○°

How an American regards the consistency of German coffee

"*Take a barrel of water and bring it to the boil; rub a chicory berry against a coffee berry, then convey the former into the water. Continue the boiling and evaporation until the intensity of the flavour and aroma of the coffee and chicory has been diminished to a proper degree; then set aside to cool. Now unharness the remains of a once cow from the plow, insert them in a hydraulic press, and then you should have acquired a teaspoonful of that pale blue juice which a German superstition regards as milk, modify the malignity of its strength in a bucket of tepid water and ring up the breakfast. Mix the beverage in a cold cup, partake with moderation and keep a wet rag around your head to guard against overexcitement.*"
Mark Twain, A Tramp Through Europe.

———
○○°

57 Cup design, water-coloured pen and ink drawing by Wassily Kandinsky. Halle, Staatliche Galerie Moritzburg. Top: "Cup handle—green-smoke". Centre: "The form for all cups"; centre right: "Interior base (cup)". Bottom: "Saucer".

The range of themes is indeed broad, extending from Charles de Groux's "Coffee Roaster in a Wintry Alley", the scenes from the life of the Belgian workers by Alexander Struys and Hendrik Luytens, to pictures by the German proletarian artists, such as Fritz Junghans's "Woman with Coffee Mill" (Ill. 56).

The process by which coffee established itself in the private sphere between the 17th and 20th centuries has been fully reflected in cartoons, and to a certain extent by painting, but the real theme which has never ceased to fascinate artists is in fact not the personal sphere, but rather the public coffee-drinking ambience, that of the coffee-house (see pages 228–230).

The preparation of coffee in cookery books from the 17th to the 20th century

Coffee—and tea—gradually also became featured in contemporary specialist publications. One of the first books to deal with the preparation of coffee on any major scale, which went further than the mere repetition of the reports of other 17th-century writers, is that of the Frenchman Nicolas de Blegny dating from 1687 (Ill. 58). He even provides recipes which he had possibly tried out for himself. Based directly on laboratory experiments, Jacob Spon respectively Dufour (cf. postscript to the reprint of 1986) in 1685 assembled all the information required for the layman on the preparation of coffee (Ill. 4). Similar booklets came onto the book markets of England and the Netherlands between 1650 and 1700, devoted specifically to the subject. Most of them were written by authors who had a direct interest in editing such publications, among them coffee-house keepers, coffee traders, or physicians who propagated coffee.

In 1682, exactly a century after Rauwolf had first mentioned the drink, there appeared for the first time in a relevant German work the *Diaeteticon* by Johann Sigismund Elsholtz, instructions on how to prepare coffee beans. Elsholtz, who had studied in Padua, grouped coffee, together with tea and chocolate, under the heading of new kinds of foreign beverages which "not only in Holland, but in our parts, too, are becoming known among notables".[38] Elsholtz devotes precisely two printed pages to coffee, which he writes as "coffie", suggesting that he made use of English sources. The assertion reported by Adam Olearius that coffee consumption reduces the libido (cf. p. 9 f.) is dismissed by Elsholtz or his English source with short shrift as "a jolly tale".

In 1685 there appeared in Vienna the first coffee recipe book which can be treated with any seriousness, the *Bevanda Asiatica* by Luigi Conte Marsigli. Having been taken prisoner by the Turks in 1683 and having worked for some time as a *kahveci* or coffee-maker, upon his return Marsigli provided a comprehensive account of the correct way to prepare coffee (roasting, pulverizing, brewing). He also gained much of his knowledge from a Turkish publication which he first had translated into Italian and then extensively used for his own book.

Coffee was accorded more attention in family and household literature of the time than in contemporary cookery books. That such comprehensive works as the *Vollständige Nürnbergische Kochbuch* (Complete cookery book of Nuremberg) of 1691 or the *Freywillig aufgesprungene Granat-Apffel* (The pomegranate which opened voluntarily) of 1709, make no mention at all of coffee, or limit themselves purely to the advice that every cook should also have some knowledge of coffee, has to be explained in the first instance within the context of courtly culinary literature in general of whose tradition these books form a part. A major reason for the omission of coffee from the leading cookery books was also the continuing uncertainty as to the true "powers" native to the coffee bean.

Pronouncements by physicians on the subject were so contradictory—one would describe the predominant quality as dry, another as moist, the third as warm, the fourth as cold—that it is not surprising that coffee was mainly mentioned in a dietary context. Thus coffee can be found as early as 1700 in one of the finest household manuals, in Andreas Glorez's *Vollständige Haus und Land-Bibliothec . . .* (Complete compendium on household and agricultural matters; Regensburg, 1700). Situated between a slimming suggestion using cherry stones and a description of the extraordinary powers of wild thyme, the author introduces almost unheralded three passages: How the Turks prepare their coffee/Preparation of the drink/Consumption. One can see that he himself is still not quite sure where coffee should be included in his system. In addition to recommendations as to the best method for roasting the beans and the vessel most suited for the purpose, he describes—and this is the most interesting part—an experiment with the drink which he carried out on his own body over a period of several months. For a four weeks' time he "imbibed" coffee every morning, thereafter two times per week and then eventually just once a week. In fact he does not provide any account of the outcome of this experiment, and neither does he mention why he started to limit himself in this way in the first place. The most likely explanation is that his supply of coffee was running low, for he had no reservations of a medical nature, otherwise he would no doubt have referred to them. Coffee drinking caused him as little injury as it had the Turks who drank it "constantly", as he wrote, and continuing in this vein, "Its main quality is cold and dry . . . it is good for the eyes . . . for colds and discharge/and is excellent in preventing gout/and the dropsy."[39]

In Germany, coffee does not assume a special section in cookery books (neither does tea) either in the early stages when it first became known, or later. If it is mentioned at all it is generally extremely briefly and mostly within the context of dietary warnings or suggestions as to how one can prepare visitors' coffee or make coffee go further. The proverbial German love of coffee cannot with all the will in the world be gathered from its cookery books, for instance the many different ways of preparing the drink are treated with bland indifference, as for instance in the case of "a few Hamburg housewives" writing in their *Hamburgisches Kochbuch* (Hamburg cookery book) in 1830, who reported that the methods of filtering coffee had long been common knowledge and that further instruction would be superfluous. If one compares English and German cookery books around 1850, it can be observed that the English devote far more space to coffee. In Frederick Bishop's *The Illustrated London Cookery Book* (1852) there are some nineteen different coffee recipes, whereas German books of the same period generally contain about three or four at the most.

After 1840, some German authors sought to overcome this deficiency by translating French and English coffee recipe books, and with a greater or lesser degree of modification, published them under their own name. A so-called *Kaffeebüchlein* (a booklet on coffee) published in Coburg in 1841,[40] bore the significant sub-title "a counsellor for the rich and the poor". *Der wohlservirte und elegante Kaffeetisch*[41] (The well-served and elegant coffee table), published in 1847, for the first time offered advice for the setting and presenting of a stylish table, at least according to its title. Since 1800 in most bourgeois households the coffee table had pushed the sumptuous dinner party into the background. A quick glance into this booklet, however, reveals that it is really more concerned with a description of the various different kinds of coffee plus a report on the latest coffee machine, which had been published in Paris in the previous year under the

LE BON USAGE
DU THÉ
DU CAFFÉ
ET
DU CHOCOLAT
POUR LA PRESERVATION
& pour la guerison des
Maladies.

Par Mr DE BLEGNY, Conseiller, Medecin Artiste ordinaire du Roy & de Monsieur, & préposé par ordre de sa Majesté, à la Recherche & Verification des nouvelles découvertes de Medecine.

A PARIS,
Chez { L'AUTEUR, au College des quatre Nations. la Veuve D'HOURY, Quay des Augustins. Et la Veuve NION, ruë des Mathurins.

M. DC. LXXXVII.
Avec Privilege du Roy.

58   Title page of Nicolas de Blegny's guide to the best methods for the preparation of tea, coffee and chocolate. Rostock, Universitätsbibliothek.

°o⊙o°

Newspaper announcement, Hamburg, 1713
"At Samuel Heyl's, bookseller, in the St. Johannis Church, a singular tract can be obtained, going by the title: Reliable instruction on the correct and healthy preparation of the coffee drink drawn up from experience by one who takes the drink every day. In 8 volumes for 3 shillings."
Freytagischer Nordischer Mercurius, *Hamburg, 20 January, 1713, p. 8.*

°o⊙o°

authors' names Giraud and Dausse. At last, in 1864, Johann Rottenhöfer, the cook to the Bavarian royal household, provided what by then had become a much-needed guide to the formal coffee table. For the decades that followed, *Der elegante, wohlservirte Kaffee- und Theetisch* (The elegant and well-served coffee and tea table) became the standard book on the subject, also containing an international flavour with the author describing at length the manner and mode by which the family sits down to coffee in England and America.

If one considers the seemingly endless range of culinary literature of the 20th century, then one is forced to the conclusion that little has changed in their treatment of coffee as cookery's poor relation. Specialist books on the subject continue to be a rarity, in fact they can be counted on the fingers of both hands. Today the most comprehensive and accurate books about coffee are to be found in the place where coffee will probably, if at all, only become established at some time in the future—namely Japan.

Contraband coffee

If one day a history of smuggling will be written, then the smuggling of coffee will assume a major place in it. Smuggling is carried on all over the world wherever international trade is being conducted and where tariffs, duties and other charges levied upon it are being made.

Even today, with but a few exceptions we cannot say when and where the first coffee was illegally carried over an international or domestic customs barrier. But the first ships officially permitted to leave the Arab trading port of Mocha with cargoes of coffee, already had "partners" who were transporting coffee out of the country without official sanction. And neither did the unloading of coffee in the European ports in the second half of the 17th century always follow the procedures laid down by the authorities. In fact we can say that wherever sole importing or exporting rights and privileges existed, they would to a greater or lesser extent be deliberately flouted. And because the foreign goods of whatever kind—coffee, tea, cocoa, tropical fruits, porcelain, silk etc.—were subjected to the highest tariffs on their way to the consumer, the smuggling trade was the most profitable of all and was carried on with matching energy. Like the legitimate trade itself, coffee smuggling was carried on both on the large and small scale, by the centner or ton and by the pound, and the profit made correspondingly large or small, either at the expense of some monopoly holder or of the State itself.

We have already made mention of the smuggling of coffee seeds and saplings, but such largely individual and isolated acts are nothing in comparison to the scale of the smuggling of the end-product, either then or now.

We cannot refer to any precise figures as to how much of the coffee consumed in Europe had passed legally or illegally through the customs barriers of the respective countries. But by way of reference the following comparison can serve as a guide: In 1780 in England it is said that two million people made their living through smuggling. Of some seven million kilos of tea, nearly the half was contraband. A similar picture is thought to have existed in respect of the illegal importing of coffee into Germany at the end of the 18th century, when the country was divided up into hundreds of different customs and tariff zones. From 1750 onwards the imposition of trade restrictions and bans on raw coffee arising from the official mercantilist philosophy of the State, acted as a direct encouragement to smuggling. The trade was then assured complete success by Napoleon's continental blockade from 1806 to 1812.

Carlo Goldoni writing in his autobiography, 1787
"At the bridge of Lago Sucro, a mile from Ferraro, where the customs post stands, I had forgotten to present my trunk for inspection, and at the exit of the hamlet, I was halted by a passing patrol.

I had a small supply of chocolate, coffee and candles about my person, all of which were contraband goods and had to be confiscated. In addition there was a considerable fine to pay, and in the papal States the customs officials are not to be trifled with."
Carlo Goldoni, Mein Theater—mein Leben, *Berlin, 1949, p. 333.*

The forms used by the smugglers to transport their black market wares over frontiers were as diverse as they were ingenious, as indeed is still the case today.

The practice for an individual or groups of smugglers to struggle over the frontier at dead of night with a sack of coffee slung over the back was just as commonplace as the legal crossing through a customs barrier with concealed contraband. Coffee smugglers with nerves of steel would stand in mourning dress carrying light baggage at the customs point, present what little they had for checking and if necessary the payment of duty (sometimes a couple of pounds of coffee) and then gesture silently to the accompanying coffin in which their wife lay, who had died of smallpox. Naturally no customs official would dare open the coffin for fear of infection, and in this way it was possible to carry at least two centners of coffee across the frontier without paying any duty. During the 18th century repeated use was made of this trick with the coffin, and it never seemed to fail. Similarly when a leper's bell sounded on the other side of the barrier, and a while later four muffled men appeared with a coffin swaying on their shoulders, no customs official would ask to see inside the coffin to examine the corpse. They would as quickly as possible ensure that they put as great a distance between themselves and the bearers of the coffin and once again two or three centners of coffee had entered the country illegally.

In Germany, smuggling particularly flourished—almost reaching farcical proportions—in the second half of the 18th century, when the country was divided up into a seemingly endless number of principalities, with each country issuing its own decrees, possessing its own capital, passing its own laws, and imposing its own import and export duties, taxes and fees—separated by a myriad of customs barriers and state frontiers. The princes of these territories, in eager imitation of their example Frederick II, monopolized the coffee trade. The customs laws, which after 1800 became increasingly based on the Prussian model in the German States, imposed the severest penalties for engaging in smuggling (ranging from fines to loss of goods, and in cases of repeated infringements even imprisonment), but the great profit to be made from the smuggler's trade proved a constant temptation to break these laws. And coffee by the sackful was to be found over and over again in the wanted lists issued by the customs officials or in the records of confiscated goods which had been found hidden, for example in a barn. Following the setting up of the German Customs Union in 1834 the unofficial guild of smugglers extended their lucrative trade to the frontier between France and Germany. On both sides of the frontier, customs officials, high and low ranking, were by no means inured against bribery, and not infrequently they were directly involved in smuggling themselves. Everywhere along the frontier there were situated notorious smugglers' haunts where raw coffee would be temporarily stored and transferred.

Two examples selected from more recent times serve to illustrate the two extremes of coffee smuggling, on the one hand a multi-million concern, and on the other a means for the little man to earn a bit of extra money. At the end of the 1950s, coffee was considerably cheaper in the Netherlands than in the Federal Republic of Germany: At less heavily frequented frontier crossing-points young girls would cross the frontier into Germany, taking with them a small traditional Dutch doll. They passed the customs officers clutching the dolls in whose wide skirts were concealed a kilo of coffee, for which there was a ready demand on the western German side. Dogs were also used on this border, ambling between the two countries with a canister of coffee strapped to their backs, to be met on the German side and then sent home without their load. Later on, specially

Ludwig Börne's competitive coffee recipe

"... he publicizes a coffee recipe ... This might be highly laudable, when Germans of noble birth show a concern for the material interests of the German common folk, and by means of disseminating good cookery books attempt to still the fractious tongues of the rabble. In this sense the coffee recipe is a work of virtue, not of grace, and a bourgeois writer, although not presentable at court, can nevertheless present a coffee recipe. However, if a coffee recipe is truly to be a matter of grace, then in this respect I can rank myself here not only as the equal of Prince Pückler but as triumphantly superior. The recipe supplied by Prince Pückler is old and well-known ... It can be read in hundreds of travellers' accounts from the Orient ... I however can supply a recipe which I have not simply copied from elsewhere, but which I have invented by myself, a chocolate recipe ... It was on the day that I was studying the memoirs of the Duchess of Abrantes, that I read that for breakfast ... a chocolate had been served which was so frothy and mild that a mere quarter of an hour before luncheon it was possible to have drunk eighteen cups of the drink, without in any way reducing the appetite. I had such an urge to sample this drink for myself ... and after a few days I had found out how to make it. However, this did not satisfy my craving, I aspired even higher. I invented a chocolate gas which is graciousness itself and of which one can drink a hundred cups without it having the remotest adverse effects."

Ludwig Börne, Schriften zur deutschen Literatur, edited by Walther Dietze, Leipzig, 1960, p. 254f.

trained dogs were used by the customs officers, spaniels with a particularly fine sense of smell, who would be sent to track down the canine contrabandists.

For some time coffee smuggling on a gigantic scale has been flourishing along the border between Brazil and Paraguay. For Brazil, coffee is the most important export commodity. Organized gangs operate in the frontier regions of the country, offering the coffee farmers up to fifty percent more for their coffee than the Brazilian Coffee Institute. Hence these gangs always have a ready supply of coffee, for which in Paraguay they receive more than double the bulk purchase price, sometimes even triple. In 1982 losses sustained by the Brazilian government as a result of coffee smuggling, the main destination of which was Paraguay, totalled nearly one thousand million dollars. It is obvious that such an enormous quantity cannot be destined for the domestic Paraguayan market alone. It is not hard to fathom the identity of the real organizers behind this trade, when it is borne in mind that in the middle of 1982, Paraguay sold 280,000 sacks of coffee on the New York Coffee Exchange, although according to estimates by Brazilian economic experts Paraguay's own domestic production had not even amounted to 100,000 sacks over the whole year. The State, in this case the Stroessner dictatorship, emerges as the chief beneficiary from this dubious trade, and it is apparent that here the attempts towards some sort of international regulation of coffee production and export have been completely thwarted to suit the national interests of the Paraguayan bourgeoisie.

Other similar kinds of smuggling activities, albeit hardly on such a massive scale, are registered every year by the International Coffee Institute. They fall under the laconic heading of "statistically unquantified exported quantities". In cases where the official export figures fall for a coffee-producing country, then the question which comes most readily to mind is the purchase price in the neighbouring countries. Uganda for example countered smuggling in neighbouring Kenya and Zaire in 1981 most effectively by drastically raising the State's bulk purchase price by nearly three times for Arabica and Robusta coffees.

COFFEE-HOUSES
AND THEIR CLIENTÈLE FROM THE
17th TO THE 20th CENTURY

"We'll meet in the coffee-house" or "He can be found in his usual café"—such suggestions or declarations have ranked among the common features of everyday public life for nearly three hundred years.

Just as the drinking of coffee has become one of the accepted forms of behaviour of the middle-class family and forms a firm part of the general etiquette surrounding social visiting, so too "going for a drink of coffee", to go in search of an establishment serving coffee to the general public, is also subject to certain norms which have evolved with time, and which differ fundamentally from the traditional habits of wine and beer drinking. The reasons for visiting a coffee-house have always been of a highly varied nature. They derive from the characteristics and expectations of specific social groups for which, over the course of time, the coffee-house trade with the establishing of different kinds of coffee-houses has catered, in satisfying the most diverse of needs. The variegated nature of coffee-houses, their evolution in a number of different directions and their greatly differing kinds of services has meant that the concept of the typical coffee-house is subject to factors of time, place and national and social features which are in turn correspondingly varied. Taking into account respective historical conditions, and both domestic and foreign points of view, reflected in the standpoint of different social strata, the coffee-house has a hundred different faces which can be grouped into about a dozen truly typical forms.

This diversity, particularly in terms of furnishing and interior design and the social composition of the clientèle, has entailed that the coffee-house has been the object of the most varying interpretations, which spring from a particular class-based assessment of a concrete coffee-house type or personal and subjective viewpoints and reservations. For example an examination of the bourgeois coffee-house in all its finery at the end of the 19th century gives rise to the tendency to consider it as the embodiment of bourgeois parasitism and a symbol of decadent consumption.

Ever since 1750, the cry has regularly gone up every forty or fifty years that the "great age" of the coffee-house is passed. Such a lament was to be heard in 1750 in London, at regular intervals in France between 1790 and 1871, and from 1914 on repeated occasions throughout Europe. On each occasion such assertions have been based to some extent on a correct perception of the situation that a certain type of coffee-house has lost its place as epitomizing the culture of a now by-gone age. But all claims of this kind have overlooked the central object of the coffee-house trade, that it is in the first place a commercial undertaking. Although it has sufficient flexibility to provide a suitable ambience

From taverne à la mode to mirrored luxury café— the changing character of the coffee-house from the 17th to the 19th century

A Turkish coffee-house, circa 1920

"The customers in the coffee-houses also sleep there incidentally, they sleep in these warm and dark cattle stables, laying the inevitable saddle under their heads. Such a state of affairs is as natural as kissing in the cafés of Paris. The coffee-house is a workplace, a dormitory, a dining room and even a bathroom for any number of Turks.

One corner of the coffee-house is the direct preserve of the barber. The razor refreshes the cheeks and the coffee elevates the soul. The guests bring their own food with them—garlic, maize, water melons . . . conversation will revolve around the evil eye, sheep born with two heads and other no less wondrous occurrences. Here, too, for the price of a few piasters a learned scribe will write a petition, not only to the governor, but addressed to Kemal Pasha himself, concerning the pension for an invalid or the reduction of taxes. Here one can order a drink of coffee in the morning and remain seated until nightfall. One can also drink nothing at all and simply order a water pipe—placid and sumptuous like one of Molière's enemas in which the water bubbles melodiously with every puff. The coffee-house is open at all times and to all—like the mosque and death itself."

Ilya Ehrenburg, Visum der Zeit, *Leipzig, 1982, p. 249.*

for artists and all kinds of men and women of culture, these latter by no means account for the majority of its clientèle.

Declared extinct a hundred times over, and just as often resurrected, the coffee-house trade presents itself in such shimmering array of guises as to render any definitive description of its real character over the times impossible. If the history of the coffee-house is to be considered in unqualified and unconditional terms, then there are really only two cardinal criteria which can apply for any kind of definition:

1. The coffee-house or café is a public, mainly catering establishment, which bears this description or a combination thereof.
2. Coffee is among the drinks served in such an establishment.

All other features frequently claimed to be common to the "typical" coffee-house possess a restricting character, only ever embracing a limited number of contemporaneously existing types of coffee-houses, representing a differing point of view under respectively differing conditions—not infrequently with a particular purpose in mind.

The history of the coffee-house and its clientèle, on account of its tremendous wealth and diversity, cannot be either chronologically or systematically elaborated. For this reason no attempt will be made to assemble a continuum of the various phases of this history. We will restrict ourselves to a selection of themes and attempt by means of generalizing examples to highlight the essential nature of the coffee-house, its multitude of individual, social and cultural functions, in short its cultural and historical relevance.

THE COFFEE-HOUSE OF THE EAST   The coffee-house with which the 16th and 17th century travellers to the Orient became acquainted was an undistinguished small room, a free-standing wooden hut, an open tent or a small street stall. A charcoal fire—open or in a simple tile oven—in a street-level room or in a cellar opening onto an alleyway, rugs and carpets, a few wooden benches in the room and outside on the street, such was the total furnishing of the oriental coffee-house which the travellers compared with the bottegas, taverns, inns etc. of their own countries. The beans were roasted and pulverized in front of the guests, and the coffee then brewed or boiled according to the custom and practice of the particular country. In the old Turkish coffee-house which can still be found today in its traditional form in parts of rural Turkey and throughout the Balkans (Yugoslavia, Bulgaria, Albania), copper jugs stand on the edge of the tiled oven, which is kept going the whole day long, until they are used, i. e., when a spoonfull of coffee powder is added, and the jug placed in the middle of the hot plate and the coffee boiled.

A characteristic feature of the coffee-house of the East, whether Egyptian, Turkish, Syrian or Afghan, is the bench made fast to the wall, upon which the guests make themselves comfortable, their legs crossed under them. Apart from the primitive coffee-houses got together out of wood and clay, which stand alongside the caravan routes, the oriental coffee-houses are always protected from the sun and the wind. Often they also provide a good lookout-point, for example on raised stilts on a lake, or a nesting-place for swallows on a cliff face as on the Yugoslav coast, or even installed as a bird's nest at the top of a tree—this latter however being merely a tourist attraction built in the 19th century.

This type of oriental coffee-house has existed unchanged down the centuries to the present day, and a familiar and commonplace picture in many parts of the Arab world, Turkey and throughout the Balkans is the sight of an exclusively male gathering sitting behind an open shop front opposite a tiny coffee stove, passing the time drinking coffee, smoking, occasionally playing some board game or pondering (Ill. 69–73).

The early travellers to the East, in addition to the coffee-house, also encountered mobile coffee stalls everywhere. Coffee sellers plying their coffee from house to house carried in a large copper jug or a container on their back, were a common sight in the 17th century, as they still are today. The coffee pedlar would carry cups with him as well, in the same fashion as the water or lemonade seller. Another part of their equipment were small portable charcoal burners in the glowing ashes of which stood copper jugs with ready-to-serve coffee. Once the pedlar had found some customers, he could put down his load on the spot for a pleasant chat and a smoke from a water pipe, for this latter was also part of the standard equipment of the roving pedlar.

THE EUROPEAN COFFEE SHOP

For more than a hundred years, the coffee-houses which opened in Europe after 1645 onwards (Venice), either resembled completely their oriental counterparts or they took the form of traditional taverns where also coffee was served. In similar fashion the mobile coffee stall also established itself from the outset in Europe. "Coffee ambulances" were present at every market and fair during the 18th and 19th centuries, and "flying coffee stalls" were set up wherever there were customers. In Italy and on the fringes of the Ottoman empire (e.g. Armenia) the first coffee-houses had a markedly oriental appearance. In the major cities of Europe where foreigners ran the first coffee-houses, such establishments were decorated in the style which their owners knew from their own countries. The first coffee-house to be set up in Paris on the occasion of the September fair of 1672, a wooden booth, was in "Armenian" style (cf. Ill. 66), another similar one which opened a short while later was described as "Persian", while others were "Greek" in appearance. In these early days the only features matching the current fashion for the Orient in these small, simple booths, was the fact that one might have to sit on the floor and could smoke long Armenian or Turkish water pipes.

The transformation from the Italian *bottega* to the *bottega da caffè*, from the French *taverne* to the *taverne à la mode*, or to the *maison du café*, from the *Schenke* to the *Caffeeschäncke*, or from the inn to the coffee-house, was not that great—in England (1650 Oxford, 1652 London) and in the Netherlands (1664 The Hague) at least, it consisted of nothing more than a change in title and the serving of the latest fashionable drink. In England, particularly, it appeared to be the case that the transformation of the commonplace inn or ale-house to a coffee-house was completed with a change of name and the payment of a one penny entrance charge. The celebrated Will's Coffee-House for example had formerly been an inn bearing the name "The Rose". In the early days it had all the appearance of a normal tavern. Only gradually were the various rooms altered to suit the new requirements of the establishment. There was the area where the guests sat and ate, not in the uniform compartments with their high back-rests which were to become so typical of the English coffee-house, but at tables which were scattered at irregular intervals around the room and were placed together or separated according to individual requirements. In the fireplace of the room, coffee pots stood in the glowing embers, and by as early as 1700 the cashier, initially the only respectable woman in the establishment, was already installed in her cubicle.[42]

"In accordance with my resolve, I am continuing my correspondence partaking in the process of my breakfast in a coffee-house where I slept the previous night." Such was the

Daniel Defoe, writing from the English provincial town of Shrewsbury in 1727

"I found there situated around the town hall the greatest number of coffee-houses I have ever seen in one town. However, when you enter they are in fact alehouses. They clearly believe that the name coffee-house has a better sound to it!"
Quoted in William H. Ukers, All About Coffee, New York, 1922, p. 78.

59 English coffee-house. Contemporary copperplate engraving, c. 1700, in: William Harrison Ukers, *All about Coffee*, New York, 1922. The incomplete inscription "The Coffeehous Mor(1)" can be open to a number of interpretations. It could be a reference to Mol's Coffee-House, Exeter, Devonshire, which was opened in 1655. London coffee shops which began with the letters Mor include Morat Ye Great Coffee-House and Morat Coffee-House. The cashier seated at the left-hand side of the picture sold tokens (from 1/2d to 2d), which the coffee boy would collect when refilling the bowls. Each coffee-house had its own tokens.

60　An early portrayal of a German coffee-house, 1698, most probably a print of an English or Dutch original. Title copperplate in: *Das Curieuse Caffee-Hauss . . .*, Freyburg (Leipzig), 1698. Zurich, Zentralbibliothek.

tenor of a letter written by Georg Christoph Lichtenberg on 17 October, 1775 from London. So was it then possible to sleep in a coffee-house as well? However misguided such a question might appear today, in the England of the early 1700s, and indeed even to the end of the century it was a matter of course to be able to sleep in a coffee-house. The lodging-houses soon moved with the times and began to call themselves coffee-houses. In America even before 1700 it was customary for the landlord to keep rooms, for there, too, the first coffee-houses resembled those of the old country, that is to say like all European guest-houses, combining lodgings and refreshment in one establishment. In Denmark overnight accommodation was also available at the coffee-house. In 1706, for example, the travel guide *The finest European journeys* recommended lodgings in an Ålborg coffee-house.

That the coffee-houses in Germany were small and modest affairs at the turn of the 17th century, is evidenced among other things by their names: coffee cellar and coffee parlour. The German *Kaffeehaus* and the Englisch coffee-house are adaptions of existing names of *Wirtshaus* and *Gasthaus* or ale and gin or beer-house. The French word *café* first gained universal currency in the 19th century, although in France itself it is mentioned in the context of the institution of the coffee-house for the first time in 1694, that is to say more than three decades after the opening of the first coffee establishment. Later, the French were to make a fine distinction between the *grand café* and the *petit café*.

In the Netherlands in the second half of the 17th century, the *koffiehuis* was also a small parlour, in the same way that today the *koffiehuizen* are, lined with brown wood, filled to the ceiling with endless curiosities and junk, and ideal and congenial drinking places.

It is not only the names which show that the first coffee-houses were simply refurbished public houses, for the interior decoration and layout of these establishments also revealed their origins.

In the 18th century the *bottega da caffè* was typical for Italy, and similar establishments outside Italy were given the description "Italian-style" or "all'italiana". A contemporary, reporting from Vienna in 1781 wrote: "The coffee-houses are in the Italian style on the ground floor, and one enters them from the street like a shop."[43] In fact, to be more precise, the Italian style was Venetian. The basic outline or position of the establishment was both characteristic of medieval drinking parlours as well as showing evidence of oriental influence. In general they consisted of elongated rooms at ground level, furnished around the walls with wooden benches, in front of which stood wooden tables. Access was gained by a single door, and the only light came from the one bay window.[44] Sometimes the interior would be embellished by the presence of wicker chairs, but this would be the only additional decoration. The 18th-century Café Greco was a typical example of such an establishment. Originally it consisted only of a narrow room scarcely eight paces wide, against whose walls were placed wooden benches. Even Berlioz describes the world-famous haunt of artists as "a ghastly tavern" (Ill. 139).

COFFEE TENT AND COFFEE PAVILION　The oriental influence can also be discerned in the first coffee tents, kiosks and pavilions, which with their quadrangular, sexagonal and circular outline can be found from the 17th century onwards, ranging from the most simple to the most luxurious in design. The rounded outline (to suit the seating arrangement in the tent), offering an all-round view, was an added comfort to the guests, lending such places the character of a lounge. Turkish coffee pavilions sprang up alongside

Chinese tea-houses in the grounds of stately homes. Here can be seen the creation of illusion and the fashion for the oriental as is also the case with the effortlessly elegant blend of both forms of décor in the "cabinet chinois pour le café" designed by François de Cuvilliés in the grounds of the German palace of Falkenlust near Brühl, representative of many similar creations.

The coffee tents and pavilions set up along well-frequented walks on the outskirts of towns alongside garden cafés achieve their major significance in the context of the cultural history of the coffee-house, by simple virtue of the fact that they represented the first public houses of any description which could also be visited by women of the upper strata. In the year 1789, the Italian Giovanni Milani, owner of the famous Café Milani in Vienna, opened a tent of this type on the Burgbastei, where he served lemonade and ice cream. The success was instantaneous and the further development to the open-air café, the *café-confiserie* and the confectioner's shop was merely a question of time (Ill. 61, 79, 81).

Refreshment pavilions were also incorporated into town architecture (Ill. 85) but with few exceptions they were unable to hold their own as permanent establishments, and their presence, like the tents before them, was restricted mainly to town gardens and

Old English coffee-house, circa 1700

"We stumbled through a dark entrance . . . and climbed up a few steps, which brought us to a traditionally furnished room, where a throng of wildly gesticulating fellows were busily engaged like a swarm of rats in a dilapidated cheese store room. Some went, some came, some scribbled, some gossipped, some drank, some smoked, others quarrelled . . . On a small bookstand . . . hung a parliamentary decree against drinking, conspiring and all kinds of swearing. The walls were hung with gilded containers . . . These contained a multitude of rarities such as nectar, ambrosia, mead, golden elixirs, favourite pills, snuff, beauty waters . . . all as infallible as the Pope . . . so that, had my companion not told me that it was a coffee-house, I would have taken it indeed for some charlatan's parlour or the consulting room of some celebrated quack."

Edward Ward, The London Spy, London, 1704, quoted in Hermann Westerfrölke, Englische Kaffeehäuser als Sammelpunkt . . ., Jena, 1924, p. 14.

Der Caffee Garten.

61 Coffee tent in a coffee garden, *c.* 1820. In Vienna, such summer cafés were known as "poison huts". Copperplate engraving by Christian Gottfried Heinrich Geissler. Leipzig, Museum für Geschichte der Stadt.

parks. During the course of the 19th century, their seasonal existence became a common feature of the urban landscape—tents in the Zoological Gardens (Tiergarten) of Berlin, the Bodega Kiosk in Zandvoort or the Café-Kiosk Tomaselli in Salzburg.

COMBINATIONS OF CAFÉS WITH RESTAURANTS AND CONFECTIONER'S SHOPS Apart from a few exceptions, up until the first half of the 18th century the coffee-houses of Europe and North America had not rid themselves of their public-house character (Ill. 59, 76, 77). But this began to change noticeably during the second half of the century, and particularly at the beginning of the 19th century. One coffee-house after the other opened—now indeed occupying two floors or a house of several storeys, with terraces and balconies—either rented to this end or purpose-built. At the beginning of the 19th century, alongside the traditional coffee parlour, tent and pavilion, there appeared the coffee salon, which attained its apogee of classical décor during the Empire and *Biedermeier* periods (Ill. 102, 103). What the Sicilian Procopio Cultelli had begun in 1689 in Paris with his Café Procope (mirrors on the walls and marble surfaces on the tables—remains of a former high-class bath-house) was now imitated in a number of luxury establishments during the 18th century. But it was during and after the Congress of Vienna, and then even more extensively after 1850, that such a style was further developed and perfected. Unashamed luxury cafés were established, as typified by the "Silbernes Kaffeehaus" in Vienna. Opened by its proprietor Ignatz Neuner in 1824, it continued in existence until 1848, serving largely as a gathering-place for the Viennese literati. In the "Silberkammer" not only was the tableware (pots, jugs, cups, spoons) made of real silver, so too were the salvers, cake dishes, coat-hooks and door handles. Only the finest and most expensive woods were employed for the billiard tables. Expensive wall coverings and finely-chased oil lamps complemented each other in elegance and unrestrained luxury.

With the advent of the restaurant in France after 1800, combinations of the café and the eating-house became increasingly frequent. The precursors of such café-restaurants already existed in Germany in the 18th century, examples which come most readily to mind being the "Zum Hirschen" in Würzburg and the "Gast- und Kaffeehaus" in Baden-Baden. In Vienna, after 1811, coffee-house keepers were permitted to serve small warm dishes twice a day, in order for their establishments to survive, for between 1811 and 1813 there was a complete lack of coffee beans on account of the continental blockade.

Following the lifting of this blockade, increasing numbers of confectioners and pastry makers acquired permits to serve coffee, and thus the *Café-Konditorei*—a combination of confectioner's shop and café—was born, from then on to become an indispensable part of the colourful European coffee-house scene. The rise of the hotel trade, the continuing specialization and mutual overlapping of various types of catering establishments further promoted this development, and the different combinations of form which the coffee-house could take appear almost limitless (Ill. 63).

Whatever differences might have existed, from the middle of the 19th century Paris and Vienna led the world with their coffee-houses, giving rise to the so-called French and Viennese cafés, more significant for the rest of Europe and the world for their name rather than for the creation of any particular style.

Let us take a brief glance at two coffee-houses which represented exceptions in the 17th and 18th centuries by virtue of their sumptuous luxury, which was not merely restricted to furnishing, mirrors and interior decoration. Whereas the coffee-fountain[45] installed in the "Gekroond Coffyhuys" in Amsterdam was already considered a masterpiece of craftsmanship, its sophisticated mechanism was far surpassed by facilities of the Café Mécanique in Paris. Here each guest sat at a table of the kind normally found only in a fairy-tale or as the ingenious mechanical plaything of some royal household, the only difference being that here a whole coffee-house was filled with such devices. Mocha was pumped up to the tables through the hollowed-out table legs, where it could be poured directly into the coffee bowls.

HOTEL-CAFÉ AND COFFEE PALACE   After 1800, with the middle classes becoming increasingly seized with a love of travel, and with the invention of "tourism" (the word appeared for the first time in 1811), the era of the modest inns and hostelries was now past. The golden age of massive hotels beckoned on the horizon, an age which has continued unrelentingly to the present. From the very outset, these "palaces of the upper middle classes"[46] possessed a multi-purpose character, offering in addition to accommodation a number of different services and amenities. Among these, the restaurant and the café together with a multitude of other facilities, such as gaming rooms, are regarded as an almost obligatory feature. Nearly every hotel possessed its café, accessible both from the hotel itself and from the street, in other words open to the public. Hotel-cafés range in character from the coffee rooms of the English hotels of the 18th century, and the modest coffee parlour of the German overnight lodgings of the 19th century to the imposing hotel café-restaurants of the *belle époque*, which at the turn of the 20th century were incorporated on a scale appropriate to the size of the establishment in every major city of the world.

62   Parisian coffee waiter, *c.* 1848. Wood engraving from an original by Charles Albert Arnoux (Bertall) in: Jean Anthelme Brillat-Savarin, *Physiologie du goût*, Paris, 1848.

In the English hotel, the coffee room was in fact the lounge for the guests. Before 1800 it was devoid of all comforts, not infrequently taking the form of mere partitioned compartments, in which there was barely room for the bed, or the hammock brought by the guest himself. All the meals would be served in the coffee room, and anyone who so wished could spend the whole day here. During the 19th century, the open coffee room remained typical for the English hotel, and in some instances can still be found today. Modest and tastefully appointed, and in no way comparable to the hotel café-restaurants of the continental hotel, they epitomize English refinement and congenial "simplicity". We can also find the coffee room in the American hotels of the same period. As early as 1770, there are reports of such premises in "The Globe" on New York's Broadway, where over their morning coffee or tea each guest would be handed a copy of the *New York Herald*.

With the decline of the *table d'hôte*, and the simultaneous increase in the opportunity to dine *à la carte*, and with the setting up of restaurants and similar establishments gastronomy began to specialize into different fields which were to reach their high point in the multi-functional café-restaurants of the big hotels and in the beer and coffee palaces of the turn of this century (Ill. 83, 84, 88, 155).

In general there was little to distinguish the hotel-café from other types of coffee-houses. In terms of furnishing, amenities, opening times etc. it conformed to local tradition and custom and of course to the character of the respective hotel to which it belonged. Thus it is little wonder that the most exclusive and luxurious cafés (Ill. 89) at the turn of the century were to be found in the major hotels, or in other representative buildings which served similar "stately" functions, and that the grand café was located

Café Pupp in Karlsbad, end of the 19th century

"Pupp is in fact not just an elegant coffee garden, it is also a feature on the scale of the Tuileries, from which towers the 'Grand Hotel Pupp', a huge castle in the style of the Gothic Renaissance; all around are terraces, verandahs, gardens, all covered with tables for dining and drinking. Illuminated by the light of thousands of lamps, in the evening the whole effect is like a fairy-tale."

Theodor Fontane to his daughter Martha on 17 August, 1893.

in the grand hotel. One need only consider the immense labour costs and overheads required to lend these ever more elegant establishments the feudal character expected—and paid for—by their guests. Here, where service was writ large, from the marbled lobby to the sumptuous restaurants and gaming rooms, from the selection of dishes and drinks to the number of personnel, the individual attention accorded each guest was on a similarly lavish scale. The cafés of the hotel palaces which were built around the 1900s were in many respects similar. And that to the modern eye many of them seem to suffer from a monotony of extravagant elegance is very much a reflection of the spirit of that age, of a not infrequently disastrous blend of decoration and ostentation. Parallel to their acquisition of great wealth, the upper middle classes adorned their "castles" and "palaces" in correspondingly rich style—which was often far from tasteful. Ponderous gilded stucco ceilings and imitation marble were obligatory features for all cafés of this type, rendering them indistinguishable in their profligate décor the world over.

Apparently also symptomatic of this development was the relatively limited choice of names for the many hotels of this type and for their cafés. In the major cities of Europe and North America as well as in the traditional spas and watering places of the upper classes, and not forgetting the coastal towns of the colonies, we find over and over again the "Hotel Central", the "Metropol", the "Monopol", the "Bristol", the "Royal", the "Victoria", the "Continental", with their café-restaurants attached. Apart from the specific categories of hotel which lay behind certain names (for example, Bristol and Monopol), their designation was intended to convey an imperial cosmopolitanism.

Noteworthy in this respect are the changes of name to which hotels and cafés—and by no means only these—were subjected to adapt to changes in the political climate of the times. For instance during the Franco-Prussian war of 1870/71, and the First World War, in Germany the "Café Français" or the "Hotel de France" was altered to a more patriotic sounding name with astonishing rapidity. For instance the "Französischer Hof" in Baden-Baden became the "Frankfurter Hof", the "Café Piccadilly" in Berlin became the "Kaffee Vaterland", the "Royal" in Hanover and in Kassel became "Königlicher Hof" and "Fürstenhof" respectively, the "Savoy" in Cologne was transformed to the "Grosser Kurfürst".

Although there was no fundamental difference between the hotel-café and the coffee palace, there was one decisive distinction held in particular probity by contemporaries, and this lay in the respective clientèle of the two types of establishment. Thus, for example, the members of the Academy of Sciences in Berlin would meet on Thursdays in the café of the Hotel de Rome (refurbished in 1876), because "there was a more refined and tranquil atmosphere there than in the newly-opened Wiener cafés"[47].

A special feature of first-class hotels in the United States in the second half of the 19th century was the existence of two separate entrances, one for ladies and one for gentlemen. Deriving from the traditional segregation of the sexes at the *table d'hôte*, there was a strict separation in the ladies' and gentlemen's café. In other words men were only permitted to enter the ladies' café upon the invitation or in the company of a woman. As late as 1907 the commissionaire of the Hotel Astor barred entry to a gentleman to the elegant and modish ladies' café where afternoon teas with music were a special feature.

Eventually cafés were also belatedly incorporated into the old-established hostelries which had survived so many eventful years. In what is probably Europe's oldest hotel, the Hôtel Cour St. George in Ghent, built in the 14th century, adjoining the venerable old rooms is a separate café. In the Hôtel des Trois Rois in Basle, the coffee terrace, upon which both Goethe and Napoleon drank coffee, stands directly at the Rhine.

Finally, mention shall be made of some examples of the better-known hotel-cafés which are still in existence, for instance the old-established Café Nádor in Pécs (Hungary), part of the hotel of the same name, which was built one hundred and fifty years ago. When seated in the "Nádor", a visitor can dispense with the history books when seeking to ascertain the extent of the Ottoman empire, to which after all Europe is indebted for coffee. The view from the window of the coffee-house to the imposing mosque opposite is sufficient instruction.

The world-famous Café Américain in Amsterdam (Ill. 106), a gathering place for exiles and the haunt of artists, forms part of the Hotel American, built by Willem Kromhout in the finest *art nouveau* style.

The interior is still in its original state, right down to the lighting and murals, the latter already more than sixty years old. The no less distinguished Poolsche Koffiehuis in Amsterdam is located in the winter garden of the Grand Hotel Krasnapolsky.

The Café de la Paix (1872) in Paris (Ill. 126), which never ceases to evoke scenes of artists' and writers' gatherings in the minds of foreigners and natives alike, is part of the grand hotel of the same name which, with its originally seven hundred rooms and seventy salons, at the time of its construction was one of the world's largest hotels. And the exclusively *art nouveau* Café Evropa in Prague (Ill. 88) forms, together with two restaurants, part of a hotel which in former times bore the name "Erzherzog Stephan".

63   Café Français (Felsche) in Leipzig. Wood engraving from a contemporary drawing, end of the 19th century. The installation of the gas lighting in 1839 cost 623 talers and 14 groschen. Leipzig, Museum für Geschichte der Stadt.

64 Advertisement for the Café Thonethof,
pointing out the special feature of electric
lighting; in: *Wiener Almanach*, Vienna, 1900.

LIGHTING   Until well into the 19th century, the coffee parlours, cellars and houses
were lit during the evening and night time by the mode of lighting customary for the
times—by candles, oil lamps and the glow of open fires (Ill. 59, 60, 66). The candles
were placed in candelabra or on large stands, which were put in front of metal mirrors
in order to enhance their light, or on the table at which the guests sat. Oil lamps hung
on the walls or on pillars.

The dim light afforded by all these fixtures was a frequent source of complaint on the
part of customers, levelled primarily at the proprietor who sought to save money by providing only the bare minimum of lighting. And in coffee-houses lighting was more necessary than in most places. Writing from Vienna in 1792, a contemporary commented:
"The best-known coffee-house for those who enjoy reading newspapers is the
Kramersche in the Schlossergassel. But for my part one visit sufficed. On every table
two lamps burn from morning till night, by the light of which one is expected to be able
to peruse the newspapers."[48] In some parts it was the custom—in similar fashion to the
lodging-house—to include the cost of lighting on the customer's bill. Once he had paid
in advance he could order as many candles as he wished. In the Hotel Biedermeier in
Berlin, the price of a candle was the same as that for a coffee or a tea—five silver
groschen.

If the introduction of illumination by gas light (Ill. 63, 83) at the end of the 19th century resembled some kind of revolution, the almost contemporaneous development of
electric lighting as a viable possibility was indeed a true revolution. In Germany the
Edison Company (Deutsche Edison Gesellschaft)—which later went on to become
AEG—took up the patent of the celebrated inventor, and in 1883, one of the first sixty-
five subscribers to Berlin's electricity supply was the proprietor of the Café Bauer, who
thereby anticipated considerable financial reward from the installation of the brilliant
lighting in his fine establishment, a prediction fully vindicated by the tremendous increase in custom which followed in the wake of this sensation. And the fact that now and
then the lights went out due to the overheating of the generator which he had housed in
the neighbouring cellar, in no way diminished the attraction of "applied electricity". It
was to take only another few decades for gas light to be replaced by electric illumination
in every coffee-house in Europe. And from this moment on, no coffee-house proprietor
of any worth would neglect to draw particular attention to the fact that his premises were
equipped with electric lighting (Ill. 64), in addition to the usual attractions of "attentive
service", "reasonable prices" and the "latest billiard tables and bowling alleys".

SEATING   In 1849 for the first time a Vienna coffee-house was enhanced by an item of
furnishing which had immediate and dramatic effect, and which from then on was to
dominate all types of coffee-house styles and contribute in no small fashion to the spread
of the so-called Viennese coffee-house. The item in question was the Thonet chair. Together with marble tables, which had been introduced previously by Procopio Cultelli
in Paris and had in the meantime lapsed into obscurity, during the second half of the
19th century, combining comfort, convenience and elegance, the Thonet chair became
a kind of obligatory feature of all coffee establishments throughout Europe and North
and South America (Ill. 65). With the complete fitting out of the Daumsche Kaffeehaus
in Vienna with these bentwood chairs (Type No. 4) in 1849, and the order for a further
four hundred chairs by a Budapest hotel in the same year, the way stood clear for Michael
Thonet's unique design to make its triumphal progress around the globe. A series of suc-

65   Pavement café in Paris at the end of the 19th century, equipped with bentwood chairs. The placing of potted plants around the perimeter of the premises was a commonplace in all cities, generally requiring the payment of a special fee by the proprietor. Wood engraving in: *Le Journal amusant*, Paris, 15 March, 1872.

cesses at world exhibitions promoted the rapid export of his chairs to France, England and further afield. Only a small family business in 1850, by 1856 Michael Thonet had expanded the firm and transferred his premises to Moravia, a heavily-wooded region and possessing a ready supply of cheap labour. By 1860 he was employing three hundred workers, who were turning out some two hundred chairs per day. The business flourished and demand rose constantly. By 1896 his Number 14 design had topped an export total of forty million!

Bentwood settees and chairs proved themselves ideal for every kind of coffee-house, simple and luxurious alike. Thonet chairs were selected by Adolf Loos for his design of the interior of the Café Museum in Vienna in 1899, which with its sober modernity stood in stark contrast to the normally eclectic taste prevailing in the 1890s. According to him "since the time of Aeschylus there has been nothing more classical"[49].

The spread of Thonet's chairs as the ultimate in coffee-house furniture was not restricted to the West. The complementary processes of influence and adaption which we have previously noted in the context of the imitation of oriental coffee-pot forms by Europeans, can now be observed operating in the opposite direction, by which this feature of European furnishing now made its way to the East. Thonet chairs are to be found, for example, standing at the marble-covered tables of the Café Pierre Loti in Istanbul, and the daily newspapers hang from newspaper stands. In addition to these items, in Cairo's Café Fishâwy are to be found magnificent oval mirrors. The glasses in which the coffee is served are fully reminiscent of the French tradition. To the eye, the only difference here is that oriental water pipes are smoked. A more fundamental difference lies in the composition of the clientèle. Whereas formerly it consisted of representatives of the colonial authorities, today alongside upper-class members of the local population it is chiefly made up of foreign tourists.

It is typically the Thonet chair and its imitators which represent the feature uniting the small-town coffee-house in Slovakia or the village café of rural Greece or Portugal, and the Café Sperl (Vienna), the Café Reitschule (Munich), Café Einstein (West Berlin), the "Zurich" (Barcelona), and the "San Marco" (Trieste). However, the genuinely original chairs from the firm's founder will not be found in any of the finer establishments of the West today, to find such examples one would have to travel to the remotest towns and villages of Bohemia, Moravia, Slovakia and the mountain huts of the Carpathians.

MIRRORS   In Paris, the city of the mirror, the true birthday of the fitting-out of coffee-houses with mirrors goes back to the year 1702. As had been the case with the marble panels, on account of their worth and the grandiose impression they would make, Procopio Cultelli took the mirrors from the former bath-house and installed them in his coffee-house. But the fact that during the 19th century the use of mirrored panelling became increasingly frequent in coffee-houses cannot be attributed directly to their use in the first coffee-house in France erected on the site of a former bath-house. The continuity of this phenomenon is really nothing more than a sign that mirrored halls and galleries, once the centre-pieces of formal architecture in feudal times, had now gained more general currency on a wider social scale. Although the expense lavished on installing mirrors in the Café Militaire (Ill. 90) in Paris in 1770 might still have all the appearance of an aristocratic affair, nevertheless it can be said that the more the coffee-houses took on the character of bourgeois *salons*, the more importance attached to mirrors. From Vienna, for instance, we hear in 1789: "Of the coffee-houses two in particular stand out as excellent, the Milani coffee-house and that at the Hauptmaut . . . The vestibule of the former resembles a chamber of mirrors, for thirty mirrors are suspended there. This particular coffee-house is filled with customers the whole day long."[50] As with other public gathering places where the desire of the bourgeoisie to show themselves off at their best is manifest, after 1850 mirror arrangements became increasingly a component of interior decoration, and this is demonstrated above all in the mirrored opulence of the cafés of the *belle époque*.

But there are other factors which make the mirror so attractive and so advantageous for the interior design of public rooms. One of the most important of these is the illusion of size which can be engendered by their use. When one considers that some of the coffee parlours of the 17th and 18th centuries were mere vaults, which only gradually increased in size after 1800, eventually by the end of the 19th century culminating in the massive mirrored establishments, it is little surprise that this illusion of size was utilized to the full. A second reason for the installing of mirrors on the walls of coffee-houses, a place of coming and going and a place to satisfy the need to see and to be seen, was that mirrors aided considerably a view over the premises, and the possibility to observe other patrons without oneself being observed in the process.

FROM STREET BOOTH TO MIRRORED LUXURY ESTABLISHMENT   The range of catering establishments bearing the name coffee-house or café with which most localities of the coffee-drinking countries were extensively served by 1800, extended from the simple street booths to the most luxurious establishments with their mirrored walls. All the various types we have mentioned co-exist from now on alongside each other, each frequented to a greater extent by one particular social group.

The refined and elegant coffee salon made its appearance at the beginning of the 19th century during the Empire period and later into the German and Austrian *Biedermeier*, but coffee rooms and coffee parlours continued to exist alongside these as before. From the middle of the 19th century the newly-established large coffee-houses follow the many neo styles in appearance. The influence of historicism made its presence felt in the coffee palaces, to be subsequently replaced by *art nouveau* elements, but the bourgeois coffee salon continued to exist nevertheless. Apart from a few standard features, at no time has a universal coffee-house style gained any international currency. In general the design of coffee-houses has owed more to the local and national conventions of traditional catering establishments than to respectively prevailing, and to some extent short-lived, decorative fashions.

In Portugal, for example, where even the tiniest village possesses its coffee-house, the walls of such establishments are nearly always lined with tiles. This feature was even exported to the Portuguese colonies but is otherwise unique in the world.

It is well-nigh impossible to make any generalization about the features which typify the Italian, English, French or Viennese café. Anyone attempting such an exercise with reference to furnishing or service for instance in the 18th century, is meaning something different to that of the first half of the 19th century, and both periods have nothing in common with such aspects in the second half of the 19th century. The features involved are highly variegated; they can derive from both the nationality of the proprietor and from the nationality of the majority of the customers (particularly in the 17th and 18th centuries). They can also stem from other aspects such as details of decoration or furniture (mirrors, chairs), the functional division of the various rooms (gambling, reading, billiards, etc.), the type of gastronomic or other services (such as the provision of music) which have been regarded as typical beyond national frontiers and boundaries of time, playing a by no means minor role in the designation of a particular name.

The foreign coffee-house keeper in the 17th and 18th centuries

What then did the first coffee-makers in London, Paris or Vienna look like? We have no pictures of them, but nevertheless we do know that they somehow looked different. Wherever one looks, the first coffee-houses to be set up north of the Alps were established by proprietors who came from abroad, and they were to continue to come for more than fifty years. It was Greeks, Armenians, Turks, Lebanese, Egyptians, Syrians or people from the Balkans who, picturesque in their outlandish costumes, sought to make their fortune through providing the public with coffee.

In England, although coffee was already being drunk in the first half of the 17th century among private circles in London, particularly those with good foreign connections, it was not until 1650 that a contemporary was able to report from Oxford: "In this year a Jew by the name of Jacob opened a coffee-house . . . and some persons partook of the unusual drink there."[51] And in 1654, Anthony Wood from whose journal we quote, refers to the opening of a second coffee-house in the town: "Cirques Jobson, a Jew and a Jacobite, born in the vicinity of Lebanon, sold coffee in Oxford in a house between Edmund Hall and Queen's College Corner."[52]

It was doubtless foreign students who were in possession of coffee-making equipment and who also had access to further supplies of the beans. Among their guests were their fellow-students as well as this Anthony Wood, who as a researcher in ancient history sought out conversations with such individuals from distant lands.

66   Coffee-house in traditional Armenian style in Paris, pre-1700. The garçon at the door is wearing a typical oriental costume. At the table in the foreground, two ladies, two gentlemen and an abbé in conversation, to the left a game of tric-trac, and to the right card players. Title copperplate engraving in: De Mailly, *Entretiens dans les cafés de Paris et des differends qui y surviennent*, Paris, 1702.

The first coffee shop in London was opened in the year 1652 by a Greek by the name of Pasqua Rosée, "in the Church-yard in St. Michaels Alley". He had acted as servant and coffee-maker to an English merchant on the latter's return journey from Smyrna to London, and by way of reward was given premises for serving coffee to the public. In order to enlighten the populace about the beverage, Pasqua Rosée distributed a broad-sheet[53] containing all the essential information concerning coffee, in particular its invigorating properties. Each year new coffee-houses were set up, and by 1700 there were more than two thousand. A number of them continued to be set up by foreigners—for instance the "Grecian" in Devereux Court, established by the Greek Constantine— but in the meantime the majority were being run by local men and women. Although they might have borne such names as "The Turk's Head", "Smyrna", "Sultaness" or "Morat Ye Great Coffee-House", this is no indication that they were established by foreigners.

In Paris it was an Armenian by the name of Pascal who first offered the drink at three sous per cup in his *maison du café* in 1672. In the following years the people of the city were also served by a mobile coffee stall operated by a limping Greek, who charged two sous for three small cups. In 1689, the Sicilian Procopio Cultelli, who had come to Paris from Venice and who for some time had been Pascal's assistant, opened his first stall in the Rue des Fossés (St. Germain), where he remained until 1702, when he moved to the Café Procope which still stands to this day.

In Vienna, the first people to serve coffee from permanent premises (arcades) were two Armenians, Isaak de Luca and Johannes Diodato.[54] Diodato was a member of the Armenian merchant's family already mentioned above, which had settled in Vienna in 1666. The wares which they brought with them consisted of $17^{1}/_{4}$ centners of groceries, and it is possible that they included coffee beans.

In 1690, Diodato acquired the civic rights of the city of Vienna, and having a keen eye for business he mingled everywhere where deals were to be done and money made. With unerring commercial acumen, in 1685, having already obtained the right to trade in Turkish goods, he acquired the privilege to be the sole purveyor of the "Turkish drink" for a period of twenty years. With customary astuteness he interpreted this as also giving him the right to sell tea and sherbert in addition to coffee.

The first coffee shop in Vienna was thus opened on 17 January, 1685, always assuming that Diodato had not already maintained such premises long before and only retrospectively obtained a permit (i.e. in order to exclude any imminent competition). Teply is of the view that Diodato's coffee shop was located in the so-called 'Hachenbergisches Haus' until 1701, when mention is made of a coffee establishment in the Schwanfeldnersches Haus on the Stephansplatz, which seems to have been run by Diodato.

Diodato ran his coffee business himself between 1685 and 1693, but from that year his wife took over because he had to leave the city in some haste, having already spent some time in prison and barely escaping with his life. This respected and prosperous man had come under unfavourable scrutiny, his relations with the Turks being rather more intimate than was acceptable to the Viennese authorities. He spent nine years in Venice, returning to Vienna in 1701.

In the intervening period the coffee-maker's trade had become well established, and it is quite possible that Diodato would have been greatly astonished at the fate which had befallen his "sole" privileges. They belonged neither to him nor his wife anymore. The number of coffee-houses had grown every year, and every "little kitchen rat" was engaged in making coffee, either for his own consumption or to make a living. In particular from 1700 onwards coffee was being almost universally consumed throughout the city, for a Turkish embassy had been set up in Vienna, whose daily coffee requirement for its personnel totalled 25 kilos. Within a matter of a few weeks this had risen to centners, and by the end of the ambassador's stay which lasted 273 days, several tons had been consumed. The public functions, the tents which were accessible to the local population, made it a certainty that Turkish traders would have seized upon the opportunity to pass on some of the coffee to the people of Vienna for them to try, thereby earning a little extra for themselves.

Isaak de Luca, like Diodato an Armenian, acquired Viennese civic rights on 23 March, 1697, and two months later he married the daughter of one of Vienna's most respected citizens, winning in the process the opportunity to gain access to the coffee-making trade. On 2 December, 1697, together with two others, Andreas Pain and Philipp Rudolf Kämberg (probably also Armenians or baptized Turks), De Luca obtained a trading concession granting the sole right to sell tea, coffee, chocolate and sherbert. The extent to which this permit, granted without demur, was also an act of defiance on the part of the city fathers against the great number and variety of trading concessions issued by the royal household, and which ran counter to the interests of the city, may only be speculated upon. A complaint from Diodato's wife has not been preserved, and in any event such a step would barely have been possible, for royal concessions were inalienable and granted to one person only. What is certain, however, is that following his return from Venice, Diodato was no longer the central figure of the coffee-making trade. And, furthermore, it would also appear that neither was he among the eleven coffee-makers who formed themselves into a cooperative in 1714. On the contrary, his royal concession was declared legally invalid, having by now expired, despite his continuing to run a coffee-house. He did not belong to the civic coffee-makers, and it is possible that he ran one of the coffee-houses which were exclusively patronized by Greeks, Turks and Armenians, which enjoyed a less than respectable reputation.

That all the forefathers of the Viennese coffee-house trade were Armenians is not so surprising inasmuch as the individuals who brought the trade to the city, as we have seen, were nearly all foreigners (Ill. 66). Neither is it any surprise that they should have changed their premises as often as their counterparts in Paris or Leipzig, for they made plenty of money in a relatively short time, and hence moved their establishments more frequently than other catering places, renting larger premises or even straightaway buying whole houses in which they then proceeded to serve coffee.

Foreign coffee-house proprietors established the trade in other cities under similar conditions. An Italian from Milan, Frantz Minetti, who traded in tea and coffee, took a cure in the fashionable German spa Rastenberg in Thuringia in 1696. To this place the ailing and lame pilgrimaged from everywhere to seek a miracle cure from the "Fountain of health". The busy Italian hastily had a coffee-house erected and prepared beverages from the much-desired mineral water, thus in his way guaranteeing a successful medical treatment. In 1700 in Salzburg, two Italians, Caribuni and Forno, and a Frenchman by the name of Jean Fontaine, applied for and obtained a permit for the serving of "coffè, rosolio, tea, aquavit and other alcoholic beverages"[55]. In Brünn it was a baptized Turk who established the first coffee shop in 1702, and in 1714 a Syrian, Gorgos Hatalah el Damashki (Georg Damascenus) opened the first coffee-house in Prague, in the "Goldene Schlange" (Golden Serpent).

67/68 Two celebrated propaganda pamphlets for and against the coffee-houses of London, 1674. London, British Library.

Many of the foreign coffee-makers mentioned here wore their picturesque national costumes to enhance their reputations, and also to add colour to their otherwise somewhat drab and unprepossessing premises. But born-and-bred English and Germans also adopted the habit of donning this exotic attire and serving the fashionable drink in appropriate costume. Anton Staiger, the founder of the Café Tomaselli in Salzburg, commissioned the painting of his portrait in 1753 as a "royal coffee and chocolate-maker"[56] in imposing Turkish costume.

In Leipzig, with its traditional trade fairs, novelties of no matter what kind were treated rather more matter-of-factly than in other German cities. The colourful gathering of foreigners was a regular twice-yearly occurrence in the city, and hence it is not surprising to learn that it was not newcomers who first established the coffee trade here, but rather it was the local inhabitants who took things in hand themselves. The first coffee proprietor was an individual by the name of Johann Lehmann, who from 1694 ran a stall on the market place. He was soon having to devote considerable energy to keeping competition at bay, but all to no avail, for other citizens of the town were by now also well aware of the profit to be had from such a business. For instance Carol Justafft, a Turk by birth, begged in a letter to Augustus the Strong written on 15 January, 1711, "because I know no other trade, to take me into your service as a messenger, or to grant me the high and most gracious favour that I might serve tea and coffee"[57]. But he had little chance of being taken into the circle of eight Leipzig coffee-house keepers. They thwarted this application in the same manner that they were to do with a similar application on the part of an Italian, Pietro Bartolmai, in the following year.

Alongside foreigners from the Orient, in northern Europe (and elsewhere, too) it was increasingly the English, Dutch and French who featured as the founders of coffee-houses. They established such premises not so much for the delectation of, say, the people of Hamburg or Danzig, but rather out of consideration for the fact that when on their travels, the British or the Dutch could not go without their coffee or with the opportunity to peruse the newspapers. Unfortunately here, too, we do not have access to precise dates. The first coffee-house in Hamburg is supposed to have been opened by the Dutch physician Cornelius Bontekoe (the commercially astute advocate of tea and coffee, and later personal physician to the Prussian Court) in 1679 or 1680 (Ill. 14). Other sources point to an English merchant having been the first to grace the people of Hamburg with their first coffee-house. In Weimar, the first concession was granted in 1737 to a Frenchman named Louis, the courtly billiard-master at the archducal palace.

Even today the significance of the founding of such "national" coffee-houses by the alien proprietor in foreign parts has barely been subjected to any research. One thing, however, seems certain that the coffee-house trade involving such "English" coffee establishments in France and Italy, "French" and "Dutch" houses in England etc. played a major part as a gathering point for foreigners on their travels and for middle-class scholars doing their grand tour, a place traditionally occupied by the national hostelries and lodging-houses which had gradually lost their significance through the advent of the hotel trade. The first step on the way to giving the hotel and catering trade a fully international character, a process which was to be completed through the development of the world exhibitions in the 19th century, was taken it would seem by the coffee-makers of the 17th and 18th centuries, who also prepared the way soon to be covered so thoroughly by the Engadine confectionary trade, which spread after 1800 particularly in the towns of Germany, with the setting-up of the Swiss *Café-Konditorei*.

The opening of coffee-houses in England and the Netherlands, in France, Italy and Germany was not only greeted with mistrust from many quarters, in fact, the "triumphal march" of coffee and the coffee-house, as it was so aptly described by Heinrich Eduard Jacob, was opposed from the very outset. This progress was held back, in some cases decisively, by bans and proscriptions which were imposed by the authorities at various times from 1500 until well into the 18th century. The motives behind such bans on the consumption of coffee on the part of authority were manifold, two reasons, however, predominate over all others down the centuries:

Firstly, coffee-houses were shut on account of their being regarded as "breeding grounds of unrest", as gathering places for conspiratorial individuals, as meeting places for disaffected subjects who were a threat to public order and morals and, if not this, then at the least they were seen as institutions promoting indolence and idleness.

Secondly, coffee-houses were forced to close because brandy distillers and the keepers of wine and ale-houses regarded them as competition, and took action against them on the basis of their prior rights.

Both reasons were in some places directly connected in a manner barely explained even to the present day, that is to say the wine and ale-house keepers, both private and commercial, were not reticent in their choice of methods for eliminating this unwelcome competition. Among the weapons at their disposal were the reservations about the new drink expressed by members of the medical profession in the pay of the brewers, and also the increasingly vociferous political and moral disparagement of the new trade.

The first ban imposed for reasons of State came as early as 1511 in Mecca. The coffee-houses were closed because according to the reigning ruler of the city, their existence threatened the authority of the State. But a mere eight days later the decree had to be rescinded, because the reigning sultan in Cairo did not share this view. In fact twenty years later, when not only the sultan drank coffee, but apparently a whole number of coffee shops had set up business, a similar ban was imposed in Cairo itself. This was to be repeated in Istanbul in 1568, coffee-houses having greatly increased in number in the city since 1557. But this ban was also ignored. In the intervening period opinion in the Islamic countries had settled the question of whether or not the drinking of coffee was compatible with the teachings of the Koran. Previous reservations on religious grounds, behind which beyond any doubt other interests lay, too, were dispelled. Consumption of the new drink was now not only accepted, it was positively encouraged in order to combat more effectively the prohibited drinking of wine. From then on there was no hindrance to hold in check the further spread of oriental coffee shops. By now such obstacles existed in all the countries of Europe. As soon as the consumption of coffee was thrust into the centre of public attention, a variety of opponents would appear on the scene. The decades-long discussion in the East as to the compatibility of coffee with the precepts of the Koran was excluded from the outset in Christian terms thanks to the intervention of Pope Clement VIII, who, having sampled the drink in about 1600 brought to him by Venetian merchants, he declared it to be a "Christian drink", which should not simply be left without further ado as the sole preserve of the Turkish arch-enemy. From henceforth his learned followers spared no effort in searching for evidence to support this papal assertion in the Scriptures (see page 12).

In wine-drinking Marseilles, where coffee had been known from about 1644, a public debate arose as to whether the consumption of coffee was injurious or not. After much putting together of learned heads, the medical fraternity finally came out with the asser-

Coffee-houses—"breeding grounds of political unrest" and unwelcome competition to other inn-keepers in the 17th and 18th centuries

o**O**o

The closing of the coffee-houses in the 16th century

"The following instruction is issued to the Cadis of Istanbul and Galata: Repeated orders have already previously been dispatched from on high, to the effect that all coffee-houses and Tartar bosa breweries and wine-houses situated in Istanbul and Galata are to cease trading. It has now come to our attention that wine-houses and coffee-houses are once again in operation in their former fashion . . . and that vice and dissipation prevail. To this end, in like manner to those formerly, this order is in force, and I decree: upon arrival of this communication, all . . . wine-houses and coffee-houses which are situated in Istanbul and Galata shall be prohibited . . ."

Renewed enforcement of the ban on the serving of wine, coffee and bosa, dated 23 May, 1568. Quoted in Friedrich Rauers, Kulturgeschichte der Gaststätte, Vol. 2, Berlin, ²1942, p. 1272 f.

o**O**o

Pasqua Rosée encounters problems; London, 1652

"*The Greek soon had attracted so much custom that the beer sellers and inn-keepers of the surrounding neighbourhood felt compelled to present a petition to the Mayor complaining against this threatening rival on the grounds of his being 'no freeman'. Hodgers, an alderman of this borough, installed his man-servant Bowman, a citizen of England, as a fellow partner. Within a short time this latter took over the running of the coffee-house for himself, after Pasqua had been forced to leave England on account of 'some misdemeanour'.*"

Hermann Westerfrölke, Englische Kaffeehäuser als Sammelpunkt . . ., *Jena, 1924, p. 6.*

Pamphlet against the drinking of coffee

"*The humble petition and address of several thousands of buxome good women, languishing in extremity of want.*

Since it is reckoned among the glories of our native country to be a paradise for women: the same in our apprehension can consist in nothing more than the brisk activity of our men who in former ages were justly esteemed the ablest performers in Christendom. But to our unspeakable grief we find of late a very sensible decay of that true Old English vigour . . .

The occasion of which we can attribute to nothing more than the excessive use of that newfangled, abominable, heathenish liquor called coffee, which ridding Nature of her choicest treasures and drying up the radical moisture has so eunuched our husbands and crippled our more kind gallants that they are become as impotent as Age, and unfruitful as those deserts whence that unhappy berry is said to be brought."

Pamphlet published in London, 1674, kept in the archives of the British Library, London.

tion that the drink was detrimental, if not positively injurious, to human health. Clearly this declaration was based less upon medical knowledge of the physiological effects of coffee (at this time extremely sketchy) than far more on the realms of invention put into the mouths of the doctors taking part in the discussion by wine traders, who hoped to deal a deadly blow to their rival coffee importers and coffee-house keepers.

Neither did it look as though coffee would have a completely unhindered passage to general acceptance in the British Isles. With coffee having been known in Oxford since 1637, the first public coffee shop was opened in the same city in 1650. London had its own coffee-house two years later, and thanks to a regular supply of the raw product from abroad, it was soon followed by many more, despite the numerous complaints of the proprietors of ale and gin-houses. The tremendous popularity enjoyed by the coffee-houses, the apparently unusually clear heads of the disputants and not least the possibility of an extra source of taxation revenue, led in 1663 to a law being passed by the authorities, that all coffee-houses had to obtain a trading licence, and those without such a licence would be closed. After ten years the coffee-house had become an institution in the forefront of public life, and unlicenced establishments had proliferated as if there had never been any law passed, a fact which greatly displeased Charles II, who decided upon drastic measures. On 29 December, 1675 he issued an edict on the closing of coffee-houses, which not only applied to London, but extended expressly to Wales and Berwick-upon-Tweed. Perhaps Charles had assumed that the power of the Royal word would best put an end to the heated public debate concerning the relative merits and demerits of coffee-houses (e.g. "Women's Petition against Coffee" and the subsequent "Men's Answer"), which was more motivated by economic than ideological considerations (Ill. 67, 68). The reasons for the proclamation as enumerated—that coffee-houses were frequented by idle and disaffected persons, that many tradesmen were kept from their lawful calling and affairs, that they were a seedbed for the devising of false and malicious and scandalous reports to the defamation of His Majesty's Government etc.—reveal in their full detail the true interest which really lay behind it.

The proclamation was supposed to come into effect on 10 January, 1676, but it did not because its issuing had aroused such a storm of outrage the scale of which put the hitherto heated debates far into the shade. The proclamation was rescinded in the first week of January after the coffee-house keepers had undertaken in writing "to be wonderful good for the future, and to take care to prevent treasonable talk in their houses"[58]. Campaigns to suppress coffee-houses in England on anything like this scale were never repeated, instead a policy was adopted of renewing licences at regular intervals upon payment of the appropriate fee.

In the Netherlands, and particularly in the Northern Provinces, there were no such major interventions or bans on the part of the State which applied on a countrywide scale. The setting-up of coffee-houses occurred within the framework of the regulations and requisite permits of respective towns. In the Spanish provinces closures did in fact take place particularly during periods of armed conflict, as this example from the end of March 1699 in Antwerp shows: "Last Friday, in this city through the posting of royal proclamations, a ban was imposed on the maintaining of coffee-houses or the serving of coffee, tea, chocolate and on gambling, upon payment of a fine of 500 guilders and 5 years banishment."[59]

As had been the case in France and Italy with the wine traders and in England with the brandy distillers, in the towns of Germany around 1700 it was the ale-house keepers

69 Coffee- house in Baghdad. Wood engraving by Eugène Flandin in: *Le Tour du Monde*, Paris, 1861.

70 Turkish volunteers (*bashi-bazouks*) in a coffee-house in Trebinje, Bosnia-Herzegovina, *c.* 1875. Wood engraving from a drawing by F. Kanitz in: *Illustrirte Zeitung*, Leipzig, 21 August, 1875.

71   Algerian coffee-house, erected for the
Paris World Exhibition of 1878. Wood en-
graving from a drawing by L. von Elliot in:
Illustrirte Zeitung, Leipzig, 20 July, 1878.

72 Tartar coffee-house. Steel engraving, mid-19th century. The pipes were supplied by the coffee-house proprietor (in the background left). Music (left), board games (centre) or declamatory entertainment were characteristic features of such a coffee-house. Private collection.

73 Modern-day Arab street-side coffee-house in Minyet el-Qamh, Egypt.

74 Smoking Turk. This painted tin figure was a typical trade sign of Vienna coffee taverns in the 18th century. Vienna, Historisches Museum.

75 Portico of the coffee-house "Zum Arabischen Coffe Baum" in Leipzig, dating from about 1725.

Gold, Thou bright Son of Phœbus, Source
Of Universal Intercourse;
Of weeping Virtue Sweet Redress,
And blessing those who live to bless:
Yet oft behold this Sacred Trust
The Tool of Avaricious Lust.

No longer Bond of Humankind,
But Bane of every virtuous Mind.
What Chaos such Misuse attends!
Friendship Stoops to prey on Friends,
Health, that gives Relish to Delight,
Is wasted with y' wasting Night.

Doubt & Mistrust are thrown on Heaven,
And all its Power to chance is given.
Sad Purchase, of repentant Tears,
Of needless Quarrels, endless Fears,
Of Hopes of Moments, Pangs of Years!

Sad Purchase, of a tortur'd Mind
To an imprison'd Body join'd!

Invented Painted & Engrav'd by
Wm. Hogarth, & Publish'd June y' 25 1735 According to Act of Parliament
Sold at y' Golden Head in Leicester Fields Lon. Plate 6

76   White's Coffee-House in London. Copperplate engraving by William Hogarth from the cycle "The Rake's Progress", folio 6, 1735. "This is White's notorious coffee-house, about which any of our readers with even the slightest acquaintance of English literature will have heard . . . This is the establishment where frequently the value of a nobleman's estate rests on the turn of a card or the throw of a pair of dice, and once this has gone, it will be followed by houses, and often then by golden shirt buttons . . . it is the place where penury and luxury can change places in an instant; it is the source of a thousand evils and miseries, of duels, of despair, of incurable insanity, of frenzy and suicide . . . Here is the interior of White's coffee-house. A fire broke out here on 3 May, 1733, and Hogarth availed himself of this event to portray the establishment for the London public of the day . . . The expression on the faces and figures making up the company dominate the scene, diverse as they may be, and encompass the major part of the range of human emotions. Empty futility of the basest kind, true moral degradation and nihilism . . . cold-blooded detachment in the face of good fortune and comfortable complacency in the midst of the clamour of curses from the unlucky ones upon whose ruin it is based . . . It is dreadful! If one could hear it now, . . . the clatter of tipped-over chairs, the clink of large numbers of guineas, . . . and the cumbersome sliding of piles of money to and fro across the table; curses and imprecations drawing on all the reserves of the language and delivered at full volume; the accompanying barking of dogs, and in the background to all this, cries of murder and fire! What was one supposed to think was in progress here? A gaming party indeed? If it were not for the clinking of coins one could be led to believe that one was witnessing some profane debate on the subject of human rights, or a more spiritual discussion concerning the attainment of eternal salvation, or at the very least one could think one was listening to some droll conversation in the realms of the dispossessed—in the madhouse. In reality, however, it is indeed a gaming party!"

William Hogarth/Georg Christoph Lichtenberg, *Marriage à la mode and further commentaries*. (German-language edition: *Die Heirat nach der Mode und weitere Erklärungen*, Berlin, no date, pp. 108 and 195f.).

Invented Painted Engraved & Publish'd by H B Hogarth March 25 1738 according to Act of Parliament.

MORNING

77 Tom King's Coffee-House in London.
Copperplate engraving by William Hogarth
from the series "The Four Times of the Day",
folio 1, 1738.

78 Mobile coffee vendor in France. Coloured
copperplate by Louis Philibert Debucourt,
1821.

79 The coffee tents in Berlin, *c.* 1790. Etching by Daniel Chodowiecki in: Georg Hirth,
*Kulturgeschichtliches Bilderbuch aus vier Jahrhun-
derten*, Munich, 1925.

80   Viennese coffee-house waiter
Coloured lithograph, *c.* 1800.
Vienna, Historisches Museum.

Ein Wiener
Marqeur.

Garçon caffetier
de Vienne.

C.P.S.E.M.   Publié à Vienne chez Artaria et Comp.

81 Garden café in the Jardin Turc, Paris, a favourite meeting place for promenaders, *c.* 1810. Aquatint from an original by Jean-Jacques de Boissien, 1810. Paris, Bibliothèque Nationale.

La promenade du Jardin Turc.

82　Café de la Bourse in Brussels, end of the 19th century. Wood engraving from a drawing by L. von Elliot in: *Illustrirte Zeitung*, Leipzig, 10 February, 1877.

83　Café Bauer with festive illumination provided by gas lamps. It was here in 1883 that the "Bauer" became the first Berlin establishment to demonstrate "applied electricity" to the general public. Wood engraving from an original drawing by Gottlob Theuerkauf in: *Illustrirte Zeitung*, Leipzig, 13 April, 1878.

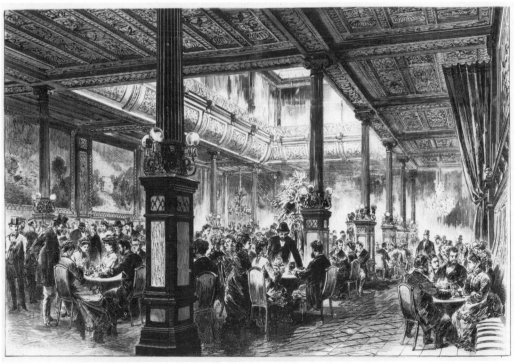

84 Sumptuous interior decoration in the
Café Bauer in Leipzig, *c.* 1900. Leipzig,
Museum für Geschichte der Stadt.

85 Café-Kiosk Schrangl in Vienna. Post-
card, *c.* 1900. Vienna, Historisches Museum.

86 Café A Brasileira in Lisbon. This coffee-house, opened in 1904, rates as one of the finest *art nouveau* cafés in Portugal, and is a protected building.

87 Café Slavia in Prague, restored to its original appearance and re-opened in autumn 1983.

88 Café Evropa in Prague's Hotel Evropa.

89 Menu cover from the Café-
Restaurant Luitpold in Munich,
c. 1900. Munich, Café Luitpold.

89 Menu cover from the Café-Restaurant Luitpold in Munich, *c.* 1900. Munich, Café Luitpold.

90 18th-century mirroring. The reconstructed interior of the Café Militaire by Charles Ledoux in Paris, 1762. Paris, Musée de Carnavalet.

91 20th-century mirroring—reflecting pillars set in wood and steel in the café of the Palasthotel, Berlin. Designed by Dieter Tucholke, 1980.

92 Café Van Ouds de Vriendschap in Utrecht. As is the case in many historical restaurants in Holland, the traditional built-in bar has been preserved.

93 Café Monico in Amsterdam, with a verandah-like frontage, one of many similar kinds of methods adopted by the coffee-house trade since the 18th century to create outdoor seating.

94 A coffee shop in Amsterdam, a typical combination of coffee parlour and restaurant to be found today in nearly every city as a response to the "fast food" needs of customers.

who viewed with displeasure the opening of coffee shops. Like any other group with vested commercial interests, both between themselves and against outsiders the members of the catering trade jealously guarded their livelihood and were quick to protect it from any unlawful encroachment. Hence the irritation with the arrival of this new trade can be understood. For around this time (1700) as had been the case for centuries before, all beverages (ale, wine, brandy) attracted generally large profits. And the fact that it was the cheapest drink of all, namely water, which was being mixed with coffee powder and elevated to the status of high fashion and a luxury drink, was not only a thorn in the flesh of the city fathers and the tax collectors, it was above all an irritant to established landlords. The dates of the establishing of coffee shops in the towns of Germany are centred around 1700 and are contemporaneous with the dispensing of tax-based privileges—in the majority of cases following upon conflicts between them and proprietors of other premises, but because of a lack of research we know too little to provide further details of individual complaints brought by ale-house or wine-house keepers.

But we do know that it was not only the inn keepers who regarded the coffee-houses as unwelcome competition. Ordinary citizens also feared for their profits. Not a few people supplemented their income by means of the non-commercial sale of ale and spirits. This customary right, which could be obtained from the local council for the payment of a small fee, was even essential to the survival of some sections of the populace (including teachers and pastors). Although this way of making a living was becoming increasingly restricted anyway, nevertheless the setting-up of coffee-houses and the spread of the drink as a whole was opposed in the early stages by a group with genuine vested interests.

Despite the superior power of the opposition groups of traders and other citizens ranged against them, the coffee shops won their place alongside other branches of the catering trade. But this did not mean that their problems were over. Once a coffee-house proprietor had managed to obtain a concession or even a trading privilege, he in turn was then fully preoccupied with keeping unlawful competition at bay, this time from among his own kind. The fact that coffee is so simple to prepare tempted many to set up business and to try and obtain a licence, or simply to sell the drink illegally.

We have already related above the story of what happened to Johannes Diodato in Vienna, but we will continue here by way of example our account of the Viennese coffee-makers' trade, being representative of similar processes taking place all over Europe. The problems of the formation of a particular trading group were, it would seem, universal. In Vienna the Court coffee-makers were banded together against the civic coffee-makers, and in turn both groups were joined in opposition to those on the outskirts of the city, in the case of Vienna those who had set up business at the toll bridge, which on account of its location would be particularly heavily frequented by travellers. Here one coffee stall stood alongside the other (initially permanent premises were not permitted to be built for defensive reasons), and their proprietors formed together into an association which was not to amalgamate with the others until the beginning of the 19th century. But once the word got around that an individual was seeking to obtain a sole purveyor's privilege, all coffee-makers and coffee-house proprietors would unite as one against him. Following his return to Vienna, Diodato attempted on two occasions to win back his sole privilege, for which purpose he deposited an immediate advance payment of ten thousand guilders with the Court chancelry. A certain Peter Koch, apparently bent upon a similar venture at the same time as Diodato, guaranteed a monthly payment of two thousand guilders. But it would appear that the city and the Court had enough money already, for neither reacted favourably to these applications. A state of monopoly control could never be achieved by one individual, for those affected, i.e. those who would have had to have closed their premises, used every means at their disposal to thwart such an attempt. And in such cases the funds which could be assembled by way of bribes for the relevant influential officials were far in excess of anything which could be put up by the person with monopoly aspirations.

In concluding our consideration of the rivalries between the individual branches of the catering trade, let us take a brief look at what in fact was being offered by the proprietors of coffee-houses to their guests in the 17th and 18th centuries. Wherever one cares to look in fact, to London or Paris, to Amsterdam or New Amsterdam, to Vienna or Leipzig, one encounters the surprisingly simple fact that there was never a single coffee-house where exclusively coffee was served. From the beginning, tea, chocolate and various wines and spirits were served—little wonder that the distillers in particular feared the contraction of their profits (Ill. 103, 104). And in the same manner that Johannes Diodato had so liberally interpreted the term "Turkish drink" to include coffee, tea and chocolate and sherbet, so Procopio Cultelli's premises in Paris also offered in addition to these four drinks flavoured wine and maraschino, ices and a variety of pastries. The bitter arguments with the brandy distillers, who proceeded to resort to the illegal serving of coffee, was gradually resolved in the fashion that had been adopted so judiciously by Maria Theresa in Vienna in 1747 who, to put an end once and for all to the endless strife, permitted both brandy distillers and coffee-makers from henceforth to sell the drink of their competitors, a position which has remained unchanged to this day.

95 Regulations for the creation of "order" in the coffee-houses of Leipzig issued in 1704. Leipzig, Municipal archives.

"It is one of the virtues of the coffee-house that all day long and throughout the night, too, one can sit among people of all classes," observed Charles Louis de Montesquieu in a letter in 1721. He was describing a social situation which had already been perceived by many from about 1700 onwards as a particularly special feature of the coffee-house. Of course this was not completely the case in any coffee-house, it had simply become apparent that the otherwise complete lack of social contact between the aristocracy and bourgeoisie was more easily broken down in such an establishment than elsewhere. For in the coffee-house it was possible in a relatively relaxed fashion and without any of the constraints of social etiquette, to discuss and converse with other people in an atmosphere of clear-headedness. Whereas up until this juncture the different estates and strata had led strictly segregated social lives, the coffee-house suddenly offered the opportunity for the aristocracy and the middle classes, foreigners and non-citizens under particular circumstances to gather in the same locality at the same time. In practical terms, however—as indeed is often the case today—this meant in the majority of cases that

> firstly, different groups preferred to frequent different coffee-houses, and
> secondly, different groups frequented one and the same coffee-house at different times of the day, in other words that the regular customers by day were different to those in the evening and during the night.

That De Montesqieu was able to describe one of the advantages of the coffee-house to be that he could sit among people from all social classes there, might have applied by about 1720 to England (London) and France (Paris), by virtue of the fact that there were already so many establishments of this kind that it was possible to proceed from one coffee-house to another and indeed to encounter people from all classes in the different premises.

In London, in particular, the coffee-house around 1700 with its variety of customers was a microcosm and a theatre of the daily life of English society of the time: "Every profession, trade, class, every party has its favourite coffee-house. The gentlemen of the law discussed legal science and scholarship or complained about the latest case . . . at Nando's or in the Grecian close-by to the Temple . . . the City met to confer on the rise and fall of shares and to agree upon the latest insurance rates at Garraway's or in Jonathan's. The academics exchanged the latest university gossip . . . at Truby's or in Child's . . . the soldiery gathered to air their grievances in the Old or at the Young Man's . . . The St. James's and the Smyrna were the headquarters of the Whig politicians, while the Tories frequented the Cocoa Tree or Ozinda's, all situated in St. James's Street. The Scots had their meeting place in Forest's, the French at Giles's or in Old Slaughter's in St. Martin's Lane. The gamblers would play dice in White's and in the chocolate-houses around Covent Garden, the artists graced the neighbourhood of Gresham's College and the leading wits gathered at Will's, Button's or Tom's in Great Russell Street, where piquet would be played after the theatre and the highest quality conversation prevailed until midnight . . . the military came together at the Old Man's, while the rich burghers and merchants gossiped over the rise and fall of shares at Lloyd's. At Robin's and Mrs. Rochefort's foreign emissaries and bankers would meet to discuss affairs of mutual interest. Friends of the arts honoured Don Saltero's coffee-house in Cheyne Walk with their presence."[60]

Until well into the 19th century, the declared aim of the by now universal trade was to provide a stopping place for all, regardless of their social status, and this was to be particularly proclaimed in the country where in the 18th century it applied least, namely in Germany's coffee-houses. We know from several sources that here, where in any event there were far fewer coffee-houses than in London, Paris or Amsterdam, not every establishment was open to all. The cryptic representation of a German coffee-house from the 1770s provides a perfect illustration of this fact (Ill. 104).

For example, in Germany until the establishing of coffee-houses and ladies' rooms after 1800, and in Austria not until as late as 1840 with the growth of the so-called *Konzertcafé*, cafés with musical entertainment, only one form of coffee premises had any kind of democratizing effect, and that was the coffee garden. At the beginning coffee pavilions and tents, as well as the gardens maintained by some proprietors during the summer months, were the only establishments which a woman could visit without putting her reputation at stake. The Sunday excursion to some nearby destination or somewhere more further afield, which became a common feature of family life during the 19th century, encouraged the growth of the kind of coffee-house, particularly those situated in the vicinity of the burgeoning cities. By 1900 Berlin was completely surrounded by a ring of such gardens. Here notice boards bore the inscription "Family coffee-brewing available"—which meant that a family would bring its own coffee powder and the landlord would supply hot water, a last relic of a typically Berlin response to the coffee laws imposed by Frederick II (cf. p. 41 f.).

In proportion to the speed with which the coffee shop emerged from its fledgling state and succeeded in ridding itself of the trappings of the *taverne à la mode*—a process which, as we have already seen, lasted several decades in some countries—and developed as an institution catering for the most varied sections of the public, coffee-houses with widely differing character came into being, which over the course of time assumed a multitude of descriptions in line with their most prominent feature, some extra service they offered or their location.

If one looks at the period between 1650 and 1789, and considers the advanced countries such as the Netherlands, England and France, one can perceive that, as a public institution, the coffee-house lent major impetus to the evolution of the bourgoisie from a class in itself to a class for itself, and to the latter's emancipation from the aristocracy and clergy, by virtue of the external framework it provided for the organizing and intensifying of bourgeois self-awareness in all its variegated and mutually contradictory manifestations. The Netherlands and England—the two countries which provided the main backdrop for the first fifty years of the cultural history of coffee-houses in Europe—already had their bourgeois revolutions behind them. They had already been using the non-intoxicating drink as a welcome positive contributory element in enhancing bourgeois productive power for several decades by the time that with the increase in coffee-houses in Paris (six hundred by about 1750) they, too, became a breeding ground for the awakening consciousness of the middle classes.

The quite open references to the State and clerical authorities both living and dead which were now to be heard as loudly in the coffee-houses of Paris as they were already in London, and the criticisms both minor and major of Absolutist policies, showed clearly the kind of intellectual forces which were starting to influence the course of world history. Of course, the existence of the coffee-house was not the pre-condition for the emergence of the bourgeoisie—to claim so would be to overestimate its role—but prominent supporters of bourgeois emancipation took their place here, and the chief significance of the coffee-house lies in its role, however restricted that might have been, as a public gathering place, which was accessible to all, of a kind which had previously not existed at all.

Between the 17th and the 19th centuries, the urban social structure underwent major changes. The constant influx of sections of the rural population, the separation of home and the workplace, the dissolution of the traditional formal craftsmen's eating and drinking habits and their replacement with loose-knit gatherings around the ale-house, the increasing possibilities for the individual enjoyment of leisure time etc. were all concomitants of the relentless upsurge of the bourgeois capitalist economy. And the demand of the middle classes to enjoy its share of the "life of ease" of the nobility was given further impetus by the simultaneous demand for education and entertainment.

In the following we will demonstrate that the coffee-house was the birthplace and home of the movement for the emancipation of the middle classes whose informal and formal groupings of particular circles of individuals were

1. associated over a long or short period with the coffee-house public (artists and writers, for instance, used to frequent coffee-houses over hundreds of years), or
2. relatively rapidly disassociated themselves from the public coffee-house, in turn to reappear as institutions, establishments or similar in their own right (for example political parties or middle-class concert societies) or
3. withdrew from public life as independent bourgeois institutions, having first constituted themselves in the coffee-house (clubs, associations etc.).

Against this background, the significance of the coffee-house as a public venue for the birth of journalism and the press, for the spread of the sciences, literature and the arts among the middle classes, for the emergence of bourgeois musical life and not least as forming the core of the emancipatory movement against the privileges of the aristocracy and the clergy, the development of an individualist political awareness, becomes self-evident.

At the same time the coffee-house became a catering establishment which, apart from providing the obligatory service of offering a variety of drinks, meals and pastries, was driven to provide additional services. For, given the relatively cheap price of the eponymous drink, no coffee-house proprietor could possibly hope to make a living from the serving of coffee alone. Games (cards, chess and billiards), entertainment (music, singing, and later cabaret) and culture (newspapers, magazines, reference works) were constantly on offer for the guests, thereby rendering the coffee-house as a qualitatively new element of the catering trade by satisfying simultaneously the need for information and diversion. This twofold character can be regarded as the origin of the multifarious nature of the trade as a whole, and at the same time as the reason for the resultant ambivalence which can be manifest for example in the seemingly contradictory atmosphere of a particular coffee-house to whose clientèle one belongs, and with which one identifies or consciously rejects.

Between the individual forms taken by coffee-houses, there are many duplications of function, and the democratizing consequences of the existence of the public coffee-house are far too diverse as to permit any kind of generalized picture. Thus, in principle the coffee-house is open to all members of the public, but the trend towards their being centres of specific intellectual activities, the creation of special facilities for regular customers, and the setting aside of rooms to hire at the rear of the premises means that already this is no longer the case. Gatherings of societies, associations or clubs behind firmly closed coffee-house doors signifies the presence of a public place nevertheless denying access to the public as a whole, and at the same time the establishing of such organizations in the coffee-house indicates that the latter itself has evolved into an institution of bourgeois life in its own right.

"Schools and universities are not half as good as the very worst coffee-house"— the education of the middle classes in the coffee-house

MEN OF LEARNING   Today the embodiment of concentrated collective education is the university or the academy. But as the age of the universal man of learning went into decline in the 17th century, and the sciences became increasingly specialized, their main proponents were to be found to a considerable extent in the coffee shops of London and Paris. In London, for instance, such establishments not without justification became popularly known as "Penny Universities". Some of these "universities" rated as places of pronounced academic distinction, where communication rather than being directed towards gaming and light entertainment was specifically oriented towards the continuous acquisition of knowledge. For example the Grecian Coffee-House (today the Devereux Court Hotel) was particularly renowned in this respect. Around 1700 it was mainly frequented by the members of the Royal Society, which had itself emerged from an Oxford coffee-house club founded in 1655. No less distinguished personages than Hans Sloane (founder of the British Museum), Edmund Halley and Isaac Newton were among its regular guests. It is evident too that their thirst for learning went far beyond the bounds of archaeology, astronomy and mathematics, when one recalls the story that one fine day these three gentlemen dissected a dolphin which had been caught in the Thames before an enthusiastic crowd of onlookers in the coffee-house.

But what was possible in the coffee-houses of England, France and the Netherlands in terms of the open exchange of knowledge between men of learning, was quite out of the question in similar establishments in Prussia. Not until 1755 was such a house founded in Berlin which in fact actually bore the name "Gelehrtes Kaffeehaus", and which had the declared objective of contributing to the growth of scientific and philosophical knowledge. But even this establishment—where incidentally billiards was also played—had more the character of a club. The membership fee was two talers, and the weekly meetings were open to members only. Basically it was really nothing more than a place of recreation for the Royal Academy of Sciences, membership of which was strictly subject to the personal decision of the King of Prussia.

Bourgeois consciousness takes shape in the press, London, 1711

"Recently I heard how I had been criticized in a coffee-house, on the ground that my epistle to Crassus was apparently an allusion to a great man who is still in high office and in all likelihood will remain so. And how would it have been had I indeed had this end in mind? I cannot accept with what right I could be criticized for such mild reproaches."
Jonathan Swift, in: The Examiner, No. 30, 1711.

JOURNALISM AND THE PRESS   Coffee-houses have been in existence on the continents of Europe and North America for some three hundred and fifty years, and the press (here for simplicity's sake meaning both journals and newspapers) has patronized these places for just as long. The history of the modern-day press commenced in the 17th century, and underwent a dramatic upsurge in the 18th century, and not a few historians attribute the coffee-house as the birthplace of journalism.

The growth of bourgeois consciousness and the emancipation of the middle classes from the aristocracy and the Church, which at the turn of the 17th century is also reflected in the setting-up of a variety of journalistic ventures, in England and France is quite evidently associated with the presence of particular coffee-houses. Until then the traditional forum for the exchange of news was the market place, the Sunday church service, or the post station, especially, however, the inn. The emergence of the coffee shop soon rendered such localities redundant. The public which frequented the latter consisted on the one hand of academics, writers and philosophers etc., who engaged each other in debate and discussion. From their ranks appeared the first newspapers, which in turn assisted the formation of a corresponding learned, literary and, later, political public. On the other hand, there were the political tub-thumpers, who eagerly enquired after every new development in all fields, to which they would thereafter even more eagerly add their own suitably "sober" comment.

Whereas in London already before 1666 the coffee-houses had become well-frequented places, in the following years their popularity increased enormously up until the 1670s. Almost every week a new coffee-house would be opened, or an already existing establishment turned into one. As has already been mentioned, by about 1700 there were between two thousand and three thousand in the city (a figure claimed by contemporaries, verifiable sources today put the number nearer five hundred), and according to the English historian Macaulay, around 1685 many of these coffee-houses had their own speaker, who would lead discussions and skilfully entertained the assembled customers with their eloquence and erudition (of whatever kind), and whose power of oratory in every case attracted large audiences—and a correspondingly large patronage for the landlord. Doubtless, too, the content of their discourses was quite different to that which could be heard from the pulpits of the day. The open discussions which were conducted here by such evidently "sober" minds aroused the displeasure of the representatives of the monarchy, not least the Church, resulting in the attempts, already mentioned, to close down the coffee-houses (see page 108).

In Hamburg, too, warning voices were to be heard as early as 1688 that the coffee shops and public houses, where much of the talk centred around the "latest developments" in England and France, were places to be avoided, so that those tempted to visit such places would not run into the danger of coming into contact with "more curious intelligence than that disseminated by their pastor"[61]. The example of Danzig, where in 1707 a ban was imposed on the distribution of hand-written newspapers in coffee-houses (printed matter was permitted)[62], contravention of which would result in a 50 taler fine, demonstrates clearly that the coffee-house had assumed a firm place in urban life as a seedbed for the emergence of bourgeois public opinion.

The members of the public who gathered in the coffee-houses of London were doubtlessly of as many opinions as there were coffee-houses, and there was no prevailing *public* opinion as such. This was only to emerge gradually after 1700. Richard Steele and Joseph Addison, two brilliant critics of the everyday-life of the middle classes, who created the first journals highlighting the morals of the day, conceived this complex question of the formation of general opinion in a subtle manner in their publications, by permitting no precedence to any one particular group patronizing the various coffee-houses. Steele presented the contents of his *Tatler* (1709–1711) in columns dedicated to coffee-houses. In the first issue which appeared on 12 April, 1709 he proclaimed that all reports of gallantry, of pleasure and entertainment would appear under the report from White's Chocolate House, poetry would be featured under Will's Coffee-House, scholarship under the "Grecian", news from home and abroad was contained in the article from St. James's Coffee-House, and sundry other items which he had to offer would emanate from his own residence.

These were houses which were known to all, and the bourgeois and commercial readership to whom the subject matter of these weekly journals was primarily directed, were able to recognize themselves in their pages. It was receptive to the kind of news in-

Benjamin Franklin in London, 1725

"My pamphlet by coincidence came into the possession . . . of a surgeon by the name of Lyons and thus became the occasion for mutual acquaintanceship . . . Lyons also brought me to Bathon's coffee-house, to Dr. Pemperton, who promised me the opportunity of an introduction to Sir Isaac Newton, something which I desired highly; however, he did not keep his word."
Benjamin Franklin, Autobiography.

"Oriental" trade signs in 17th-century London

SIGNS: HOW TO FIND IT OUT

As you along the streets do trudge,
To take the pains you must not grudge,
To view the Posts or Broomsticks where
The Signs of Liquors *hanged are.*
And if you see the grat Morat
With Shash on's head instead of hat,
Or any Sultan *in his dress,*
Or picture of a Sultaness,
Or John's admir'd curled pate,
Or th' grat Mogul in's Chair of State,
Or Constantine *the* Grecian,
Who fourteen years was th' onely man
That made Coffee *for th' great* Bashaw,
Although the man he never saw:
Or if you see a Coffee-cup
Fil'd from a Turkish pot, hung up
Within the clouds, and round it Pipes,
Wax Candles, Stoppers, *these are types*
And certain signs (with many more
Would be too long to write them 'ore,)
Which plainly do Spectators tell
That in that house they Coffee *sell.*

The Character of a Coffee-House by an Eye and Ear Witness, *London, 1665, p. 2.*

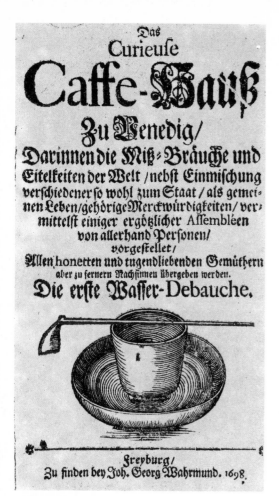

Das Curieuse Caffe-Hauß Zu Venedig/
Darinnen die Miß-Bräuche und
Eitelkeiten der Welt/nebst Einmischung
verschiedener so wohl zum Staat/als gemeinen Leben/gehörige Merckwürdigkeiten/vermittelst einiger ergötzlicher Assembléen
von allerhand Personen/
vorgestellet/
Allen honetten und tugendliebenden Gemüthern
aber zu fernern Nachsinnen übergeben werden.
Die erste Wasser-Debauche.

Freyburg/
Zu finden bey Joh. Georg Wahrmund. 1698.

96 The first German coffee-house treatise, Freyburg (Leipzig), 1698. The authorship is attributed to Sinold Balthasar von Schütz (Faramund). Zurich, Zentralbibliothek.

cluded in these weekly journals, which were designed to elevate the taste and manners of their readers. A far more likely reason behind the arrangement adopted by Steele could have been the fact that a popular format, intelligible to all, would prove attractive and stand out from the veritable flood of news publications. In this respect his calculation was certainly right, for the sheet had a weekly circulation of four thousand, enormous for those days, and each issue was eagerly snatched up.

The Spectator also featured the topics currently under discussion in the coffee-houses, thereby in the process also acting as a prime factor in the emergence of public opinion. *The Guardian*, the third most prominent weekly journal of the day, was purely and simply the house news sheet of Button's Coffee-House. The first issue appeared when Addison opened the establishment. An additional effective element in the desired objective of creating public opinion was the "Reader's Letter-box", in the form of a lion's head which from July 1713 was fixed to the premises of Button's Coffee-House. The close interplay between the public meeting place and socially-coalescing means of communication is here unmistakable.[63] Every expression of opinion on the latest issue of *The Guardian* could be posted into the lion's "most wide and voracious mouth", and each week Addison would reply to the correspondence in his "roaring of the lion" column.

From England and the Netherlands (where the journalism of the Enlightenment—both academic and literary—was also associated with the coffee-house), the idea of weekly journals with moralistic treatises migrated to the bastions of the German Enlightenment, Hamburg and Leipzig. In fact at the moment they first started to take root there, their actuality in England had already faded.

In Germany the coffee-house had no part to play in the evolution of newspapers. The publications which had been distributed since the middle of the 16th century containing the latest news of wars and trade and other notable happenings in all their astonishing profusion and variety, were purely information sheets with sparsely-worded items of news. And even the scientific journals which began to appear in Leipzig during the last quarter of the 17th century—which included Otto Mencke's *Acta eruditorum* (1682), Christian Thomasius's *Monatsgespräche* (1688), Wilhelm Ernst Tentzel's *Monatliche Unterredungen* (1689)—came into existence without benefit of the coffee-house as a birthplace.

After 1700, when with a greater or lesser degree of success, attempts were made throughout the German States to set up newspapers, the coffee-house—inasmuch as it now existed—also began to play a role as a clearing-house for news. And it would appear that the coffee-house played a particular part, under the evident influence of its English counterpart, with the advent of light literary journalism—albeit to a far lesser extent as a place of production, but nevertheless as a factor in its dissemination. The first German newspaper which might have been established in a coffee-house, but which was certainly indebted to one for its existence, was the *Das Curieuse Caffe-Hauss Zu Venedig . . .* which appeared in Leipzig in 1698, and which closed in 1707/1708 with a successor (Ill. 96). Divided up into three diversions, it described fictitious coffee-house discourse, whose themes included fashion, the love of reading, beard styles (a highly topical issue of the day!), and political diatribes. The author of the journal, which appeared in a limited edition only and which today is a rarity of the first order, was Ernst Ludwig von Faramund, a minor figure of the early German Enlightenment, who usually appears under one of his pseudonyms—Philipp Balthasar Sinold von Schütz. The author's desire to devote his journal to encourage all "honest and virtue-loving spirits to further reflection" was doubtlessly rather premature for Leipzig's conditions, for there the coffee-house, a public house in the widest sense of the term, still bore a low reputation, and a counter-publication promptly appeared entitled *Das Ausgefegte Caffee-Hauss Zu Venedig . . .*

Two decades later, by which time the coffee-house trade had become thoroughly established in the towns of Germany, the situation appeared quite different. In 1724 in Hamburg a ten-men patriotic association was formed (among which were Barthold Hinrich Brockes and Michael Richey) from whose ranks emanated the weekly *Der Patriot*. Of all such journalistic ventures this emancipatory publication had the largest circulation and the largest readership (up to five thousand). It appeared weekly from 5 January, 1724 to 28 December, 1726. The members of the association would meet once a week to discuss such issues as the law, morals, government and economics. Their meeting-place was a Hamburg coffee-house whose name is unfortunately unknown to us today. These meetings simultaneously took the form of editorial meetings for the next issue of the journal.

Among the customers of the coffee-houses of Leipzig was Johann Christoph Gottsched, editor and author of *Der Biedermann*, which by the standards of the day can be regarded as an oppositional publication of the Leipzig early Enlightenment. Following the example of the English weekly journals, Gottsched already had his first successful journalistic venture behind him in the form of *Die Vernünftigen Tadlerinnen* (circulation two thousand, price 6 pfennigs) as he published *Der Biedermann* on the occasion of the Leipzig Easter Fairs of 1728 and 1729. Gottsched had certainly never worked in a coffee-house himself, but he used its public context as an adjunct to argument, adding weight to an article by signing it as having been written in the Lehmannische Coffee-House in Leipzig on 1 March, 1728.

In Stockholm, where English and German papers were eagerly read in the coffee-houses, the first weekly journal appeared five years later in 1733. Its publication prompted considerable discussion. For two years, in the Altenecks Coffee-House and at Grigsby's, speculation was rife as to the authorship of *Den Svenska Argus*, with its highly critical articles. The identity of Olof Dalin, who had the while been secretly seated among the customers of these two establishments and who ranked among the initiators of the Swedish Enlightenment, only became apparent when the journal ceased publication.

Another association, somewhat similar to the Hamburg Patriotic Society, but with a pronounced literary character, met in Leipzig between 1745 and 1748. The first club of German journalists, although not possessing quite such an obviously campaigning name as its Hamburg counterpart, has gone down in German literary history for the journal *Bremer Beiträge* for which it was responsible.

The ten members of the club, who included in their ranks such distinguished personalities as Zachariä, the Schlegel brothers, Rabener and Klopstock, regarded themselves as having a common responsibility for the content of their paper. Their relationship was an extremely close one, some of them even sharing the same house. Giseke, Gärtner and J. A. Schlegel shared rooms in the Ritterstrasse, while Klopstock, Cramer and Rabener resided together in lodgings in another house in the same street. They convened their editorial meetings in one of the houses, but for the most part they met in the coffee-house, where a paper would be presented which they would then proceed to discuss and edit. Unfortunately the records do not reveal which of the fourteen coffee-

97   Title page of the Italian journal *Il Caffè*, 1764/65. Berlin, Deutsche Staatsbibliothek.

Das

Caffee.

Ober

Vermischte Abhandlungen.

Eine Wochenschrift.

Aus dem Italiänischen übersetzt.

Erster Band.

Zürich,
bey Füeßlin und Compagnie, 1769.

98   Title page of the German translation of the journal *Il Caffè*, 1769. Zurich, Zentralbibliothek.

houses that had been established in Leipzig in the meantime they preferred to visit, but it is highly probable that they would have patronized the houses of Enoch Richter and Johann August Pufendorf.

Even in Italy emancipatory press ventures had their origins in certain coffee-houses, although in the 18th century the dominant spirit of the times was still too Catholic there for a truly "enlightened" press with an inevitably anti-clerical stance to develop. More than a century of Spanish rule, the country's position as a pawn in the games of a wide range of dynastic interests and the influence of the Counter-Reformation, had all contributed to a growth of the Baroque spirit, but by the same token the European Enlightenment with its enthusiasm for education and knowledge was either stopped at its borders or treated as a foreign import to be watched over with the utmost vigilance and suspicion. An exception to this, however, which achieved recognition far beyond the borders of Italy in the middle of the 18th century, and which achieved continent-wide status as contributing to the overall development of the bourgeois ideal, was a journal entitled appropriately enough for our context *Il Caffè* (Ill. 97). In Lombardy, which had been annexed to the Austrian monarchy since 1714, Charles VI and then Maria Theresa—in a spirit of enlightened Absolutism—had given their support to a number of attempts to introduce large-scale economic reforms. For three years from 1764 to 1766 *Il Caffè* became a leading witness to this reform programme. In imitation of their English and French counterparts before them, the leading figures of the Enlightenment in northern Italy met in coffee-houses; and what had evolved over the course of decades in the former two countries, was now emulated in rapid succession in the coffee-houses of Milan and Venice. A circle was formed which called itself the Società del Caffè, consisting among others of Pietro Verri, an economist in high favour with Maria Theresa, who had performed undoubtedly major service in the reform of the economy together with his son Alessandro, and the outstanding lawyer Cesare Beccaria, a public law specialist. All of them were in addition members of the Accademia dei Pugni. Skilfully exploiting the liberal sentiments of the Austrian empress against the Jesuit censorship otherwise prevalent in Italy at the time, they were able to publish this opposition paper which won major credit with its reputation as the mouthpiece of the Italian Enlightenment. Following the example of Addison's *Spectator* which they consciously took as their model (although here the authors signed their own articles), they brought out *Il Caffè* every ten days. Its contents ranged over subjects as economics, the natural sciences, law, politics and literature. The wide-ranging themes and the incisive character of the paper's critical approach went far beyond that which could be read in the German press of the same time, which had in the meantime reached flood proportions in terms of the number of publications being produced.

It was probably the content of *Il Caffè*, in particular the contributions by Beccaria, which prompted the versatile Johann Heinrich Füssli, a committed advocate of the spirit of Enlightenment, to translate parts of the paper and issue it in Zurich in 1769 (Ill. 98). Füssli, who had visited Jean Jacques Rousseau in exile in Geneva in 1762, and who had undertaken a study-tour to Rome the following year where he made the acquaintance of Johann Joachim Winckelmann and Angelika Kauffmann, rated as an extremely clever opposition figure, and among Zurich's conservative circles was even regarded as an "undesirable subject". Like his brother, Füssli was a Republican through and through, and it was his commitment to everything which contributed to the bourgeois enlightenment which led him to publish articles from *Il Caffè* in Switzerland.

Füssli had got to know the paper in Italy, but whether he had actually made the acquaintance of Beccaria himself, whose work on crime and punishment had deeply impressed him, one can only speculate. For Füssli, who led an extremely simple life-style and whose ideal was the rejection of luxury and the "hygienic duty of moderation", the frequenting of coffee-houses was nothing short of reprehensible; in his writings he vigorously attacked social gatherings for the purpose of diversion or, even worse, the playing of cards.

From the English *Tatler* with its coffee-house rubrics in 1709 to the Italian *Il Caffè* some fifty years later, there is a broad range of examples of the interplay between the coffee-house and the emergence of middle-class journalism. But it is evident that in the German States in the second half of the 18th century, the authors of weekly journals were far less likely to be found in the coffee-house in the common cause of reason—but to the same degree were equally likely to be found in the schoolhouse or the vicarage. And from these sources stemmed the attacks against the coffee-house as a place of unseemly expression of discontent against authority. Titles such as "Weekly paper for the tea table" or "Something concerning tea and coffee for Germany's maidens and ladies", selected here at random as representative of a veritable flood of such light periodicals in the 18th century, were concessions to the coffee-drinking public in Germany accepting the attractions of the drink which in the meantime had become regarded as a luxury, but had nothing in common with the aggressive and bluntly conceived "coffee journals" which were by now appearing in great profusion in France.

During the 16th and 17th centuries the distribution of printed matter such as broadsheets and decrees in the inns and hostelries of Europe was by no means uncommon. Leaflet sellers found a ready market for their tracts and broadsheets among landlords. The desire to look beyond the narrow confines of one's own horizons was already so widespread by the end of the 17th century that landlords, "particularly in the villages", would serve free of charge "anyone who has in his possession a printed leaflet and permits the reading of the same"[64], and would do everything to come into the possession of news.

This being the case, over the course of time the coffee-house assumed a special significance in the distribution of the daily publication of news. And it was not simply a question of the reading of printed matter which had arrived on the premises more or less by chance, to be read aloud and discussed, but systematic efforts were made to obtain and distribute specific material. For the coffee-house trade, subscribing to newspapers was obligatory, for other establishments too it was still possible for some time. "Coffee shops and public houses make their living in this way, and at the same time make themselves all the more attractive for casual passers-by to visit."[65] Gradually the providing of newspapers for customers became exclusively reserved for coffee-houses. At the end of the 18th and beginning of the 19th century, in particular Hamburg, Leipzig and Vienna were renowned for the great variety of newspapers which were available in their coffee-houses.

The close relationship between coffee-houses and the press has continued down the centuries, sometimes more, sometimes less intensively, on some occasions even showing a reverse trend; but it was always present to some degree. During the 17th and 18th centuries, in many places the press actually came into being in the coffee-house itself. Information was passed on and exchanged, written down and edited, and the result was a newspaper. By the 19th century, newspapers were being more consumed than pro-

Biedermeier journalism in Berlin coffee-houses
"The sun is setting, it is evening. From the confectioneries of Stehely, Sparpagnani, Giavanoli, Josty, Courtin, and however else the free Swiss gentlemen like to call themselves who have brought cake instead of freedom to us, there emerge the celebrated political correspondents of Berlin. Their faces are lit up, they have just confected so much news to be able to assemble an article containing diplomatically veiled attacks."
Unsterblicher Volkswitz. Adolf Glassbrenners Werk in Auswahl, *edited by Klaus Gysi and Kurt Böttcher, 2 vols., Berlin, 1954, Vol, 1, p. 82.*

duced in coffee-houses, but there were still coffee-houses where political journalism was very much evident.

By the end of the 19th century, when coffee-houses had to some extent taken on massive proportions, the volume of press publications had assumed no lesser dimensions. The possibilities presented to the coffee-house as a place for the enjoyment of newspapers was virtually limitless, when one considers, for example, that in Germany alone there were some six thousand five hundred daily newspapers being published in 1887. Hundreds of these plus many more foreign-language publications would be available free of charge in coffee-houses for the perusal of customers. In Switzerland in 1913, the *Neue Zürcher Zeitung* was appearing six times a day, with two morning, two midday and two evening editions. Thus anyone sitting in the city's Café Odeon would barely have finished reading one edition before the next issue would be placed on the table by the waiter (Ill. 105).

THE BOOK TRADE   The production and consumption of the daily press in the coffee-house, particularly in the early decades in London, Amsterdam and Paris, would be attended for the most part by those responsible for its distribution outside this locality, in other words both by reputable and serious booksellers as well as by the less esteemed leaflet and picture sellers, who in the 17th century purveyed to the public with great speed throughout the country "weekly and special newspapers and broadsheet, as well as small fairy-tale books"[66], and rather more frequently, scurrilous ballads and gruesome horror stories.

By about 1700 there were booksellers in towns who set up business directly in coffee-houses, others established themselves in addition to traditional locations such as in and around churches, in the immediate vicinity of coffee-houses where circumstances permitted.

That publishers and booksellers should mainly frequent those coffee-houses, where such existed, patronized by men of letters or members of universities, is not hard to imagine. "The learned produce and the learned consume the bookseller's wares", which are made "by and for none other than the learned themselves", was the judgement delivered by Adrian Beier in his report on the book trade written in 1690, referring to more high-class literature. Trivial literature of a lesser quality was brought into coffee-houses by itinerant tradesmen or sellers of cheap goods, provided they were not barred by the landlord, who from the early days of the coffee-house onwards often enough ran a profitable line himself in the sale of books. In London, for instance, as early as 1657 books were being sold "by D. Pakeman at the Rainbow near the Inner Temple Gate", and in 1662 the witty dialogue *The Coffee Scuffle* was published, bearing the inscription "Printed and are to be sold at the Salmon Coffee-House, near the Stocks Market". There is plenty of evidence of coffee-house keepers who conducted a subsidiary trade in the sale of books until well into the 19th century in England, France and America. There is record of many complaints from outraged booksellers that the regular book trade was being ruined by the owners of bric-a-brac shops, grocery stores and coffee-houses dealing in books. Naturally these complaints contain no reference to the fact that for many coffee-house keepers this ancillary trade was essential for their continued survival.

Just as the Paris book trade was mainly concentrated around the Palais Royal, where simultaneously many coffee-houses were located, so, too, the English book trade was similarly closely associated with the coffee-house trade, both figuratively and geographically. For instance between Rainbow's and Tom's Coffee-House were situated the two bookshops of Meadow and Brotherton, a few paces further on in Cornhill there were three further bookshops (Strahan, Walther, Ascley) and two more coffee-houses, the New Union Coffee-House and the Union Coffee-House (according to the map of the city dated 1748). In this centre of the book trade, of sixteen adjacent houses there were five bookshops and four coffee-houses—hence the journey for the coffee-house customer to the bookseller's was as short as the journey for the bookshop owner to the coffee-house. For Carlo Goldoni, the stage-set of his *English Philosopher*, which depicted a square in London, consisted of course of but two shops, a coffee-house and a bookseller's.

Whereas in London and Paris, and above all in Amsterdam, the centre of the European publishing trade in the 17th and 18th century, the bookshop and the coffee-house were two intimately associated social institutions whose existence was logically mutually interwoven, this was not evident to anything like such an extent in any of the centres of the German publishing trade in the first half of the 18th century, neither in Frankfurt (Main), nor Hamburg or Leipzig. It was not until the last third of the century that a coffee-house was established in Leipzig bearing all the hallmarks of a meeting place for booksellers, and furthermore whose premises witnessed the birth of the most important institution of the German book trade—the *Börsenverein*. The establishment went by the name of Richter's Kaffeehaus, originally set up in some rooms of the Romanushaus in 1772, and then transferred to its own premises in 1794 in the Katharinenstrasse, standing there until the year 1794 (Ill. 102).

One of the last in this line of booksellers who set up residence in a coffee-house, is described by Stefan Zweig in his novel *Buchmendel*. Before the First World War, in Vienna in a "small café on the outskirts of the city, of a traditional almost quintessential character, without any of the new-fangled trappings imitative of the German-style inner-city music parlour, solid old Viennese, filled with insignificant people who consumed more newspapers than pastries", there lived a giant of bibliographic memory by the name of Jakob Mendel, "a magician and middleman of books, who steadfastly sat here every day from morning to evening, a landmark of knowledge to the glory and honour of the Café Gluck!" Glory and honour to the Café Gluck on the one hand, profitable business on the other. Neither does Zweig neglect to relate why, despite partaking only to a small extent of the café's services, Jakob Mendel was able to set up business here on a permanent basis: "For on every occasion, his numerous clients and inquirers were pressed in the friendliest manner by the staff to order some refreshment, so that the major portion of the profit from his knowledge flowed in fact into the thick leather wallet at the hip of the head waiter Deubler."[67]

In the same manner as journalists, publishers and booksellers are also to be found associated with the coffee-house as a place for the production of books, in the most diverse of ways, at times especially closely and in other times or places less perceptibly. The mutual attraction between the representatives of the production, distribution and consumption of the written and printed word becomes particularly marked in the context of the history of the coffee-house in the literary milieu of the Bohemia of Paris, Prague, Berlin and Munich around the turn of the century.

READING ROOMS AND CLUB ROOMS IN THE COFFEE-HOUSE The evolution from the coffee-house newssheets of the 17th and 18th centuries to the reading room of around 1800, and finally to the reading café of the late 19th century—which culminated in Vien-

Richter's coffee-house at the end of the 18th century

"In particular, however, in the year 1782 the population were infused with a new spirit which emanated primarily from Richter's coffee-house, renowned not only in Germany, not only in Europe, but in America and Asia too . . . Here, among others, the most important foreign personages gathered during the city's trade fairs, here business of the greatest significance was conducted, and here the setting up of the great association of German booksellers first took root."
Leipziger Tageblatt, *January, 19, 1838.*

99 Lloyd's Coffee-House in London, 1763, the birthplace of the insurance firm Lloyd's of London. Contemporary copperplate engraving. Private collection.

"Another almost equally important location is Lloyd's Coffee-House, which is situated in the same building whose courtyard forms the Stock Exchange. Frequency of visits in no way diminishes one's sense of wonder at this—in its own way unique—gathering place. The reader will be aware from numerous descriptions what takes place here. From early until late, the place swarms with business people and merchants. The rooms are in fact halls with a composition floor. One of the halls has a kind of cupola. Here, as in all English coffee-houses, cubicles and tables are arranged along the sides, upon which lie writing materials and thick sheaves of business letters from all over the world. Many are engaged in writing and reading; only a few are actually attending to their appetite; the majority wander around talking with each other; one sees groups gathered everywhere; one can hear from all sides the words ship, stranded, wrecked, arrival, casks, rich, good house, broken, loss and the like, and from these fragments of conversation emerges a fascinating picture of trade on the high seas. On a small table one can see a few bills and penny post letters which, apart from bearing the name of the addressee, are all addressed to Lloyd's, because people from large businesses find it convenient to open their correspondence here on the spot, being then able to make their necessary dispositions. What is most noticeable, however, are the large books of which several lie open in the various halls. As is generally known, they contain details of the arrival, departure, wrecking, seizure and battles etc. of the merchantmen and convoys, for the perusal of the public. In the newspapers these interesting communications are called 'Lloyd's book'."

London und Paris, *Vol. 5, Weimar 1800, p. 112 f.*

---

na's Café Central, a kind of library with coffee service—was a lengthy process. It brought the coffee-house trade much honour as an upholder of culture, a role which it did not always take on quite so voluntarily as might be supposed. Having come into existence with the proclaimed object of providing both information and entertainment, the coffee-house keeper gradually witnessed the emergence of a whole number of different competing ventures (for example reading societies and educational associations), which he was forced to counter by setting aside extra space as reading rooms, even when this section of his premises brought in less profit than it should. Billiard saloons, reading rooms and ancillary rooms set aside for private functions are three mutually dependent elements which, in economic terms, have assured most coffee-house proprietors their survival. One would be unthinkable without the other.

Even in the 17th century in England, groups of individuals with interests in literature, economics or politics were gathering in the coffee-houses, sitting separately as clubs or associations, and making a major contribution to the evolution of bourgeois society. The Rota Club, a group devoted to the propagation of republican ideas, met for a whole year in "The Turk's Head" before the overthrow of the republic in 1660, when the Royal Society which itself had evolved from the Oxford Coffee Club for the dissemination of royalist ideas made the Latin Coffee-House its headquarters.

Of the "unpolitical" activities undertaken in coffee-houses, perhaps the most famous is the fascinating story of the birth of Lloyd's of London. Edward Lloyd, proprietor of a coffee-house bearing his name (Ill. 99), made a profitable business out of the gossip and news circulating among the customers of his establishment. He carefully recorded the news of events on the Seven Seas filtering back to his coffee-house via the many mariners, ship owners and exporters who congregated there. Having systematically compiled these maritime reports, he published them in the form of a newssheet by the name of *Lloyd's News*. Soon he became involved in the business of obtaining passes, taking commission for the setting-up of voyages, and trading in insurance contracts and freight bills. This lucrative sideline was transformed into the main business of the establishment by Lloyd's successor who, together with about a hundred private insurers, founded Lloyd's Coffee-House and were responsible for the publishing of *Lloyd's List*, which first appeared in 1738. Over the course of time, the coffee-house trade gradually receded into the background, and from the exclusive financiers' club in Lloyd's Coffee-House, there emerged the Lloyd's of London, one of the largest insurance undertakings in the world.

One can only speculate how many clubs, associations or societies were brought into being by a group of regular coffee-house customers getting together, or indeed how many were actually resident for a certain period in a certain coffee-house, particularly when one considers, for example, that among the groups regularly convening at Merchants' Coffee-House in New York in the 18th century, were the Independent Rangers, the Federal Republicans, The Society of Arts, Agriculture and Economy, the New York Committee of Correspondence, the New York Marine Society, the Chamber of Commerce of the State of New York, the Whig Society, the Society of the New York Hospital, St. Andrew's Society, the Society for the Promotion of the Manumission of Slaves.

Outside England and North America, too, during the 17th and 18th centuries, only a door separated the regulars' table from the consciously organized format of intellectual exchange or social gathering, which in the 18th and 19th centuries took on institutionalized form as a club or association. This was the door which led to the reading room or to one of the side rooms in which by the end of the 19th century nearly all the social groups of an increasingly stratified bourgeois society had sat at least once, as a means primarily of asserting their identity, or to a lesser extent to do business with one another.

In Germany, the coffee-house as a club venue was still the exception during the 18th century, but by the middle of the 19th century it had become the rule. During the course of the 18th century, following England's example, the German middle classes gained in self-confidence and awareness, and by means of a great number of patriotic, literary and economic and other associations, began to depart from the established order, replacing it with new social structures. *Delectare et prodesse* (delight and benefit) might have been the unwritten motto of the coffee-house enlightenment in England, which the advocates of the German Enlightenment eagerly sought to transplant into their own intellectual world, but barely had this noble emancipatory ideal been taken out of the bastion of liberation which were Frankfurt on the Main, Leipzig and Hamburg, and into the provinces and assumed formal character, than the "edification" element became somewhat less in demand. In the age of so-called refinement, of the cult of friendship, of the awakening of national sentiment and patriotism, the coffee-house was not yet the place for the cultivation of such ideals. For patriotism is synonymous with love of one's fellow man, with the acquisition of education and the duty of enlightenment and as such includes admonitions of virtue, simplicity, moral rectitude and the shunning of luxury. In some puritanical associations this is even incorporated into their statutes. Thus, for instance, Paragraph 2 of the Historical and Political Association, founded in Zurich in 1762, reads:

"The venue for meetings should be a public place such as a guild house, and for the duration of a meeting no tea, coffee or wine should be drunk by any member, and neither should tobacco be smoked."[68]

100 Meeting of the deaf and dumb association in the Café Schiller, Vienna. Wood engraving from an original drawing by W. Grögler in: *Illustrirte Zeitung*, Leipzig, 14 October, 1865.

Of course such strictness was not imposed everywhere. But even "respectable" reading societies which had been set up in a coffee-house (because such a facility had been offered by the landlord himself, or indeed had been directly set up by him), had to suffer the suspicion for several decades of being in competition with such puritanical institutions as museum and reading societies.

In the course of time the initial aversion to coffee-houses as a meeting place shared by the founders of associations in Germany began to diminish, not least because the coffee-houses themselves had in the meantime polished up their image as café-restaurants and salons, and were doing everything they could to attract to their premises literary and arts societies, social and amateur clubs, welfare and trade improvement associations, sports and collectors' clubs, choral societies, chess and bowling clubs, in fact every kind of group or association which existed in the middle of the 19th century.

In Ulm, for instance, as early as 1825, the "Liederkranz", the town's first song club which had evolved from a Freemasonic lodge, was meeting every Thursday in the Spangenberg'sches Kaffeehaus. By 1835 it was being rivalled by the song-club "Sängerkranz Amitia", which met on Mondays, and from 1836 onwards the same establishment played host to monthly gatherings of the citizenry, "by means of discussions and lectures on manufacture and commerce, to acquaint themselves with the latest developments in these fields"[69]. From this burghers' gathering evolved the Trade Association and the Chamber of Commerce which soon after their formation moved out of their coffee-house venue.

In 1863, according to the account of two travellers we read that nearly everything in Leipzig on two legs belongs to some sort of society, and that nearly every one of the twenty-nine coffee-houses in the town housed at least one, but in most cases several of these important and highly stratified leisure-time associations, which in the 19th century formed a major feature of everyday-life in many countries.

A cursory glance world-wide at the self-portrayal of the catering trade in contemporary advertising literature, from New York to Budapest, from Buenos Aires to Istanbul, provides sufficient evidence that at the latest by the middle of the 19th century, nearly all large coffee-houses were simultaneously the meeting places of clubs and societies (Ill. 107), as the following examples demonstrate: In 1898, the Café Louvre in Vienna is the venue for the philatelists club, in the Café Schiller the deaf-mute society meets on Sunday mornings (Ill. 100). The Marienbad Cycling Club meets in the Café-restaurant Zischka. In Budapest, the Central Carambol Club meets at the Café Elite. In the early 1900s, a German cards club has its meeting place in the Parisian Café de la Terrasse, and last but not least, the German Workers' Association meets on Saturdays at the Café Procope.

Games and entertainment in the coffee-house

To entertain and to be entertained, to educate oneself and to be educated—there is an almost limitless range of possibilities for the customer to enjoy entertainment and education in the coffee-house (Ill. 109). Like the catering trade in general, the coffee-house facilitates the two most basic kinds of sociability in the broadest sense, those in which the customers themselves play an active part, and those where they passively listen or watch.

Dice, cards and board games as well as musical forms of entertainment were to some extent taken over into the coffee-house from other traditional establishments and

Preceding page:
101 "All that's to be read is read." Berlin
Reading Café, painting by Gustav Taubert,
1832. Berlin (West), Berlin Museum.

102 Richter's Coffee-House in Leipzig,
birthplace of the German Booksellers' Association. Copperplate engraving by J. Wagner,
1794. Leipzig, Museum für Geschichte der
Stadt.

103   Stylized portrayal of a Vienna coffee-house. Coloured chalk lithograph by August Strixner from an original by Carl Joseph Geiger, 1839. Vienna, Historisches Museum. The illustration is folio 24 from the series "Der Mensch und sein Beruf oder Lexikon aller Stände" (Man and his vocations or a lexicon of all estates), 1835–1841. The accompanying commentary explains: ". . . the coffee-house keeper requires a certain tact in dealing with his customers in addition to a precise knowledge of the different kinds of coffee . . . It can be readily appreciated that the other items provided by the coffee-house keeper require a similar precision and industry. Almond milk, ices, different sorts of tea, all fine liqueurs, punch, lemonade, grog . . . are the commonest items with which one is served in coffeehouses."

104 Allegorical depiction of a German coffee-house, *c.* 1770. Sepia drawing by an unknown master. Dresden, Staatliche
Kunstsammlungen, Kupferstichkabinett.
Everything can be bought, that is to say, entry
is open to all who can pay, and the wide-open
door in the centre of the picture bears the inscription "Frei und Franc", or "open house"—
but the proprietor, his fist clenched and his demeanour given emphasis by the dog snarling
at his feet, appears to be attempting to refuse

entry to a new arrival who is trying to force his
way in, pointing in the process at the tariff list
hanging on the wall. Judging by his outward
appearance, this individual does not seem to
belong to the same class as the rest of the company gathered here. He is unshaven and wears
no wig, he has patched trousers and seems to
be carrying a wooden tankard in his hand,
which all indicate that he belongs to a lower
class whose presence here is undesirable. The
table of charges hanging on the wall, which

bears the prices for coffee, tea, chocolate,
punch, various wines and schnaps, is faithfully
reflected on the five tables around which they
are grouped. Closer inspection reveals that this
coffee-house clientèle is by no means so refined
as would first appear to be the case. At the
coffee and tea table a young couple are seated opposite to each other. The scene would
seem almost affectionately portrayed, were it
not for the preacher standing over them, his
gout-ridden hand upraised in a blessing, and

were it not for the arrangement of the hands and the glances of the people standing around them, which alone are an indication that something else is in progress here than what is apparent at first sight. The saying "The cuckold's cap is his who wavers, as his wife accepts another's favours", is directly applicable here. Under the table where the wine drinkers are seated geese and a vulture can be seen. On the table itself a rat gnaws at the globe, and a monkey reaches out to a quill pen. The symbolic

use of the animal figures provide an indication of the true character of the company, which can only be sketched here. The pig, shown eating acorns, is meant to represent ingratitude to God. The vulture is allegorical for the legacy hunter, possibly a reference to the young man raising his glass in a toast. The monkey is a general symbol of evil and depravity, particularly avarice. A couple is shown standing in front of the window to the right of the picture. The man is resting his arm on the hip of the

woman, and the inscription over the window is a clear reference to the fact that love, too, can be bought. Perhaps this coffee room is even part of a house of "ill-fame". The more one looks at the scene, the more questions it poses. One thing, however, remains clear, namely that this establishment is not open to all, however much this impression is intended to be conveyed by the ambiguous tone of the list of charges.

ODEON

MENTOR · VERLAG · ZÜRICH

105 Poster advertising the Café Odeon of the Hotel Odeon in Zurich. Lithograph by Hugo Laubi, 1920. Zurich, Kunstgewerbemuseum, Plakatsammlung.

106 Café Américain in the Hotel American, Amsterdam.

107 Café and club-house of the Jockey Club in Paris. This palatial establishment, erected in 1865, comprised—in addition to a public café on the ground floor—a large billiard hall, a dining hall, four gaming rooms and a sports hall, where portraits and photographs of famous jockeys were hung, and all English and French sporting papers were displayed. Wood engraving in: *Illustrirte Zeitung*, Leipzig, 14 October, 1865.

specifically encouraged, to some extent new forms and variations were developed and took on a new quality. Simple card and board games (Ill. 66) were replaced by more complex ones; rope-trick performers and bear and other animal trainers, travelling people who would perform in or outside public houses gradually disappeared to make way for "salon" appearances of singers and conjurers, acrobats and the like, until these too in turn left the coffee-house to be replaced by variety and cabaret. Regardless of the form taken by this coffee-house entertainment, whether provided by the customers themselves or by outsiders, in all cases it served to enhance the social atmosphere and to encourage the public to spend more time on the premises, resulting in justifiable anticipation of a greater consumption of food and drink on the part of the landlord. ⌋

CARDS AND DICE   According to an edict issued by Frederick II in 1787 "inn keepers and coffee-house keepers, sellers of wines and ales and in general all those engaged in the carrying-on of businesses where the public gather who tolerate the playing of proscribed games on their premises . . ." are strictly required to cease, failure to do so resulting in a fine of three hundred talers or a three months' imprisonment. "If they have set aside closed rooms for such games or otherwise sought to conceal them, the penalty will be doubled." Even the marqueurs were required to report customers indulging in games of chance to the police authorities immediately—failure to do so would resulte in their being subjected to corporal punishment! In the first instance it was specific card games which were banned by this royal decree, because they not only resulted in time-wasting but also encouraged the thirst for profits. Laws had been in force in Prussia since 1714, of a kind very similar to those in France, Austria or other German States. Between the 16th and 18th centuries, such bans existed all over Europe, and in no century were they less adhered to than in the 18th century, which bears the distinction of being known as the "century of gaming". Sufficient evidence of this is provided alone by the multitude of card games which were prohibited or the addiction to gaming present in many localities. As early as 1714, coffee-house keepers in Vienna were being threatened with fines of up to one thousand ducats if they permitted on their premises the playing of "Bassetta, Trenta Quaranta, Landsknecht, Faro, Färbeln, disorderly games, dice, Banco and Bassa Dieci". In Prussia in 1787 a ban existed against "Bassette, Lansquenet, Faro, Quinze, Cinq & Neuf, Passe à dix, Trischacken and dice", and which in addition to the so-called Biri-biri game applied to all games of chance with cards, dice or other symbols, "be they already invented or yet to be devised".

With the continued consolidation of the bourgeois age, the gain in economic strength and not least the completely novel positive value attached to useful labour, production and competition the coffee-house during the 18th century, being synonymous with "gaming-house", came under considerable attack from contemporary critics (Ill. 76). Not infrequently this censure came from those who would sit for hours over one cup of coffee in the reading room, helping themselves to the newspapers provided free of charge by the proprietor, while in the strictly segregated back-room players would be huddled over the forbidden card games from which the landlords had a share in the proceeds.

At the end of the 18th century private gaming declined markedly, or at least lost much of its social significance. State-run lotteries proved adept at channelling off the fruits of the general addiction to gambling into the appropriate coffers. In France even before the Revolution lottery cafés existed whose proprietors on the one hand supported the State's gaming monopoly, and on the other made their own profit through the sale of tickets. In the meantime the middle classes were devoting themselves to ever more serious and useful pursuits. "Europe puts on its working clothes. Cultural life is dominated by social responsibility, educational aspirations and scientific criteria."[70] The preoccupation with gambling became a pleasant diversion to while away the leisure hours. The enormous sums spent on gaming were reduced to a more tolerable level, enhancing the attractions of bridge, whist and taroc as coffee-house pastimes without representing any significant drain on the pockets of the good burghers patronizing such establishments. In the course of time there developed in the coffee-houses of Hungary and Austria, particularly in Vienna, a highly sophisticated taroc game, whose exclusivity became a symbol of everyday-life in the Austrian coffee-house. In Vienna, the coffee-house gaming rooms were sometime simply called taroc rooms, as was the case, for example, with the Café Griensteidl.

BILLIARDS   In addition to card games—both permitted and illegal—another attraction which drew customers to the coffee-house was billiards, although in England, in contrast to France and Germany, billiards was rarely played in coffee-houses, the preferred pastimes consisting in the main of reading newspapers, and of card and board games. In Germany, billiards was a regular feature of coffee-house life by as early as about 1700, with money being staked on the outcome in the same fashion as cards. The game was constantly accompanied by scandal (when, for example, a player exasperated by luck threw a billiard ball through a closed window or set about his opponent with the cue) which prompted the intervention of the authorities. There was no ban on the playing of billiards in coffee-houses, because from the outset any proprietor wishing to set up a billiard table on his premises had first to obtain a special permit. Every coffee shop opened, for example, in Leipzig during the 18th century obtained such a permit (Ill. 95). The intense competition between the owners of billiard parlours and the coffee-house keepers which this occasioned, led to constant conflict between the two groups. On the one hand the billiard-hall proprietors accused the coffee-house keepers of permitting the unlawful playing of the game on their premises, and failing to comply with opening times, although basically their complaints boiled down to the fact that the coffee shops were for the most part more attractive to customers than the modest billiard halls (Ill. 102). By the same token the coffee-house keepers complained equally vociferously in defence of their concession, because for the coffee-house proprietor of the 18th century the hiring of billiard tables to customers was a prime source of regular income. And the price for a game of billiards was by no means cheap, being the equivalent of a cup of coffee, and what with the passion of the game prevailing at the time, this meant a considerable extra profit for the landlord.

After 1800 the playing of billiards in coffee-houses increased dramatically. All newly-opened coffee salons and café-restaurants incorporated a separate billiard room, which by the end of the century had expanded to billiard halls.

Billiards enjoyed considerable popularity in France, the birthplace of the game and so too in the Habsburg empire (Ill. 107, 109, 112). The first billiard café in Vienna was the Hugelmannsche Kaffeehaus which was established in about 1765 on the Schlagbrücke, which soon was to become a Mecca for exponents of the game. Following refurbishing in 1820, it emerged as the "billiards university" of Europe. It comprised a magnificent billiard hall on the ground floor with three tables, on the first floor were two further billiard rooms, where leading players of the game of Austria and Hungary gathered to demonstrate their prowess. Billiards was also a means of attracting the customers to the "Silbernes Kaffeehaus", already mentioned above. This latter establishment was a meeting place for Austria's national poets, who came here rather less for their role as poets than for their skill at billiards, the two most prominent being Nikolaus Lenau and Eduard von Bauernfeld, regulars for many years.

CHESS   A charming museum piece of European cultural history is the intimate connection between the coffee-house and the game of chess. Separated by an interval of about five hundred years, both derived from Islamic culture, but in Europe, free of their oriental origins they entered into a noteworthy combination as a form of diversion for the middle classes. The "royal game", with all its connotations of intellectual superiority had for centuries been an obligatory part of courtly accomplishments, thereafter becoming a game much loved by the aristocracy, until after 1700 it gained considerably in popularity, culminating in the 19th century with its general acceptance by nearly all social groups. In the same manner that coffee accelerated thought processes, chess sharpens mental acuity and deductive capacities. The campaigning psychology of the game as well as its aesthetic attractions, which undoubtedly also exist for the spectator, are probably the reasons why the coffee-house became the setting for the first public appearance of the Muse of chess.

The enthusiasm for chess among the middle classes first became apparent in the coffee-houses of England and France, but it reached its peak in the coffee-houses of the Austro-Hungarian empire during the course of the 19th century. In England the popularity of the game continued unabated even with the decline of the coffee-houses and the advent of the tea room. Thus a Viennese writing around 1900 reports that although tea was to be had cheap in the many tea-houses of London, nevertheless there was rarely a seat to be had on account of their all being occupied by chess players.

At the beginning of the 19th century, the most popular chess café in London was Old Slaughter's Coffee-House, and in Paris the Café de la Régence. This latter is the subject of many anecdotes which are preserved in French literature. When one reads the list of celebrated names who have played chess in the "Régence" one gets the impression that all the great men of France sharpened their wits here, including among them Rousseau, Voltaire, Diderot, Robespierre and Napoleon. Those who admire Napoleon can still see the table at which he played chess. The game has been played continuously at the "Régence" by both beginners and experts alike for more than two hundred and fifty years. In the second half of the 18th century, the leading light of the café was the musician François André Danican, who, had there been such a title at that time, would surely have been the world champion chess player. He has gone down in the history of the "Régence" and of chess under the name of Philidor. With the brilliance of his play it was he who first brought the intellectual fascination of the game to the attention of the great minds of his day. In the "Régence" he was regarded as invincible, and generally he conceded a rook to his opponents, among whom was Rousseau, at the start of a match. In fact Rousseau himself was also no mean chess player, himself conceding a similar handicap to Prince Conti.

One hundred years later the chess room of the Café Central in Vienna was to achieve equal renown as a venue for chess tournaments, and many reports of the games played there have found their way into Austrian literature, being given by no means gentle treatment. Top-class players were to be seen here, as well as more dilettante exponents,

Café de la Régence, Paris, circa 1750

"When it is too cold or wet, I seek refuge in the Café de la Régence and divert myself by observing the chess players. Paris is the place in the world, and the Café de la Régence the place in Paris where the game is played at its best . . . there one can witness the most sophisticated moves, and hear the crudest of language."
Denis Diderot, "Rameaus Neffe", in: Erzählungen und Gespräche, *Leipzig, 1953, p. 175.*

Café de la Régence, Paris, as experienced in 1954 by the Soviet Grand Master Mark Taimanov

"Full of anticipation we entered this unique chess museum in France. And how great was our subsequent disappointment! Of the old Café de la Régence only the memories remained. The chess tables have disappeared. The picture of the great practitioners of the game on the walls have been replaced with canvasses of banal subjects. Napoleon's chess table stands in the corner of a dark corridor, the carved figures scattered over the floor. The glory of chess sold off for commercial gain. 'Commercer!' explained the proprietor of the establishment with a shrug of his shoulders. 'Chess players are unprofitable customers, they drink one cup of coffee and sit there for hours on end. We are left with but one choice, either chess players and go bankrupt, or greater turn-over and commercial survival.'"
Heinz Machatschek, Zug um Zug. Die Zauberwelt der Brettspiele, *Berlin, 1972, p. 23 f.*

to be comparable with the Café Kaiserhof in Berlin, where Emanuel Lasker played chess and where preference was given to tea, with the Café Saffran in Zurich, the Café Arco in Prague or in Rome the Caffè Antonini. The chess room of the "Central" is also the subject of one of the most celebrated coffee-house anecdotes ever told. Receiving the horror-struck communication that a revolution had broken out in Russia, an Austrian minister reacted dimissively with the exclamation: "Away with you, who is going to make a revolution in Russia? Perhaps Herr Trotsky from the Café Central?" But truly between 1907 and 1914, it was not only chess which Trotsky had been playing in the Café Central!

FROM MAQAM TO CONCERT CAFÉ   In several oriental countries, music was already a customary form of entertainment by about 1600, and in some the only form, for example in Iraq, where the celebrated *Maqam* or poems were recited by the five *chalgis* (a singer and four instrumentalists) seated in a semi-circle on their *dais* in the *ghavakan* (coffee-house). The guests could sit for hours on end, listening to the *Maqams* with their monotonous rhythms and constantly repeated melodies, while smoking their water pipes and taking the occasional sip of coffee (later tea).

We know from the writings of several travellers that the coffee shops of Turkey in the 16th and 17th centuries were not only places of repose and dignity, but also places of musical entertainment. Pietro della Valle was of the view that the purpose of the music was to ensure that the customers would be induced to drink the boiling hot coffee more slowly, but a French traveller was probably nearer the mark when he wrote in 1685: "Music is provided from the string and wind instruments, provided at the landlord's own expense, who hopes thereby with the constant playing and singing to attract customers to his premises"[71].

In European establishments, too, musical entertainment was nothing out of the ordinary. From time immemorial travelling musicians made their way from public house to public house, for dancing or simply for diversion, although from our point of view today the quality of their offerings was probably not particularly high. Certainly there was nothing resembling concerts as such, for up until the end of the 17th century public music performances did not take place. The enjoyment of instrumental music was restricted to churches, to the households of music enthusiasts from among the aristocracy, or to some extent to private circles, of considerable importance among the latter being the private middle-class concert societies of the 16th and 17th centuries, for example the *Collegia musica* in Germany, the philharmonic academies in Italy and the musical "consorts" in England. From them emerged the institutions of public concert performances whose members were willing and able to pay money for the arts, in order to end the dominance of the aristocracy and the Church in this field, too. This step forward into the public sphere on the part of the nascent bourgeois musical life, which brought about the process of democratization of music as a whole, was associated at the end of the 17th and the beginning of the 18th century by two, one might say quite banal factors; firstly there had to be found the musicians who were prepared to play for the Third Estate, and secondly but no less important, suitable premises had to be found, either provided by a music enthusiast or hired, for at that time there were no public concert halls. The public-house keepers, in particular the landlords of coffee-houses, saw their opportunity and placed premises at the disposal of musicians and music lovers, premises which for several decades were to prove adequate for the latters' needs.

From Leipzig in 1720 there is a report of two regular *Collegia Musica*, one of which played on Thursdays between eight and ten in the evening in the wine cellar of the town hall. The other played on Friday evenings in Zimmermann's Caffee-Hauss, similarly from eight o'clock to ten o'clock in the evening, under the direction of Johann Christian Vogler, the organist. After Johann Sebastian Bach took over the *Collegium Musicum*, public performances continued to be held at the same time at "Zimmermann's" from 1729 to 1740.

We do not have any detailed knowledge of the kind of music played by the students and professors of the *Collegia musica* in the coffee-house. The "Kaffeekantate" (Coffee Cantata) which was composed in 1734, with the text by Christian Friedrich Henrici, was almost certainly premiered by Johann Sebastian Bach at "Zimmermann's". Bach himself was a fervent coffee drinker.

Despite the significance of the coffee-houses of Leipzig for the birth of the public appreciation of music (indeed, it can be said that this period in the city's musical life was at the same time part of the international musical culture), nevertheless this period of the coffee-house being the venue for serious music was really only a marginal episode in the overall evolution of the public concert performance. The smoke-filled rooms of the coffee-houses sufficed for a certain length of time, but then they began to be too small to cater for the dramatic increase in the popularity of such performances, and furthermore what was more important, too modest in form. In Germany, the performers of serious music had already moved out of the coffee-houses by the end of the 18th century, to the more exalted concert halls of the 19th century, to be replaced by military orchestras, or more frequently by light orchestras from southern Europe, "imported from Austro-Hungary or from beautiful Italy", as the opening announcement of Berlin's Café Kranzler put it in 1825. Johann George Kranzler, cook and confectioner, himself a native of Vienna, was well aware of what would please the public of Berlin: "Service from gentle hands" and "orchestras from beautiful Italy", played their part in ensuring that within space of a short time, this establishment became the "Valhalla of the Guards lieutenants" who, monocled and with their legs resting on the iron railings of the terrace, with stylish naughtiness surveyed the ladies and gentlemen who strolled below.

The coffee-houses of Paris and Vienna were the birthplace of two quite contrasting forms of coffee-house music. At the same time that Johann Sebastian Bach and his students were providing two hours of music one evening a week in a coffee-house, in Paris the first *café chantant* was founded. In the year 1731 in the Café des Aveugles, located in the cellar of the Café Italien (Palais Royal), there appeared the famed and beautiful Rosalba, accompanied by her blind musicians, who entertained the customers daily until midnight. The law reforms by which public singing was permitted in cafés, were eagerly greeted in the home of the chanson. Within a short time the proprietors of quite a few cafés engaged male and female singers and musicians and transformed their establishments into *cafés chantants*, thus becoming the home of chanson societies which were springing up everywhere, who could gather there to give free reign to their love of singing. The repertoire of the performers depended upon the social composition of the customers. During the French Revolution, in accordance with the particular political inclinations of the guests, satirical ballads would be sung against the aristocracy and the clergy. Later in the cafés most frequented by the aristocracy the songs would be directed at the Jacobins and the sans-culottes. It has been estimated that some three thousand chansons were composed between 1789 and 1794. What had begun fifty years before as

A scene from the window of the first floor of the Café de Foi in Paris in the year 1787

"*An endless throng of people, an astonishing confusion of wagons, small traders with wares of every description who plunge between the horses and the cartwheels, chairs on the pavement for those who want to observe and for those who want to be observed themselves, cafés with an orchestra and Italian and French singers, pastry cooks, cooks, inn-keepers, marionettes, acrobats and street hawkers, announcing the arrival of giants, dwarfs, wild animals, monsters of the sea, wax figures, androides and ventriloquists . . .*"
Carlo Goldoni, Mein Theater—mein Leben, *Berlin, 1949, p.467.*

a diversion for the entertainment of the customers provided by outsiders evolved during these years into a richly productive form of self-entertainment. The chansons sung here and on the streets became one of the most effective weapons of revolutionary and reactionary propaganda.

The highly conflicting political songs which re-echoed out of the *cafés chantants* in no way conformed with the desire of the Directoire for public order in stormy Paris. But it was the Emperor Napoleon I who first intervened in any decisive way: All "musicos" where disrespectful songs concerning his policies or personage were sung had to close down, an edict which was certainly not universally adhered to, but which entailed that in effect the coffee-house was no longer available for the chanson societies as a public platform.

During the 19th century, having in the meantime been subjected to further bans, the *cafés chantants* experienced a number of revivals, particularly when, following the abolition of the monarchy and the setting-up of the Second Republic in 1848, for a period of five months there was no censorship. The repercussions were immediate; the celebrated chanson "Le Pain" was not only sung on the Champs-Elysées, it was also to be heard at the gatherings of the Goguettes, who regularly met in the wine bars and cafés, and among those opposition chanson societies which had been banned during the reign of the citizen king from 1830 to 1848. By virtue on the one hand of the final banning of the Goguettes by Napoleon III in 1853, and on the other the burgeoning on a massive scale of the public entertainment industry, the *café chantant* in its traditional form relinquished its status as an important centre for home-made musical entertainment, in favour of the *café-concert*, which in turn evolved into a multi-functional entertainment establishment, where the customers only played the role of spectators.

Before turning our attention to the range of entertainment provided by the *café-concert*, the following observation should be made: Just as the *café chantant* is subject to various interpretations, so too the *café-concert* is a wide-ranging term. Although both expressions refer in the first instance to the building or the premises of a café or café-restaurant, at the same time they are not infrequently applied as a generic term to the forms of entertainment chiefly found there, but which are also to be found in other gastronomic establishments. Thus, in the same manner that a lower middle-class tavern of the end of the 18th century can be described as a *café chantant*, because revolutionary songs were sung here, so, too, one hundred years later it is just as possible that a beer garden or English tea garden could be given the description of *café-concert*.

The real birth of the French concert café took place in 1867 with the passing of a law permitting artistes to perform in costume in the coffee-houses. The till then obligatory evening dress could now be replaced by the down-to-earth dress of the street entertainer or by theatrical costumes, something regarded with contempt until then. The appearance of costumed singers, dancers and acrobats at the Café d'Apollon around 1770 now underwent a dramatic revival. Over the course of the next three decades there evolved the French "caf'-conc'", whose facilities comprised a broadly-based combination of gastronomy and wide-ranging musical entertainment, the latter dominated by the chanson. The various male and female performers who appeared in the *cafés-concerts* were distinguished according to costume and the content of their songs into *chanteurs genre anglais* (English songs were all the rage in Paris!), *diseurs*, *gommeux*, *gambillards* and *chanteurs réalistes*. The quality of entertainment provided by the *cafés concerts* of Paris reached its peak with the artistic offerings of Eugénie Buffet, Yvette Guilbert and Aristide Bruant, the creator of the naturalistic chanson.

108 Café-concert in a French provincial town. Contemporary illustration from an original by Léonce Petit, *c*. 1860, in: François Caradec/Alain Weill, *Le café-concert*, Paris, 1980.

Within a short time singers of the concert cafés were joined by other forms of entertainment, which either were created for such places or made their home temporarily there. Among these were cabaret and variety as well as all other entertainment of the "parterre" genre, ranging from weekly satirical cabaret to acrobats and jugglers, and to acts of performing animals. Only the satirical literary cabaret acquired any kind of permanence in the coffee-house, the others looked further afield for opportunities to present their acts to the public, and after the First World War the *café-concert* was finally superseded by the music hall, the variety show, revues and honky-tonk parlours.

The fifty years between the Second Empire and the start of the First World War saw the emergence of the concert café as "a national form of theatre"[72], which moulded the face of French cultural life, and these fifty years have gone down in the history of world music as the Golden Age of the French chanson. In fact the *café-concert* as an institution was too typically French to have any impact beyond the country's borders. Only individual chansons, or here and there the description *café-concert* made their way to England, Germany and beyond, but for the most part even those establishments which did bear the names concert café or *café-concert* were nothing comparable to those places which went under these descriptions in France.

Let us look for example at Vienna. As the musicians departed from the German coffee shops at the end of the 18th century, they took up residence in the capital of Austro-Hungary. In 1792 the Viennese coffee-house keeper Martin Wiegand became the first of his trade to obtain official permission to provide musical entertainment for his customers. His business successor Kleopha Lechner continued the tradition. The summer concerts in her two coffee tents attracted much interest. From 1797, the landlord of the Augustini Coffee-House offered his guests three times in the week (Sunday, Tuesday and Thursday) "Harmoniemusik", as he called it in his advertisements. No less a person than Ludwig van Beethoven played in the first Prater coffee-house. In 1814, for in-

Prussian legislation against cafés chantants, 1886

"*The items of musical or verbal recitation should not in their content or manner of delivery, offend against religion, morality, institutions or the State, and public deceny or public order.*

The performing of dramas, comedies, burlesque, operas, operettas and ballets is not permitted.

Each item must be submitted in the form of two identical copies, neatly and clearly written or printed.

The persons performing are only permitted to leave the stage for the purpose of collecting money, and are not allowed otherwise to mingle with the audience.

The proprietor of the premises is obliged to ensure the maintaining of order in his establishment, and in particular to prevent the audience from accompanying the singing, from banging on the tables or otherwise causing a disturbance.

Upon completion of the performance, and at the latest by eleven o' clock in the evening the female singers or other performers of the female sex shall leave the premises of the establishment in question."

Quoted in Peter Albrecht, Kaffee. Zur Sozialgeschichte des Getränks, *Brunswick, 1980, p. 33.*

stance, the premiere of his B-flat trio was performed here, the occasion at the same time representing the composer's last public appearance as a piano virtuoso.

Even had Vienna not been the place where Beethoven could premiere all his music in a coffee-house, it was the city where a particular musical genre, dance music, reached its heyday in the coffee-house. From 1819, in the Café Jüngling overlooking the Danube, which since 1791 had been a centre of Freemasonry, a string trio made up of Josef Lanner and the Drahanek brothers entertained the guests. The addition of Johann Strauss senior, who not only played the violin, but like Lanner also composed *Ländler*, quadrilles and above all one waltz after the other, heralded the beginning of the era of Viennese coffee-house music, whose popularity reached world-wide proportions during the course of the 19th century. In 1824 a string orchestra played for the first time in the open air in the garden of the first Prater coffee-house. The enthusiasm of the Viennese was so great that this form of musical entertainment became a permanent feature of coffee-houses and coffee gardens. From 1840 onwards, the soirées conducted by Johann Strauss senior in the Volksgarten, particularly in the music pavilion of the so-called Zweites Cortisches Café and the public concerts, were favourite attractions of the musical life of the city. At the end of the 19th century, a young impoverished musical genius stood at the fence of the first Prater coffee-house "in order to listen free of charge to the music"—his name, Arnold Schönberg. The export of the Viennese coffee-house to the capital cities of the world (cf. pp. 96 and 100–103) was accompanied by the music associated with it, albeit often of a lower quality than that of its birthplace.

In 1844, an enterprising Berlin coffee-house proprietor by the name of Kemper travelled to Vienna in order to provide his refined and prosperous Berlin public with "an alternative to the monotonous clink of coffee cups which can be heard a thousandfold every afternoon", through the procurement of a Viennese orchestra. "He obtained the services of an orchestra of only moderate class . . . but alone their outward appearance on account of its novelty represented something unique for the people of Berlin. The bearded sun-tanned faces, thirty of them in all, made a tremendous impact as they sat on their podium. They played alternately military music, waltzes, and in particular pieces which the whole orchestra sung in unison in the Austrian dialect, whose words were underlined by shouts, yodelling and the waving of hats. The storms of applause after the rendering of such a song can scarce be imagined. One could see from the expressions on the faces of some of the orchestra that they were surprised by the overwhelming reaction of the spectators, for such songs were a commonplace in their homeland. The whole of Berlin flocked to the Styrians . . . not only to the premises themselves which were separated from the street by a low fence, but outside, where people stood in their thousands to experience the performance without paying for entry. This was to continue for four whole summers until 1848."[73]

If one considers the coffee-house trade as a whole in different countries and in different periods, it becomes clear that as a gastronomic institution it sought in a multitude of ways to provide musical entertainment for its patrons (Ill. 72), but it was only in Paris and Vienna that it was able to attract a specific form for any length of period, from which evolved a standard feature which was to be imitated in the most varied of ways outside of these countries under the name of the French or Viennese café.

 Inasmuch as mealtime music serves the function of favourably affecting the appetite and encouraging the pleasure of conversation as long as it is restrained and unobtrusive, it represents a pleasant addition to sitting at table. But as soon as the musical fare

Unterhaltungen im Caffehaus   (VIENNE)   Les Amusements du Café

Vienne chez **Artaria** et Compag.

Propriété des Editeurs   Deposé à la Bibliotheque Imp.

109   Coffee-house entertainments—Les Amusements du Café. Coloured etching by Johann August Krafft and Johann Nepomuk Passini, *c.* 1820. Vienna, Historisches Museum.

110   Coffee-House. Etching by Max
Pechstein to Carl Sternheim, "Heidenstam", in:
Marsyas. Eine Zweimonatsschrift, Vol. 1, No. 4,
Berlin, 1918.

111   Konzertcafé. Etching by Max
Beckmann, folio 9 from the series "Gesichter"
(Faces), 1918. Dresden, Staatliche
Kunstsammlungen, Kupferstichkabinett.

112   Billiard rules from the Café Eckl in
Vienna. Chrome lithograph, *c.* 1880.
Vienna, Historisches Museum.

113   Billiards in the "Blumensträussl" coffee-house in Grein. The restaurant and coffee-
house which reputedly had existed in this venerable old town house since the 18th century
was re-furbished in 1924 in the *Biedermeier*
style.

114 Poster advertising cinema shows in the Grand Café Zürcherhof. Coloured lithograph by P. Krawutschke (Pik), 1908. Zurich, Kunstgewerbemuseum, Plakatsammlung.

115/116 Advertisement for musical entertainment in the modern-day coffee-house. Jazz
café in Amsterdam.

stumbled into Jan Michalik's confectionery where he proceeded to put about the idea of setting-up a cabaret. Situated not far from the College of Fine Arts, for some years the confectionery had been a regular gathering place for artists, whose tables were a forum for the exchange of jokes, caricatures and parodies, and at which young people sat who were later to achieve high renown in the field of art. The greatest difficulty was to obtain the agreement of Michalik to the venture. In the beginning he was by no means enthusiastic about the idea, regarding it as a slur on his establishment, but several years later he was to shake us warmly by the hand and confess: 'You have made a human being of me for the first time.'

Michalik's calling was the baking and selling of cakes. The room behind the shop was a miserable affair. But then everything was transformed. There was no demand for his cakes, and nothing could change this state of affairs, neither posters nor the shapes or names of new creations such as Dream, Manon, Goplana printed into the asphalt. For everyone knew from childhood onwards that one bought cakes at Maurizio's and nowhere else. Thanks to a chance advertisement Michalik acquired the room behind the shop . . . and for better or worse, following the beckoning of fate, he expanded the premises. The small confectioner became the proprietor of a coffee-house, and the solid man of business a patron of the Bohemia."[74]

And thus out of the former Lemberg confectionery in Cracow was born the Kawiarnia Jama Michalika (Michalik cavern), where the cabaret "Zielony Balonik" (green balloon) was created which exists still today.

In Berlin the "Neopathetische Cabaret" was established in 1910 in the upper room of the Café Kutschera, which in turn gave birth to the "Gnu" in 1911, which was located in the Café Austria.

Within a short time the unpolitical entertainment and amusement industry had taken over the name and form of the cabaret, and in Germany with the outbreak of war in 1914 it was transformed into a vehicle for jingoism and patriotic sentiment. Soon "there was not a single larger café which did not provide a cabaret in the evening. The programme was well-larded with patriotic interspersion. The cry of Hurrah! became a favourite refrain, and the theatrical tirades against the enemy plumbed the depths of tastelessness and odiousness."[75]

During the years of the Weimar Republic from 1919 to 1933, the coffee-houses of Germany presented the full range of mutually exclusive forms of entertainment which reflected the emergence of the production and reception of progressive art on the one hand, and the continued regressive development of the bourgeois entertainment genre on the other. While in hundreds of cafés the staple fare was light and undemanding entertainment, in some coffee-houses their rooms provided a platform for sharp social criticism from the left wing of bourgeois circles.

The opening of the "Grössenwahn, Bänkel und Bühne", political and satirical cabaret by Rosa Valetti in Berlin in 1920, in the first floor of the former Café des Westens, known popularly as "Grössenwahn", signified a conscious adaption of the Montmartre tradition and represented an artistic landmark of German cabaret history.

Not every café proprietor reacted quite so favourably when his house-cabaret took on a similar if not downright proletarian character. Thus in 1923, Erich Weinert was unceremoniously barred from the "Kü-ka", the cabaret of the Berliner Künstlercafé, because his political satires aroused the disapproval of the proprietor, a former Prussian officer, as did the clientèle which suddenly started to frequent the place. Not infrequently it was the bourgeois coffee-house customers themselves who came under attack, particularly at the beginning of the 1930s with their economic crisis and mass unemployment, when the term "café" took on particularly negative connotations in the proletarian rhetoric of the class struggle.

All this found eloquent expression in the 1930s in the colourful café milieu of Vienna, the bastion of the coffee-house. Under the influence and as a consequence of the world economic crisis, one satirical cabaret after the other sprang up. And while on the subject of the Viennese café, there is also the following aspect to be considered: all such cabarets had their origins in the coffee-houses, and by no means the smallest. For seven years, from 1931 to 1938 "Der liebe Augustin" played in the basement of the elegant Café Prückel on the Ringstrasse. The Café Döblingerhof played host to the "Stachelbeere", the cabaret parlour of the traditional and staid Café Dobner was the setting for the "Literatur am Naschmarkt", and the "ABC" cabaret appeared in the Café Arkade. These cabaret venues—in 1934 there were twenty-five—provided striking evidence of a typically Viennese counter-measure to the theatre laws of the Dollfuss regime. Only forty-nine chairs were set out for the audience, for seating for fifty or more would have meant that the programme would have immediately been subject to censorship. Right up to the entry of the German *Wehrmacht* into the city in 1938, these cabarets devoted their satirical energies to the combatting of Hitler and Austrian Fascism. One of the outstanding authors was Jura Soyfer, who wrote material for the "ABC" and the "Literatur am Naschmarkt". In an article in the *Sonntag* of May 9, 1937, he made the claim that these new theatres had "evolved from the experimental stage into a serious cultural element—a cultural element which was frequently overlooked in the invocations of the city's literary circles (e.g. in the Café Herrenhof) of the inter-war years.

FROM DUELLING-ROOM TO CINEMATOGRAPHIC SHOWS   A near limitless range of pastimes, entertainment and education—during the course of time the café proprietors were constantly on the look-out for new ideas to make their growing business commercially viable and attractive in order to fend off the competition of their rivals in the catering trade. The attractions of the coffee-house were enhanced by the addition of a variety of free services—letter-writing paper, smokers' utensils, telephones—which became hallmarks of the coffee-house trade. From the hundreds of possible examples, we will select just three here, demonstrating the methods by which a coffee-house keeper at the beginning, in the middle and at the end of the 19th century could go beyond the specifics of his trade in order to increase his takings and turn-over. "Everything for the comfort of the guest"—this guiding principle of the trade knew virtually no bounds, even if today some of the more outlandish ideas seem like some macabre joke. At the beginning of the 19th century, the Café Tortoni in Paris had an extra room set aside for the fighting of duels. In those days the aristocratic code of honour required that one either fought a duel or shot oneself. This simple solution was expedited at the "Tortoni" by the opportunity to settle the matter on the spot. The result of these duels, whatever their outcome, was an enormous consumption of alcohol . . . with a corresponding increase in profits for the landlord Tortoni who never fought duels but hung himself under the influence of persecution mania.

The ever more extravagant and profitable entertainment offered by the café restaurateurs to their clientèle after 1800, was soon matched by the *Café-Konditoreien*. They played their part in their own special field of the confectioner's art, which gained popularity among the middle classes and took up with the coffee shops, giving rise to the *Café-Konditorei*. Although the confectioners lacked quite such frequent opportunity to display their marvellous creation for financial gain, nevertheless when such an occasion arose they responded in magnificent and ostentatious style, as in feudal times, which in periods of social conflict brought them into considerable disfavour.

A major highpoint of cultural life during the *Biedermeier* years was the annual Christmas exhibitions of the Berlin and Viennese Court confectioners. In Berlin, among the most prominent of these confectioners were the confectioneries Josty, Sparpagnani, Fuchs and Stehely, whose proprietors or predecessors were nearly all immigrant confectioners from Austria and Switzerland, who on account of their great skills were regarded by many as sculptors in their own right. In line with their own particular gifts, at Christmas time each would conjure up creations out of sugar, tragacanth, marzipan and chocolate, cleverly illuminated dioramas on some topical joke or patriotically stirring theme which ranged from the closing of the Berlin theatres, the ice rink in the Tiergarten, the great fire of Moscow, scenes from the Battle of the Nations at Leipzig, or from the theatrical play the *Rape of the Sabine Women*.

It was little wonder that such a spectacle caught the imagination of everyone—even of Heinrich Heine, who provides us with the following description, written in 1882: "Here as in all large Protestant cities Christmas plays a central role in the great comedy of winter. Already a week beforehand everyone is occupied with the purchase of gifts for Christmas . . . evening is the time of greatest activity; then our dear children, often with the whole family, father, mother, aunt, sisters and brothers, go on a pilgrimage from one confectioner's to the other as though they were stations of the cross. There the darlings pay their two groschen admission, collected during *Kurrende* singing, and view *con amore* the 'exhibition', a whole collection of sugar or candy dolls which, harmoniously juxtaposed, all-round illuminated and flanked by four painted backdrops in perspective, present a beautiful picture."[76]

In Leipzig in 1835 it was possible for four groschen to visit the dioramic display of tasteful confectionery in the newly-opened Café français (Ill. 63), the admission price being so fixed as to "avoid inordinate crowd disturbances" as the daily press put it.

The immense popularity of the "candy pictures" ensured a corresponding subsidiary source of income for the coffee-house proprietors, as well as for the general public a visual experience which far surpassed the traditional fair-ground peep shows, and which forged the link to the now-nascent panorama, one of the most fascinating art forms for the people of the 19th century.

When at the end of the 19th century the "sugar pictures", the large and small panoramas and the newly-arrived photoramas went into decline on account of moving pictures becoming the latest attraction, once again it was the coffee-house which helped this new medium on its way (Ill. 114).

The Lumière brothers had made the first moving picture film in the year 1894, featuring their factory in Lyons. The seventeen meter long strip showed the workers leaving the factory. "La sortie des usines" had its first public showing in the Indian Salon of the Grand Café in Paris on 28 December, 1895. The film was shown to a group of thirty-five invited guests, and although the immediate reaction of the audience was not exactly overwhelming, at least the show brought the proprietor thirty-three francs pure profit. Despite this initial lukewarm reaction, in the days that followed hundreds of people flocked to the coffee-house to see this new phenomenon. One year later Emil Piron, the self-styled "Photographer of Kings", presented his film of the visit to Paris by the Russian czar, in the Café de la Paix. By 1898 the stage had been reached that films were an established feature at the Grand Café. The eighteen shows which were visited by some two thousand people, represented a watershed for the medium of the approaching new century.

"Coffee-house politics" and political coffee-houses

"Coffee-house politics" and "coffee-house politicians" are catchwords which find their way into the vocabularies of the coffee-drinking nations with particularly negative connotations, as soon as the people of the respective countries adopt the habit of the public consumption of the drink and use the occasion at the same time to exchange all the latest news. To this was added the term "political coffee-house" which for centuries has remained a label conjuring up either positive or negative sentiments, prompting disapproval or enthusiasm, contempt or proof of conspiracy, progress or reaction, democracy or monarchy, revolt or revolution, political opposition or establishment, and a locality appearing most frequently in the reports of the police or spies. At one time or another "political coffee-house" has embraced all these ideas, and at the same time the term has itself been employed in political argument.

Inns and coffee-houses have formed a focal point for political agitation and campaigning for all sections of the population. Such activity was a manifestation of the birth pangs of the nascent bourgeois consciousness, a trend strongly resisted by both the ruling classes and the educated élite (in particular the leading advocates of the Enlightenment). In the view of the privileged educated pillars of society such vigorous political activity was to be discouraged, for those conducting it lacked the requisite detachment, insight and knowledge. The "hotheads" in the coffee-houses, who lost no opportunity to add their own particular comments and criticisms to the latest news of the embattled state of the world, became a thorn in the flesh of the authorities and the Church. The mistrust of public gatherings in the coffee-houses and the eager political discussions they evoked was founded upon political considerations.

Isfahan, end of the 17th century

"*Under the arcades are situated various booths/ which open up onto the square/ where coffee and tobacco may be consumed. The benches of these rooms are arranged in the form of an amphitheatre/ and in the middle of such a place stands a basin of fresh water/ which one requires for filling the pipe with water/ when the same becomes overheated from the tobacco smoke. All Persians/ or those of them in possession of money/ never fail/ to gather at such places/ every day/ between seven and eight in the morning/ upon which they are promptly served with a pipe/ and a bowl of coffee. But the great Shah Abas, seeing/ that such places provided at the same time opportunity for gatherings/ for the purpose of discussing affairs of state/ a fact which occasioned his displeasure/ he resolved/ in order to prevent/ the minor mutinies/ which could thereby be engendered/ the following instruction: He introduced the custom/ that every morning/ before anyone entered such a place/ a mullah should go to each of these booths/ and engage the coffee drinkers and tobacco smokers in instruction on some aspect of their laws/ or on history or poetry. And this custom . . . is still practised today.*"

Jean-Baptiste Tavernier, Les six voyages de Jean-Baptiste Tavernier . . ., qu'il a fait en Turquie, en Perse et aux Indes . . ., Paris, 1676.

SEVENTEENTH-CENTURY ENGLAND The English Commonwealth was exactly one year old when the first coffee-house in Oxford (1650) became a focus of public attention. Ten years later the monarchy was once again restored, but the republican spirit had become firmly established in people's thinking. It took shape as bourgeois political consciousness, and one of its most important training grounds was the coffee-houses which, within two decades, and particularly after 1666, had multiplied a hundredfold. For several months during 1659, the last year of the English republic, a "company of gifted men" known as the Rota Club, gathered in the "Turk's Head" (Mile's Coffee-House), under the chairmanship of its founder James Harrington. "The society was in the habit of gathering of an evening around an oval table, in the centre of which was an opening by means of which the landlord Miles was able to serve his guests coffee. The purpose of these gatherings was the propagation of republican ideas, which Harrington had already supported in his *Oceana*.[77]

The influence and significance of these coffee parlours, bastions of a variety of political tendencies, which gradually began to take shape as the headquarters of different political groupings, was drastically underestimated by Charles II in 1675 when he sought to close down all coffee shops, in order to counter the "quarrelling and influence" of the parties. As we have already noted, he was unable to resist the combined interests of the coffee-house proprietors and their customers. After a warning on the part of the government that landlords should suppress the reading of all scurrilous writings, books and leaflets on their premises, and take steps to prevent any person from spreading defamatory reports against the government[78], the coffee-houses were permitted to open once again, and the political activity continued unabated. By 1700, the liberal Whigs, who advocated popular rule, were meeting in St. James's Coffee-House and in the Smyrna Coffee-House, while the conservative Tories frequented the "Ozinda" and the "Cocoa Tree". None of these professional politicians would think of visiting the headquarters of their opponents, such a thing was only done by foreigners or the forces of law and order when political discussion had reached such a heated level that daggers would be drawn.

EIGHTEENTH-CENTURY NORTH AMERICA   The goings-on in the coffee-houses of England between 1652 and about 1750 in terms of anti-feudal debate and parliamentary intrigue, must have been encouraging to the enlightened minds of the Old World, but even more so to those of the New World. In any event, the English emigrants to America must have taken good note of their possibilities, for when they sought to win their independence from the mother country a hundred years later once again the cradle of independence was to be found where the Anglo-Saxons were accustomed to conduct their political activities in the 17th and 18th centuries—in the coffee-house.

In the manner of nearly all coffee parlours and houses in North America, whether founded by English or Dutch colonists, Merchants' Coffee-House in Manhattan also possessed a so-called hearing-room, where meetings were held. "Merchants'" was the gathering place for politically interested circles. When in 1764, in order to alleviate the burdens of the English tax payer, import duties were suddenly levied in the American colonies, the colonists and merchants reacted with understandable outrage. The colonists were not represented in the English parliament, and up until then they had successfully opposed any taxation without representation. The wave of public protest took a variety of forms. In 1765 the general opposition to the English stamp duty laws was proclaimed from the balcony of the Merchants' Coffee-House, and in the hearing-room inside, the "Sons of Liberty" discussed the practical possibilities of imposing an import boycott on English goods. By 1770 the continuing opposition which took on an increasingly political character prompted some in England to recommend the lifting of some of the duties which had been imposed (e. g. duties on sugar, paper, glass, dyestuffs). Only the tax on tea remained in force, and it was this which three years later finally drove the Americans to take initiative and stage the Boston Tea-Party, when a whole ship's cargo of tea from England was dumped overboard into Boston harbour. This open act of defiance against tea duty led at the same time to a public rejection of the drinking of tea itself, and from 1773 onwards the drinking of coffee came to be seen as a patriotic act against England. Coffee, which came from the French colonies, was elevated to the national drink of America, and at the same time the drinking of tea was stigmatized as un-American. On 18 April, 1774 a group of onlookers leaned out of the window of Merchants' Coffee-House and observed while an English ship's captain was successfully prevented from discharging his cargo of tea. One month later the "Sons of Liberty" met in Merchants' Coffee-House in order to set up a committee whose function was to coordinate anti-English measures in the colonies. And it was here in this coffee-house on 19 May, 1774 that the signal was given for the birth of the American independence move-

England, 1665

"Coffee and Commonwealth begin
Both with one letter, both came in
Together for a Reformation,
To make's a free and sober nation."
The Character of a Coffee-House, by an Eye and Ear Witness, *London, 1665, p. 1.*

ment with the founding of the committee and the call for the setting up of a "virtuous and spirited Union" was drawn up. This was followed on 5 September, 1774 by the convening of the first continental congress in Philadelphia, at which the Association for the resumption of the trade boycott was constituted. Two years later the Declaration of Independence was proclaimed. The war of independence dragged on for a further six years, and for our purposes it is not without significance that on 23 April, 1789, the day on which he took office as the first President of the United States of America, George Washington, the military leader of the revolutionary army, was accorded a civic reception in Merchants' Coffee-House. The establishment was to retain its character as a centre of political life until 1804, when it burned down to the ground. The importance of this political coffee-house in the history of America is commemorated today by a plaque which was unveiled in 1914 on the occasion of the 125th anniversary of the reception for the first President of the United States of America.

EIGHTEENTH-CENTURY FRANCE   The year 1789 marked the hundredth anniversary of the opening of the first coffee-house in Paris, and the Café Procope, founded by Procopio Cultelli in 1689, still stood. Its exclusive clientèle continued to consist of men of letters, actors and aesthetes, but the times had changed dramatically. What had once been discussed here or in one of the city's many other coffee-houses by such great national figures as Fontenelle, Voltaire, Rousseau or Diderot, was now being put into deeds. Rousseau, who had already been dead for ten years by the time of the outbreak of the French Revolution, was a regular customer of the refined Café de la Régence, it was he who coined the phrase "sovereignty of the people". Voltaire, who had also died ten years previously, was a daily visitor to the "Procope" as long as he was able to stay in Paris. He subjected the State and the Church to merciless criticism and placed the whole basis of their authority in question. And finally Montesquieu, less of a coffee-house habitué on account of not being a resident of Paris, forty years ago had brought out his major work in which he spoke for the first time of the "separation of powers".

The stage was now set. The revolutionary events of 1789 had in many respects already been heralded by a number of occurrences such as hunger revolts which had taken place at the beginning of the year, the storming of the manufactures in April, the aborted assemblies of 1787 and 1788, and finally the convening of the Estates General on 24 January, 1789 which was a final attempt to ward off imminent bankruptcy of the State. The decayed pillars of the State were collapsing one by one.

By the end of the 1780s, Paris possessed more than half a million inhabitants. In addition to a vast number of smoking-rooms, eating-houses and wine cellars and to one degree or another run-down pot-houses on the outskirts, the city boasted approximately eight hundred coffee-houses. Although the map of the city which details their existence gives no indication of their size, nevertheless even if the large majority of such establishments were small, and the price of the drink by no means cheap (an industrial worker earned between twenty-five and forty sous per day, while a pound of bread cost between four and eight sous and a cup of coffee on average three sous), in comparison to other major European cities, the number of coffee-houses was considerable.

The dismissal of several ministers on 11 July, 1789, particularly Necker, provoked a storm of protest for the most diverse reasons from the people of Paris. Spontaneous gatherings took place at every street corner which were the scene of heated debates. In the Café de Foy the customers were in uproar. One of the main protagonists here, the journalist Camille Desmoulins, delivered an impassioned speech against this measure and its contempt for the popular will, and the crowd that had gathered expressed equally adamantly that it should not be acceded to. Finally, Desmoulins appealed to the tumultuous crowd which had gathered in front of the café to take to arms, a call which did not go unheeded. And when on the same evening a mass of people which had collected in the Tuileries was dispersed by the combined force of the grenadiers of the Swiss Guards and the Dragoons of the German Life Guards, there was no stopping the wave of popular feeling, and the general armed uprising began. The armouries were plundered, and the attempts to channel the anger of the people by means of the hastily assembled citizens' militia failed. On 14 July the Bastille was stormed and the French Revolution had begun.

The Café de Foy was the starting place of the revolutionary events, and in the months that followed, as the centre of activities of the *enragés* it was to be the birthplace of other important initiatives, until in the eyes of the municipal authorities things had gone too far, and the main protagonists were called to task by the guardians of public opinion in the Palais Royal. Eventually in September the aggressive agitation was officially banned, and the unlawful assemblies prohibited. Finally the National Guard was called on to intervene, the Café de Foy was stormed and the incumbents driven out of the garden of the Palais Royal.

At the end of August, Joachim Heinrich Campe was still able to report enthusiastically, ". . . here are who knows how many thousand thinking and well-informed citizens who through their debates in the Palais Royal are countless vigilant writers who, through broadsheets, short essays and books, assist the deliberations of the people's representatives and guide the considerations of the same . . . here everything is discussed, argued and decided in public—a check against over-hasty and selfish intentions."[79]

Due to the several weeks of strict surveillance which followed, for the *enragés* of the Café de Foy and the Palais Royal this much-heralded openness of discussion was suspended. With the founding of the Jacobin Club in October 1789, which embraced all bourgeois and aristocratic anti-Absolutist forces, the *enragés* of the Café de Foy now also had an organization with which they could link up, and in which they could play a substantial role. This assured the importance of the coffee-house as a meeting place, particularly as now all political activity was focussed on the vicinity of the Riding School, which in turn was near to the meeting place of the National Assembly. It also meant that the cafés in the Tuileries experienced renewed popularity. The best-known was the Café Hottot which fronted directly onto the square where the Riding School stood. The "Hottot" was frequented in particular by the deputies, including those of a more moderate political persuasion. "During the course of the year 1791, especially after the expulsion of the Feuillants from the Jacobin Club (July 1791), the moderates withdrew more and more, and the Café Hottot became the special coffee-house of the Jacobins . . ."[80] The police reports even go so far as to describe it as the centre of Jacobin agitation. Thus it can be assumed that the extreme left of the National Assembly not only met here to relax and drink coffee, but that it was also the scene of out-and-out political meetings and discussions.

Following the constituting of the National Convention in September 1792 and the transfer of the legislative assembly from the Riding School to the Tuileries Palace, the meeting place of the Jacobins was also moved. The Café Convent now took on the role of the favourite haunt of the extreme left. Moreover, the Café Italien (also called Café

Corazza after its proprietor), situated near the Palais Royal, also changed its clientèle which traditionally had been made-up of the aristocracy and of wealthy men of the world. A number of deputies set up their headquarters on the premises, including François Chabot and Jean Collot and their followers. It is also certain that the popular uprising of 30 April, 1793 and the subsequent overthrow of the Girondistes was prepared in the rooms of the Café Corazza. The political vicissitudes of the times, subjected to daily comment by the singers in the *cafés chantants*, was one of the factors which prompted the Jacobins to withdraw completely out of the public limelight. Following the closing of the Jacobin Club in 1794 they convened in private houses or in more obscure cafés on the outskirts of the city. Only after the suppression of the royalist uprising on 5 October, 1795 and the proclamation of a general amnesty did they once again emerge into public life. Within a month the irrepressible republicans had founded the Panthéon Club, an institution in the Jacobinic and Babeuf tradition. The meeting place of this new society was the Café Chrétien, named after its proprietor Chrétien, a former member of the revolutionary tribunal. Although their official headquarters was the former Convent of St. Généviève, because of the ever-present surveillance they restricted themselves to discussions of relatively harmless political topics there. Their more subversive intentions, namely the restoration and carrying-through of the republican constitution of Year 1 without any form of dictatorship, were reserved for discussion in the back-room of the Café Chrétien. Following the closure of the Panthéon Club and the arrest of its leading members in February 1796, the café lost its significance as a centre of political activity for the leading figures of the Revolution, in particular for Babeuf.

In the same way that there were cafés with a marked Jacobinic character, so other coffee-houses also served as gathering places for the representatives of other political persuasions. The aristocrats and monarchists sat in the Café Chartres (Palais Royal) and in the Café Militaire (Ill. 90), the "incorruptible" Robespierre and his followers favoured the Café Venuas. Following the withdrawal of the Jacobins, the Café Corazza became the haunt of the moderate constitutionalists, and it was here in 1795 that Count Paul Barras and the young General Bonaparte met to plan the putting down of the royalist uprising.

The ebb and flow of political developments also brought with it changes in the composition of the clientèle frequenting particular cafés. For instance it happened on several occasions that where once the extreme left had convened, the aristocrats would ensconce themselves and vice versa. It was a colourful, chequered and confused picture which the cafés of all groups and strata presented during the revolutionary years. However much they might have differed from each other in so many respects, the one thing they all had in common was that they were coffee-houses with a pronounced political character. All the tendencies were represented—Jacobin, royalist, moderate constitutional, extreme reactionary—and one encountered inside only two kinds of customer: one's friends or one's enemies.

NINETEENTH-CENTURY EUROPE During the years of the Revolution, Jacobins in other countries—Holland, Germany, Austria, Hungary or Bohemia—were also to be found to some degree resident in coffee-houses, thereby also lending the latter their political character. Georg Friedrich Rebmann reported the presence of terrorist and Jacobin coffee-houses in The Hague and Amsterdam, and the groupings were the same as in France—one met friends or one met enemies there: "Today (The Hague, 11 July, 1796)

I visited two aristocratic and one Jacobin coffee-house. In the latter I was regarded as an aristocrat for the simple reason that I was German, and in the former I was taken for a terrorist."[81]

Aristocrat or Jacobin—the extremes reflected the immense polarization which was just as drastic beyond France itself, although it must be said that here the power of the wellspring of revolutionary commitment was highly diffuse, or because of other conditions was barely present, even though some individuals did their utmost to encourage it. In the same breath that Rebmann spoke of terrorist coffee-houses in Holland, he poured contempt on their intemperate clientèle.

An indication of the negative connotations which the revolutionaries themselves attached to the term "coffee-house politics" is provided by the Jacobin town of Mainz, the source of this example being a report prepared by a spy. Georg Christian Wedekind introduced a new member to the club. Twenty members were against the newcomer's adoption, and in line with the club rules, stood up. Wedekind became extremely irritated by this behaviour and declared openly that it represented true coffee-house cabal politics, a declaration which almost cost him his own membership!

Around the beginning of the 19th century, there were political coffee-houses in nearly all the states of Europe, and in the next century they were also to form a focal point for the gathering of both progressive and reactionary groups. Although nearly all the revolutionary events of the 19th century made their mark on the coffee-house, too, even having their origins in such establishments, the overall social relevance of the coffee-house as a progressive political institution became a thing of the past. After 1800 it becomes increasingly the case that political activity is only possible within associations sanctioned by the State. A variety of censorship measures, overt and covert surveillance, state-sponsored arbitrary acts against the individual, the activities of the secret police etc. create restrictions for political opposition as a whole, particularly for any public activity. The growth of officialdom and the apparatus of State control, the most sophisticated exponent of which—remembered still today—being Count Metternich between 1809 and 1848, reduced coffee-house politics (which ultimately meant political opposition), either to the level of mere tirade or to a brief episode not infrequently terminated with exile for those involved.

In Berlin, the seat of the Prussian monarchy, the spirit of the 1848 revolution was very much evident in the coffee parlours and confectioner's shops. Derisively dismissed by some for its apparent ineffectiveness, held in terror by others as a hotbed of Jacobinism, the *Rote Stube* (Red Room) in the Café Stehely can claim a firm place in the history of political coffee-houses. During the 1830s and 1840s, the last of the so-called front rooms, the *Rote Stube* (so named on account of the red colour of the wallpaper) provided the venue for daily gatherings between four and six in the afternoon of liberals and radicals, mostly writers and journalists of the radical parties, who met here to peruse the journals and newspapers which were provided, as was the custom in most Berlin cafés, and to discuss what they had read. In addition to prominent journalists, professors and students from the nearby University, it was also a meeting place for the group calling itself the "Junghegelianer" (Young Hegelians), beyond the German borders known as Neo-Hegelians. Here they would conduct their debates on problems of philosophy and the political topics of the day, often with little concession to decorum or restraint. Religion in general and Prussian politics and ideology in particular were also the issues discussed by the Philosophical Doctors' Club which regularly convened during the week at

∘◯∘

Amsterdam, June 1796

"*By way of a change, I now went into a so-called terrorist coffee-house, where I was greeted with fierce glances, being taken for a spy of His Majesty the King of Prussia. Incidentally the people here, if they really were indeed Jacobins, had nothing in common with the French Jacobins. They all had long pipes in their mouths, which appear to be a prime requirement for the people of Holland; they blew the smoke into each other's faces, swigged gin, and every now and then would toast each other with loud exclamations of 'Gelykheid, Vryheid, Broderschap', in such a drawling dialect that I felt quite unwell.*"

Georg Friedrich Rebmann, Holland und Frankreich in Briefen geschrieben . . ., Berlin, 1981, p. 63 f.

∘◯∘

Stehely's under the chairmanship of Bruno Bauer, unsalaried lecturer of theology at the University. Between 1837 and 1841 no less a person than Karl Marx himself belonged to the Doctors' Club, and although very much a junior member of this august circle (whose members included Carl Friedrich Köppen and Arnold Rutenberg), he soon became a stimulating focal figure in the discussions, as Franz Mehring was later to note. Writing in 1841 to a friend who wished to come to Berlin, Moses Hess, a Neo-Hegelian, enthused: "You can prepare yourself to meet the greatest, perhaps the only, true living philosopher . . ., Dr. Marx." History was to prove the justification of this sentence. Another contemporary, remarking on the coffee-house debaters wrote: "Every afternoon over a cup of coffee innocuous conversations and discussions take place, stimulated by the perusing of newspapers and the events of the day . . .", and by way of reiterating the harmless nature of such political discussions in the coffee-house, he also quotes Robert Prutz: "Their politics consist of loud chatter and eating meringues at Stehely's."[82] But the end-product of these heated discussions on questions of religion, philosophy and politics cannot have been quite so harmless when one considers that it was only a few years later that Marx and Engels were to write their attack on Bruno Bauer "and his consorts", known today as *The Holy Family*, which ushered in a new era in the history of philosophy, and when one reads of Karl Marx writing to his father in 1837: "Here in the course of the arguments, some conflicting views became apparent."

Of the thirty or so coffee-houses in the centre of Vienna, it was the "Silbernes Kaffeehaus" where the first outlines of liberal opposition began to take shape. The radical poets and journalists of the 1840s gave written form to its dominant ideas: "These sentiments were also greeted favourably at 'Neuner's', where Metternich's Absolutism was similarly regarded as a suppression of all progressive impulses. Nevertheless such ideas were only aired in hushed tones for Neuner's Café itself was looked upon with disapproval by the government, because they felt that a spirit was prevailing here which posed a threat to the existing order. Indeed one might also say that Neuner's Café contributed to a considerable degree to prepare the events of 1848."[83]

These events of 1848 continued until 1852 and shook the whole of Europe to its foundations. During the course of these four years on many occasions coffee-houses were to emerge in the forefront of political history, and once again recede into obscurity to revert to their traditional role as mere politically anonymous coffee-houses. In Greece and Italy the coffee-house proprietors gave their support to the struggle for national unification and independence by providing rooms where the many secret societies could meet. Just as the landlord of the Caffè Florian in Venice permitted the romantic anarchist Carbonari to meet on his premises in the 1820s, so, too, in the 1840s in Lombardy many café proprietors took part in the great "tobacco strike" (designed to damage Austria financially), although such nationalist initiatives were bound to be detrimental to business. The history of the Risorgimento has been well recorded, but not that of its café proprietors.

The uprising in Upper Italy against the foreign domination of Austria was sparked off by a student rebellion in Padua on 8 February, 1848. The elegant Caffè Pedrocchi, situated opposite the university, was transformed into a "veritable battlefield"—the first time in history that a coffee-house itself became the object of attack as an ever clearer symbol of bourgeois reaction (Ill. 121). In future class conflicts, in its capacity as the "palace of the bourgeoisie" the coffee-house was to have to suffer no little damage with the outbreak of open conflict. But things had not yet reached this stage. The "holy war" against Austria, having begun in northern Italy and lost in Rome against France, a German newspaper commented on the retreat of Garibaldi and the entry of the French into Rome in June 1849 as follows: ". . . The French troops were accorded the friendliest of welcomes and greeted with loud cheering. Only as the troops marched past the Caffè delle belle Arte, the gathering place for the politically active of Rome, were they greeted with insults, thereby prompting the clearing of the premises with flat sabre blades."[84]

The anti-Austrian mood in Hungary was particularly manifest at Budapest's Café Pilvax. From 1847 it became the place of young Hungarian intellectuals who held regular round tables in the so-called "whispering room". At this table, which one can describe as having an overt political character, a small group of young revolutionary intellectuals regularly sat whose chief spokesman was no less a figure than the poet Sándor Petöfi, who had set up the "Society of Ten", a group with a thoroughly Jacobin programme of objectives. On 15 March, 1848, the day after the proclamation of the victory of the revolution in Vienna, Petöfi recited his celebrated "Nemzeti dal" national anthem, which he had composed the night before, to the enthusiastic customers of the coffee-house. Petöfi's goal was the establishing of an Hungarian republic, and in the wave of elation and in the expectation of coming events, the hall of the coffee-house, a long room with columns and a vaulted ceiling, on whose walls hung many pictures, was christened the "Hall of Freedom".

The coffee-houses in Berlin's Tiergarten, the so-called tents, can claim the distinction of having been the site of the commencement of the March events of 1848 (Ill. 120). On account of their position on the bank of the River Spree, the tents were the favourite gathering place of the people of the city. On Sunday afternoons, whole families would make their way down here in order to drink the celebrated *Weissbier* and to sit down to coffee.

The tents had already achieved a certain political notoriety in 1846 through the gatherings here of the so-called *Lichtfreunde* (Friends of Light) "who tried to organize a party here against pietistical tendencies on the part of the State, but which were thwarted by the intervention of the police"[85].

Two years later the coffee tents were once again to become the meeting place for opposition elements. On 6 March, 1848 a group of people got together in one of the small coffee-houses, "consisting chiefly of students, writers, clerks, artisans and workers, to draw up their demands"[85]. The intention was to issue an address of the youth to the King which would contain a number of demands for reforms. On the following day, when the group convened again in the coffee-house, their numbers increased on this occasion by a few more individuals, in order to finalize their document; the version consisted of nine concrete demands, ranging from the freedom of the press to the setting-up of a diet (*Landtag*). News that this document was being drawn-up spread, and the delaying tactics of the police on preventing the delivery of the address to the King enraged those attending the meeting. By the following day a crowd of about four thousand people had flocked to the tents, and further gatherings took place in and around the coffee tents on the ensuing days. By the evening of 15 March, the Tiergarten meeting "had already taken on a more serious demeanour and gave an indication of possible graver consequences. By meeting in this way the people of Berlin had simply assumed for themselves the right of free association . . ."[86]. The "graver consequences" anticipated by the anonymous eye-witness were not long in coming. The March Revolution which had begun with the drawing-up of the Tiergarten Address, now took its course.

Café Felsche in Leipzig, 1848

"His (Wilhelm Felsche's) greatest service to the working people of our city has been the instigation of the municipal eating-house, which he helped to set up. By a strange quirk of fate in 1848, the rioting mob smashed the windows of his establishment and threatened to destroy it on the very day that he had journeyed to Oschersleben for the purpose of setting up a similar eating-house for the working people and the poor in that town! We are told that the tumult had been caused . . . because at the parliamentary election he had cast his vote for Bassermann instead of for Robert Blum."

Leipziger Tageblatt, *31 December, 1867.*

From the 1850s onwards, revolutionary activity became increasingly less middle class and increasingly proletarian in character, and this in turn meant that the coffee-house lost once and for all in social terms its significance as a centre of political activity. The "bulwark" of the proletariat (Kautsky) were the inns, drinking parlours and bars which in France were already playing a considerable role in 1830 and in 1848: "Thirty thousand wine-houses of a political nature, to be precise . . . during the July Monarchy and the Republic of 1848 . . . spread their net over Paris," wrote the French historian Maurice Talmeyr.[87]

Of interest in our context is the fact that during the Frankfurt National Assembly of 1848, the left wing under the leadership of Robert Blum convened in the "Deutscher Hof" (from which the group got its name), while the right wing gathered in the Café Milani, symptomatic perhaps of the trend described above.

Emigrant cafés   Since time immemorial, at one time or another in all countries rebellious individuals have been forced into exile by the activities of the police authorities or the dictates of their consciences. During the 18th and 19th centuries, the favourite countries for those seeking asylum were France, England, Switzerland and the United States of America. The hospitality displayed by the French authorities was a consequence of the French Revolution, and this policy was adhered to to such an extent that after the July revolution of 1830, political emigrants were awarded an honorary pension, a facility taken advantage of by such people as Heinrich Heine in 1836 and Adam Mickiewicz in 1832. The wave of liberal thinking which had swept through Europe was also given sanction by the State in Switzerland, ensuring a safe refuge for those fleeing the persecution of Czarist Russia or the German *Bund*. For many of those who had fallen foul of the authorities in these countries, and in addition to politics, this could be for reasons of philosophy, religion and literature, their only option was emigration in order to avoid blacklisting, or to escape charges of preparing for insurrection, high treason etc., judicial consequences which hung as a constant threat over the activities of the pioneers of progress in those times. Prominent emigrants to Switzerland before 1848 were Georg Büchner, Ferdinand Freiligrath, Georg Herwegh and Wilhelm Weitling, and to France, Giuseppe Mazzini, Adam Mickiewicz, Heinrich Heine, Ludwig Börne and Karl Marx.

The list of those forced into emigration is almost limitless, ranging from major and minor political activists to the great poets and thinkers to insignificant journalists whose names have long since faded into obscurity. Depending on the conditions facing emigrants in a particular country, coffee-houses play an important role as meeting places for exiles, but in cases where—particularly in the 20th century—emigrants are prohibited from gathering in public, such a role is obviously restricted. Clubs, associations, private houses etc. are also important meeting places for emigrants, which assume an equal if not greater importance than the coffee-houses. In the 19th century two types of café are particularly prominent in this respect. Firstly there are establishments set up by the emigrants themselves, a phenomenon particularly apparent following abortive uprisings or successful revolutions and the subsequent mass exile which they promote, and secondly those which evolve into popular meeting places or residences abroad. The reasons for the emergence of the latter type are as diverse as there are cafés. Often they are those establishments where the newspapers of the homeland are available to customers, or which traditionally have always attracted visitors from a particular country, among which are now to be found many emigrants.

In exile in Marseilles, in 1831 Giuseppe Mazzini founded the secret society "Giovane Italia" (Young Italy). The members congregated in the numerous coffee-houses in the centre of the city and set about the organizing of a united independent Italy. But because Mazzini suffered from extreme left-wing radicalism like many fellow professional conspirators, the attempts failed.

Following the suppression of the uprising of 1830/31, some ten thousand soldiers, officers and politicians left Poland. In the main they made their way to France, but some also chose Belgium, England and the USA. As they marched through Germany they were accorded an enthusiastic reception by the populace and given support by a special committee set up for the purpose. In the memoirs of a Polish officer we read: "During the few days which we spent here [Leipzig] there was no time that we were not receiving visitors. We would be met on the streets and taken almost forcibly into the coffee-houses and confectioner's shops. We were treated more like gods than human beings."[88] Having arrived in Paris, the Poles, dressed in their characteristic red czapkas, would meet in particular cafés with a distinct Polish flavour of their own, and these became a regular meeting place of Polish emigrants.

The failure of the revolution of 1848 drove thousands of those who had taken part to France, England and Switzerland. In London, the German coffee-house became not only a gathering place for emigrants, it also served as a hotel for refugees. Theodor Fontane came upon this place by chance in 1852, and compared it with a "lion's den" or some fortress. His traditional Prussian loyalties somewhat ruffled, he wrote with some indignation over these German emigrants to his mother: "I shall refrain from further comment on my four-day stay at the German coffee-house, not that it was so dreadful that I shrink from the mere memory of it; on the contrary, the service and food became better by the day and were superior to the expensive boarding-house where I am now staying, particularly as far as the standard of coffee is concerned. But I forbear from further description because the days spent there were long and boring, and my spiritual fare consisted solely in the information my friend Blomeyer imparted to me concerning the prominent figures among the refugees. This information was indeed highly interesting in parts and could form the chapters for some adventure novel."[89] The German Coffee-House possessed three storeys, and the frontage extended along two windows. The ground floor contained an ale-house and porter shop where the customers were served at the counter. In the first floor was the large coffee room, in which newspapers could be read and where coffee and beer were served. On the second floor were situated the guest rooms and lodgings. Like their customers, the staff consisted of refugees from the 1848 revolution. The landlord, one Schärttner, had been the leader of the Hanau Corps, and the waiter one of his troops. Among the prominent figures from the revolution who Fontane met here were August Willich, who in 1849 had been the commander of a voluntary corps, whose adjutant was Friedrich Engels, Heise the co-editor of the *Hornisse* (Hornet), and the Grenadier Zinn who sat with him at table. Other common people were also present but the indignant Fontane declines to name them. "Every week a large meeting takes place here from Saturday night to Sunday morning. Then the French refugees join ranks with ours and over beer and brandy proclaim and affirm the fraternity of both peoples. The night before last I could hear the clamour into the early hours of the morning. It was pandemonium without equal. German and French songs liberally mixed with each other, interspersed by cries and oaths; now and then a door would slam, followed by a clatter down the stairs—it was an infernal scene!"[90] But even Fontane's Prussian heart is stirred when he sees the political emigrants: "Everyday they sit here with pale worn-out faces, at the mercy of the whims of a coarse waiter and the inclinations of their English hosts; there they sit, I say, their features etched with suffering and fervour, and dream of their great moment to come, with only one inquiry of any newcomer—whether anything is happening, whether that day has come. Their eyes light up momentarily and then subside like a flame without air."[91]

What Fontane failed to see of course was the international proletariat which was also establishing the beginnings of an organization in these often so desolate surroundings. For this was also the meeting place of the members of the League of Communists, who had taken over the welfare and organization of the refugees. August Willich, for example, was one such member.

Fontane saw the deprivation of the emigrants, but he was on the opposite side. In his advertisement for a German teacher's post he states unequivocally that he is "educated and a Prussian, not a refugee"!

In Brussels, where the German Workers' Association, set up by Marx in 1847, had taken over the organizing of assistance for the refugees, the most popular meeting place for emigrants was the Café des Boulevards attached to the hotel of the same name. Apart from the Germans, it was already a focal point for the Austrians, Italians and Hungarians fleeing the clutches of Metternich's police apparatus, as well as the French who had fled their country on account of their opposition to the regime of Louis Philippe. It was a motley collection of emigrants which met here, who had been politically persecuted in their own homelands for the most diverse of reasons and who adopted highly divergent views here, too. With the founding of two emigrant organizations in Brussels, Marx and Engels hoped to bring some sort of order to bear on the situation. Georg Herwegh, who at the same time was frequenting the Parisian Café Lemblin, a meeting place for revolutionaries from all countries, in March 1848 founded a democratic German legion, which was intended to carry out a military intervention in Germany. This idea possibly originated from the Russian conspirator Mikhail Bakunin, a *conspirateur de profession*, who was not only a frequenter of countless small cafés and political taverns, he also took his place in the fighting on the barricades. Marc Caussidière, the leader of the Paris barricades, is supposed to have said of him: "What a man! On the first day of the revolution he is simply irreplaceable, but on the second it is necessary to shoot him!" The first Russians to arrive in France in great numbers were mostly officers who had already fled their country in 1825 after the defeat of the Decembrist uprising. They established Russian cafés where they mainly or exclusively drank tea. These and similar establishments founded later, became the regular meeting places of a horde of political refugees whose numbers increased by the year, particularly after 1880, when an unprecedented number of Russian revolutionaries emigrated to France and Switzerland.

In Geneva, the Russian exiles nearly all lived in the Rue de Carouge. Apart from the eating-houses which they set up themselves, their main haunt was the café-brasserie Landolt in the university quarter. Between 1903 and 1905 the "Landolt" became a rendezvous for the leaders of the international working-class movement. Among them was Georgi Plekhanov, who had already founded the first Marxist group of Russian workers here in 1883, and Martov, who received the delegates to the Second Congress of the Russian Social Democrats which took place in Brussels and London, in the "Landolt".

Lenin also came here to play chess. In her memoirs, Lenin's wife was later to write of these years: "Nearly every evening, the Bolsheviks would gather in the Café Landolt and would sit here over a jug of beer long into the night."[92]

In Paris, the Russian exiles established themselves in a café on the Avenue d'Orléans (today Avenue du Général Leclerc). Together with other premises, it was kept under close surveillance by the Russian secret police, the Okhrana, a fact which is amply evidenced by the archive material discovered after the October Revolution.

While in June 1914 customers in the Café Fahrig in Munich laid hands on the Serbian orchestra, in Leipzig on "3 August, 1914, the second day of mobilization, a crowd of people . . . demanded the eradication of the traditional description café français"[93], and half of Europe eagerly rallied to the flag, the first of those with another view of the conflict began to leave their countries.

The outbreak of the First World War led to Switzerland, in particular Zurich, becoming a centre for pacifist emigrants from all over Europe. Apart from those hounded out of their countries for political reasons, there were also artists and writers who came to neutral Switzerland in order to draw up their manifestoes, protests and appeals against the war.

The Café Odeon became the most popular haunt of the exile artists, whose number included Ludwig Rubiner, Yvan and Claire Goll, Hans and Sophie Arp, Hugo Ball, Tristan Tzara, Else Lasker-Schüler, Stefan Zweig, Emil Ludwig, and many more. However, the true manifestation of the multi-faceted character of the emigrants, to which the artists and the—now resignative, now conspiratorial—political emigrants à la Bohème of the Café Odeon also belonged, is not the celebrated coffee-house itself, but rather the city's Spiegelgasse. Here, in 1916, dissatisfaction with the existing conditions united two extremes which could not have been further apart from each other. In the Café Voltaire (Spiegelgasse 1) a protest movement was set in motion, which was to go down in history as Dadaism. A few houses further down the lane, in the Spiegelgasse 14, Lenin lived with a "revolutionary-minded worker's family, which condemned the war as imperialist. The house was indeed truly 'international' . . ., in one of the rented rooms lived the wife of a German soldier . . ., in the neighbouring room, some Italian, in the third, an Austrian actor with a fox-red cat, and in the fourth room, we Russians."[94] Three weeks after the Dadaist movement was born, Lenin spoke in Zurich on the peace movement in the context of the national question. "The news of the Russian Revolution at the end of 1917 split our little world in Zurich into two camps—those who viewed it with indifference and those fired with excitement," wrote Claire Goll in her memoirs.[95] The most enthusiastic of all, the Russian revolutionaries, were from then on no longer to be found in the cafés of Switzerland and France. They returned to their homeland, leaving their seats in the emigrant coffee-houses at the immediate disposal of the Russian aristocrats to whom they had owed their exile in the first place.

With Hitler's coming to power in Germany in 1933, a wave of emigration was set off, to Europe and overseas, whose focus for the next twelve years was to be hundreds if not thousands of coffee-houses all over the world. Not a few of those who had left Germany upon the outbreak of the First World War in 1914, were forced to leave again in 1933, many of them never to return. The repercussions of this mass exodus for German cultural life were without precedent. Everyone associated with the progressive side of the Weimar Republic—from the fields of politics, art, literature and the sciences—left the country following Hitler's seizure of power. Not all of them were successful in their

A Russian aristocrat in Paris, 1934

". . . we are held in little regard here in Paris, this classic emigrant city, who is weary of our sort because she knows us so well. All have been gathering here for decades; the deposed monarchs and working class leaders; the Hungarians and the Russians; the Italian exiles and the Spanish; the Armenians, the Yugoslavs, the Greeks, Turks, Bulgarians, South Americans—and now, too, the Germans. Talk for a moment with one of these exiles who have been sitting around in Paris for ten or fifteen years . . . One of these Hungarian counts who was once Prime Minister and who had parted with all his property. He sat next to us in the Café 'Select' and played chess with himself."
Klaus Mann, Der Vulkan. Ein Roman unter Emigranten, Berlin/Weimar, 1969, p. 66.

flight. The eradication of science, art and literature, the "purification of German literature" was carried out with brutal expedition and German thoroughness. The elimination of every form of freedom of expression was achieved within the shortest time. The German emigrants were scattered all over Europe and later beyond. Up until 1939, the majority sought refuge in the neighbouring countries in the hope of an imminent return to their homeland. The main centres of emigration were London, Paris, Vienna and Prague, and within these cities the coffee-houses and hotels. Following the annexation of Austria and Czechoslovakia, and particularly after the outbreak of the Second World War, the emigrants began to move overseas. "We went into exile like dethroned monarchs. Some of us indeed did manage to live like kings on the Riviera. Others had to choke on the bread of poverty and subjugation," wrote Berthold Viertel.[96] This was a contradiction which could be openly observed in the cafés frequented by emigrants. One million Germans were driven into exile, and only a handful of them were able to live "like kings on the Riviera". In the same manner that the flight of German culture had both its predominantly political—that is to say anti-Fascist—side, to the same degree there was also an unpolitical aspect, and this situation was also reflected in the character of the emigré rendezvous, which not infrequently, in cases where the representatives of the two tendencies used one and the same café, led to conflicts among the exiles themselves.

The conditions faced by the exiles in all their complexity, the separation from family and friends, the general dislocation and disruption in work and leisure, the general feeling of rootlessness, the inability to communicate in a foreign language, police surveillance in the country of exile, restrictions on work, not to mention pecuniary want, meant that the cafés were to a large extent "cradles of illusions and graveyards" (Kesten), but also centres of resistance. Only a few (about a dozen) emigrant cafés between 1939 and 1945 have emerged until now from the conspiratorial veil which was of necessity drawn over them as clear focal points of political activity, but of their proprietors who permitted such goings-on on their premises we know next to nothing. We are better informed, however, about the cafés frequented by artists and writers. These were in the main coffee-houses which had already for decades served as established meeting places for the major figures in the world of the arts. Among these were the Café Américain (Ill. 106) in Amsterdam, the Café Continental in Prague, the Café Odeon in Zurich, the Café aux Deux Magots (Ill. 123) in Paris, the Café le Dôme, the Café de la Paix (Ill. 126) and the Café Select in Paris, the Café Royal in London and the Café Crown in New York. Encounters similar to the following were repeated a hundred times over: In the "Américain", Klaus Mann and Menno ter Braak met, the latter playing an important role in the debate around emigrant literature. In Prague's Café Continental Julius Fučik and Egon Erwin Kisch sat down with such anti-Fascist and proletarian writers as Willi Bredel, Hans Beimler and Johannes R. Becher who was passing through the city. Ernst Bloch, who had lived since 1933 in Zurich, visited his acquaintances daily in the Café Odeon. In September 1934 he entered for the last time to bid farewell. Commenting on his expulsion from Switzerland he declared: "A great tradition could not have been more stupidly tarnished. There remains but a crude, malevolent, myopic, bumbling, foolish, mean-spirited province. If you call upon Helvetia—to what ends could it be?"[97]

In addition to the major coffee-houses of Paris already mentioned, a number of smaller establishments emerged as notable emigrant centres. In 1934 the Café Mahieu became the venue for the "Kulturphilosophische Vereinigung" (cultural-philosophical association) founded by Hermann Skalde. More than thirty lectures were to be delivered here, not by any means signifying any political let alone specifically anti-Fascist resistance, they merely served the purpose of drawing German exiles together out of their isolation.

At the same time the Café Mahieu—in the same fashion as the basement of the Café Méphisto—became a meeting place for the members of the "Schutzverband Deutscher Schriftsteller" (Union for the Protection of German Writers), whose work had a specifically political character. It provided a forum for small groups to hear readings of works by left-wing and revolutionary writers. Another overtly political centre was the Café Mutualité: "Anyone taking the speaker's rostrum here frequently did so less as a writer than as a political being, who was not prepared to accept a fate as the victim and object of National Socialist politics."[98]

As was the case with Zurich, Paris and Amsterdam, Nice, Sanary-sur-Mer and Ascona also became centres for literary exiles, or rather the more notable among them. In Nice, so many German writers were assembled in places such as the Café de France and the Café Monnot, that Ludwig Marcuse, who was also here, was prompted to describe the resort as the "capital of German literature". The claim is not so far-fetched when one considers that, for example, in autumn 1934 Heinrich Mann, Hermann Kesten and Joseph Roth would congregate in the Café Monnot to discuss the theory and practice of the historical novel.

The concentration of élite literary figures in Nice and its surroundings (among whom were Thomas Mann, Arnold Zweig, Lion Feuchtwanger, Heinrich Mann, Bertolt Brecht, Ernst Toller, Alfred Kerr, René Schickele, Erwin Piscator, Hermann Kesten, Friedrich Wolf, Arthur Koestler, Rudolf Leonhard, Franz Werfel and Ernst Bloch) gave rise to not a little adverse comment on the part of other exiles, both working class and radical, who looked askance at the café circles and literary discussions as seemingly divorced from the reality of everyday events.

Such criticisms ranged from incomprehension in respect of the completely a-political attitude adopted by Erich Maria Remarque, whose schnapps recipes were better known in the cafés of Ascona than his novels (one could drink a "Remarque" in just about every café), to outright hostility to the snobbish gossips who frequented the coffee-houses of Nice, who surrounded themselves in an atmosphere of endless trivial debate. No doubt overall such a view was just as inapplicable as on the other hand Hermann Kesten's evocation of the emigré café as the "only place of any continuity in exile". In principle up until the outbreak of the Second World War, the emigrant café presented just the same contradictory features as any coffee-house in any age, it is merely in this case that they appear in a more extreme form.

Following the outbreak of war in the majority of western European countries, emigrants were to an ever increasing degree restricted from public life by internment or expulsion. It is particularly grotesque to learn, for example, that in some parts of Switzerland emigrants were prohibited from visiting cafés or promenades. During this period the emigrant café as a form of existence and way of life reached tragic proportions in Marseilles, a city with dozens of large and ultra-luxurious cafés as well as hundreds of more modest establishments, and which had now become the "emergency exit" of Europe for the victims of the Third *Reich*.

An authentic account of life in the cafés of this French port, the last stop on the European mainland, has been given by Anna Seghers in her novel *Transit*. Tens of thousands

Paris, 1933

"After 1933 Paris became a suburb of Berlin, only with the difference that the poets, writers, publishers and film directors lost all their importance once they had crossed the frontier . . . After the first pleasures of reunion, an oppressive mood pervaded the cafés. Conversations revolved solely around visas and residence permits . . . Torn from their careers they spent their time bemoaning their fate and recalling nostalgically the glory of times gone by. It was not easy to admit to oneself and to others that one now counted for nothing, after one had presided over some theatre or a major newspaper . . . They felt degraded and they were made to sense this. Even the waiters in the cafés looked down on them with disdain."

Claire Goll, Ich verzeihe keinem. Eine literarische Chronique scandaleuse, *Berlin, 1980, p. 204 f.*

of emigrants had collected here, impatiently awaiting the issue of a visa, a process involving an unending round of form-filling, obtaining stamps and permits, which more often than not resulted in the first document being already out of date by the time the final piece of paper was obtained, entailing starting the whole process again. Waiting became the chief occupation, most of it taking place sitting around in the cafés. "Should I sit in this café opposite the police station? I don't belong here. It is the café for those who have already got their papers in order and are waiting only for their exit visa . . ."[99]

The endless discussions which revolved around just one topic, when a ship was due to depart and if it would be possible to obtain a place on it—such discussions conducted over cups of bitter malt coffee by total strangers in every language of Europe—went on all hours of the day and night in the cafés of Marseilles. A woman hurries from one café to another, from the Café Roma to the Café Mont Vertoux, from the shabby to the more elegant—she is looking for someone. "He has been seen in many places. He has been seen four times a month in the "Mont Vertoux". The clerk from the Mexican Consulate saw him in the "Roma" as well as in the Consulate. The Corsican had seen him . . . in a café on the Quai des Belges. He also saw him again in a little café on the Quai du Port. But I alone always seem to arrive too late."[100]

A scene of hopelessness and loneliness—exile involved a different kind of despair for every emigrant. "Should I go back to the café? Have I been so infected by the fevered atmosphere that I have to become a part of it too?"[101] After the consulates closed their doors in the afternoon, things became particularly grim: "Tormented by a frantic anxiety, the refugees now thronged the Brûleurs des Loups and every other conceivable place. The air was filled with their frenzied chatter, an incoherent babble of wildly complicated suggestions and utter helplessness."[102] The cafés of Marseilles had all been transformed into emigrant cafés, only rarely could one observe "genuine French people. Instead of visas they discuss the easy money to be had from racketeering."[103] Even the Arab and African cafés, normally shunned by Europeans, now numbered European customers among their clientèle, who, driven by desperation, came here as a last resort in search of contacts and tips for ways of leaving the country illegally.

Writers, artists, musicians and their critics in the coffee-house

Since the beginning of the 18th century, the history of the liberal arts in all countries contains associations with coffee-houses which have been turned into centres of artistic creativity and communication by artists and writers, although with hindsight it is not always so readily apparent whether artists have frequented such establishments as representatives of the arts or merely as normal customers. If Mozart visited a coffee-house to play billiards, or Beethoven sat hidden in a back-room reading a newspaper, this clearly contains no significance in terms of music history. But where Robert Schumann and his circle of "Davidsbündler" regularly sat down in the "Kaffeebaum" (Ill. 75) in Leipzig to discuss the current unfavourable state of music, then it can be said in retrospect that such occasions played an extremely important role in the birth of German music criticism.

There are periods and places where the café has played only a peripheral role as an artistic institution, and others where it has assumed a central significance. Works actually completed here might have fallen into oblivion but can just as well have emerged as a contribution to world art or literature. In most cases many years have to pass before it can be ascertained what rank a particular coffee-house carries as a place of national or international relevance for art and literature.

There are coffee-houses which for more than two hundred years have served as an informal gathering place for the world's artists, for example the Caffè Greco in Rome (Ill. 139, 140), whereas others have entertained an artistic clientèle for but a few years, but nevertheless in overall terms have no less a cultural importance; one such example is the Café Guerbois in Paris. In many instances, the coffee-house has not only provided premises for an individual artist or groups of artists, it has also accommodated the representatives of complete artistic or literary epochs. On two occasions it can be said to have incorporated the spirit of the age. In England, the age of Enlightenment is associated almost exclusively with the coffee-house up until about 1750, and similarly in France up until 1789, and again at the end of the 19th century the coffee-house formed the backdrop for the European *fin de siècle*.

For more than three hundred years artists and men of letters have been regular frequenters of coffee-houses, either in an individual capacity or as a group, and on many occasions have also attracted followers from the general public in their wake. From informal and flexible gatherings (often brought about through the proximity of a café to a theatre, opera house, academy and the like) emerged more formal groupings with a marked club or association character, with clearly defined objectives. The association and society, dominant features of social life of the 19th century, also extended to the field of the arts, and from the Enlightenment to the *fin de siècle* a multitude of private literary and artistic societies or clubs were formed, and not a few of them were originally resident in the back-room of a coffee-house.

But even in places where large concentrations of artists and writers were to be found, there was barely a single café of which it can be said that its clientèle consisted exclusively of artists, writers, musicians and their hangers-on. For example in 1900, when the writers Peter Altenberg, Karl Kraus, Egon Friedell, Alfred Polgar et al. turned the Café Central in Vienna to the foremost Austrian literary café, the magnificent building, designed by Ferstel, was at the time the daily meeting place for higher-ranking civil servants from the surrounding ministries, the haunt of the aristocracy and the wealthy bourgeoisie as well as politicians and stockbrokers. The same could be said on a smaller scale of many other places, and as a phenomenon, the artists' café is in reality nothing more than a part of an otherwise "normal" coffee-house trade in all its variety, in which are to be found those with artistic and literary ambitions in great concentrations.

The frequenting of coffee-houses with its attendant ambiguities, being on the one hand a place for amusing and stimulating discussion with one's peers, and on the other a place to kill time, is also reflected in the ambivalent attitudes in respect of the literary coffee-house scene, which range from outright dismissal at one extreme to exaggerated idealization at the other.

As a general rule those writers who have indeed used the coffee-house table as their desk stand outside the boundaries of such controversies. Apart from representatives of the so-called Bohemian world, they also include—and more contrasting it would be hard to imagine—such writers as Georges Bernanos and Anna Seghers. The former, a leading figure of the literary *renouveau catholique*, chose his workplace in obscure coffee-houses: "For hours on end I crouch in dim cafés which I have deliberately sought out because it is completely impossible to remain in there for more than five minutes if one

Ecole de Paris

"I believe it was the Irish writer George Moore—or was it Stendhal?—who in reply to the question how might art be best promoted, gave the remarkable answer: 'Establish cafés!'"
René Prévot, Bohème, *Munich, 1922, p. 91.*

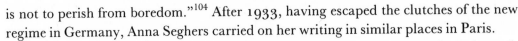

is not to perish from boredom."[104] After 1933, having escaped the clutches of the new regime in Germany, Anna Seghers carried on her writing in similar places in Paris.

The great number of gatherings of artists and writers in coffee-houses from the 17th century down to the present day renders impossible a summary be it only of rudimentary character. Even the broadest outline will not bring one any closer to the heart of the phenomenon. For this reason we will make recourse to the device of tracing the development of art and literature, pausing only at those points where artists, poets or musicians have emerged from the coffee-house to artistic achievement on a national scale, which in turn has proceeded to recognition as making a contribution of international proportions to their field. But we will refrain from any attempt at an explanation or description of why one particular café rather than its neighbour became a haunt of artists, or the extent of the role played by the respective proprietor as a "promoter" of the arts and suchlike. Sufficient information of this kind is contained in the relevant literature on the subject. An even fuller picture would be provided if at some point a systematic survey were to be made of the "ephemera" of the art world, such as letters, unpublished diaries, sketchbooks, and the compilation of all forms of credit notes or compensations for drinking debts.

ENGLAND   The intimate association between English belletrists and coffee-houses between 1660 and 1730 has already been indicated in the account of the emergence of the press, a process promoted by the writers of the day. We return once again to this juncture, for one can say without fear of exaggeration that the whole of English literature during this period is resident in the coffee-house, as once its exponents had sat in the literary taverns, for example the Mermaid Tavern in London frequented by Shakespeare, Jonson, Fletcher and others.

From 1657, John Dryden was to be found every day from three o'clock in the afternoon, ensconced in Will's Coffee-House. His towering personality captivated a dozen no less talented writers right up until his death, and attracted hundreds of admirers to his presence. For decades Dryden held court here, presiding over the literary scene like a spiritual father. He met here with publishers and translators, with actors who performed his works, and with members of the Royal Society to which he belonged.

Figures of the stature of Swift, Pope, Addison, Steele, Congreve, Wycherley, Savage, Pepys and many others frequented "Will's". The only name of distinction missing from this roll of honour is Daniel Defoe. Most of them became personally acquainted with Dryden, and Addison and Steele regularly sat down to table with him.

After 1712, Button's Coffee-House took over the pre-eminent position hitherto enjoyed by "Will's". "Button's" was a venture of Addison's very own undertaking. Daniel Button was installed as licencee by Addison in 1712, and on account of the latter in addition to his poetic talents possessing solid political interests as a committed Whig, the premises soon became a haunt of both writers and Whig supporters. With Addison at their head, a group of the regular customers of "Will's" moved "over the way" into their new domicile. One reason for this was literary and political disagreements, another was the fact that the successor to William Urwin (the founder of "Will's") was more interested in promoting his customers' thirst and enthusiasm for cards than their literary inclinations. In this he was clearly of a more practical nature than his predecessor Urwin, who was a patron of the arts and who died penniless and weighted down with debts in the year 1695.

"Button's" survived until 1719. As a centre of the literary world it was less sought after than "Will's", for like Addison most of the writers who gathered here were actively engaged in politics, and within a short time the house had taken on far more the character of a political headquarters, particularly after 1714, as many of the "major thinkers among the Whigs were pressed by the new government instead of discussing questions of taste and literature, to become involved in the political struggle"[105]. Two additional literary venues were the "Smyrna" and St. James's Coffee-House. Among others Swift was a regular habitué of both houses. In the middle of the 18th century "The Turk's Head" became the meeting place for the Literary Club, which had formed into an exclusive society from the group gathered around Samuel Johnson.

FRANCE For 18th-century Europe it was France, for France it was Paris, and for Paris it was the coffee-houses, the "stamping mills" of the metropolis, which sent the blood coursing through the veins of the bourgeoisie. Around 1750 there were six hundred cafés in the city, by 1789 there were about nine hundred.

During the *siècle des lumières*—the age of Enlightenment—from 1715 to 1789, everyone of rank and repute frequented the cafés situated along both banks of the Seine. In the Café Procope Voltaire and Diderot conducted brilliant literary debates, surrounded by performers from the *Comédie* situated opposite, although regrettably there was no-one present to record them for posterity. Among the other prominent literary figures who came here were Beaumarchais, Fontenelle and Crébillon. The by now equally renowned Café de la Régence also played host to just about all the great thinkers and political figures of the 18th and 19th centuries, to list them all would be to draw up a catalogue of the history of French thought and culture.

The significance of the coffee-house as a public institution for the literature and art of France up until 1850, can be gleaned from three works unsurpassed for the comprehensive picture which they provide: Louis Sébastien Mercier's *Tableau de Paris* (1781–1790), and his *Le nouveau Paris* (1798), and the grandiose *Comédie humaine* by Honoré de Balzac. Like no other, Balzac described the literary life in the Parisian coffee-houses from 1820 onwards, and the twilight existence at its heart. The Café Voltaire, the Café Turc and others were literary rendezvous where Balzac was also to be seen on occasions. He could even be found in the Café Tortoni, among "all the latest authors"[106], but none of these or similar haunts held his custom for long, for the world of the Parisian literary cafés "wearied and repelled him to ever increasing degree"[107].

After 1850 the coffee-houses of Paris assumed an increasing significance for the representatives of the plastic arts, both for those artists returning to the city from the provinces to which they had withdrawn during the period of the July Monarchy (for example the Barbizon School) as well as for those seeking to counter the prevailing trends in the art of the day. Not least the cafés were of importance for those artists from Europe and overseas who, with the aid of a stipend or at their own expense, had made their way to what they regarded as the art metropolis. In 1855 and 1856, the Café Molière became the daily meeting place for the followers of Gustave Courbet, who had experienced rejection from the Salon. Assembled here were Courbet himself, Fantin-Latour, Manet, Degas, and the subsequent President of the Society of British Artists, the Anglo-American painter James Whistler.

The Café Guerbois was frequented by Edouard Manet, a dominant figure who during the course of the 1860s gathered around himself everyone whom subsequent art histo-

Paris, circa 1870

"Major artistic revolutions are planned and announced with cool determination in the cafés. One needs only to mention the Café Neu-Athen in Montmartre, where fifty years ago the painter revolutionaries spent their evenings in a frenzy of creativity."
René Prévot, Bohème, Munich, 1922, p. 92.

rians have come to refer to as embodying the birth of Impressionism, whose repercussions affected artistic trends all over Europe. The group included such artists as Degas, Monet and Renoir. By the time Vincent van Gogh arrived in the city, Manet was already dead, but in the artists' quarter a dozen coffee-houses had sprung up to become the established rendezvous of impressionist painters, the most prominent of these being the Café de la Nouvelle Athènes and the Café de l'Ermitage in Montmartre. During the 1870s and 80s the latter establishment became the gathering place of the Scandinavian Impressionists, both writers and painters, among them Carl Larsson, Bernt Lindholm, Olof Hermelin, Alfred Wahlberg, and not least, of course, August Strindberg.[108]

Towards the end of the 19th century, a trend which had been in progress for decades now became readily apparent. The protagonists of art and literature had finally abandoned the surviving literary and artistic salons, and were seeking their public among the artists' taverns and cafés. The main consequence of this is an enormous increase in the number of such establishments, and from this moment on until the outbreak of the Second World War Paris was to become the centre pure and simple of international art. Nowhere is this more evident than in the cafés of Montmartre and Montparnasse.

The greatest figure of the age of Enlightenment was Voltaire, and during the 1890s in the café named after him there sat the most prominent exponent of the *fin de siècle*, prince of poetry and master of linguistic obscurity, Stéphane Mallarmé, and around him, Arthur Rimbaud, Paul Verlaine and Paul Gauguin.

Shortly after the turn of the century, the Café aux Deux Magots (Ill. 123), which since its inception in 1875 had been an informal rendezvous for intellectuals and writers of all shades, became the haunt of Pablo Picasso and Georges Braques, where they called the Cubist movement to life. After 1920 it was the Café le Dôme which emerged as the most popular meeting place for the painters, representing the whole "école de Paris".

During the years 1939 and 1940 the French writers and artists began to move away from the Café le Dôme. Jean-Paul Sartre has given two reasons for this. Firstly, the Vavin Metro station was closed down, and secondly the café was inundated by Germans who were "so tactless as to bring their own tea and coffee with them, and have them prepared in front of the French customers . . ."[109] After 1939 the Café de Flore (Ill. 125) became the new centre. Picasso, André Breton and Léon-Paul Fargue took the rest of the art world along with them. In 1940 Sartre and Simone de Beauvoir were daily visitors to the café, sitting there "from nine in the morning until midday, when we would go and eat. At two we returned, and talked to our acquaintances until four, working from then until eight in the evening. After supper we would arrange to meet there with all manner of people. This might all appear somewhat strange, but the 'Flore' was, to put it thus, our home. Even when the air-raid sirens sounded, we merely pretended to make our way down to the basement, but in fact crept back up to the first floor where we carried on with our work."[110]

The French writer Boris Vian, who belonged to these daily gatherings at the "Flore", which in the post-war era with its *littérature engagée* was to form one of the most significant episodes in late-bourgeois literature, has summed up the scene as follows: "If there had not been any cafés, there would have been no Jean-Paul Sartre."[111] However exaggerated this claim might appear, nevertheless it is very much apparent from many passages in Sartre's works that the motifs and occurrences taken from the coffee-house milieu, substantiate to a considerable degree the existentialist view of the "banality of human existence".

118   Tontine Coffee-House in New York, *c.*
1797. Wood engraving by Walter M. Aikman,
1910, from an original painting by Francis
Guy, about 1797. New York, Museum of the
City.

119 Café d'Orsay in Paris in 1847. This elegant establishment was the daily meeting place of the Deputies of the nearby Chamber of Deputies. The busiest part of the day here was between 11 and 1 o'clock when the Deputies came for their midday meal. A contemporary wrote that "the election of Monsieur Léon de Malleville, the pupil and follower of Monsieur Thiers to Vice-President in place of the present Prime Minister Herbert, was initiated there". Illustrations and quotation in: *Illustrirte Zeitung*, Leipzig, 17 April, 1847.

120 Political meeting in front of the coffee tents in Berlin on 20 April, 1848. Wood engraving in: *Illustrirte Zeitung*, Leipzig, 6 May, 1848.

121 Memorial plaque to the February fighting of 1848 in the Caffè Pedrocchi in Padua.

122 Recruiting office of the Hülsen Volunteer Corps in the Café Vaterland, Berlin, 1918. Berlin, Dietz Collection.

123 Café aux Deux Magots in Paris. Since its opening in 1875, this corner café has been a prominent meeting place for artists and writers.

124 Café La Palette in Paris, a rendezvous for emigrants and a well-known artists' café. The decorative faience tiling on the walls originates from the 1920s.

125 Café de Flore in Paris, among its regular clientèle during the 1950s were Jean-Paul Sartre and Simone de Beauvoir.

127 Newspaper reader in the Café Tommaseo in Trieste; the café, which was opened in 1830 under the name of its proprietor, Tomasso Marcato, was given its present name in 1848, following the freeing of the patriotic poet Niccolò Tommaseo. The more conservatively minded among its customers continued to call it "Al vecchio Tomasso" for long afterwards.

128 Café de Gijón in Madrid. Opened in the year 1916, this coffee-house is one of the best-known in Spain.

Following page:
129 De Engelbewaarder-Litterair café in Amsterdam.

ITALY   Italy was the destination of all those embarking on their grand tour during the 18th and 19th centuries, and anyone arriving in Venice, Naples or Rome would immediately make for the coffee-house where he would be assured of meeting his respective fellow-countrymen and could announce his own addition to their number. An equivalent status to that of cosmopolitan Montparnasse in 20th-century Paris was enjoyed by the area around the Spanish Square in Rome at the turn of the 18th century, and in particular its focal point, the Caffè Greco (Ill. 139). In contrast to the "literary workshop" character of the coffee-houses of England and France in the 18th century, the "Greco", a haunt mainly of artists and art experts was more of an international clearing house for the exchange of news, a post office and a centre for art dealers. Following the withdrawal of the English from the "Greco", it became the meeting place of the Germans who made up the majority of its customers until 1860.

"Watching the people sitting in their Café Greco, one can see what a dreadful lot they are. I hardly ever go there because I find them and their favourite haunt simply too awful. The premises consist of a tiny dark room perhaps eight paces wide, and on one side of the parlour customers are allowed to smoke tobacco and on the other not. There they sit on the benches standing around the room, their broad hats on their heads, large bloodhounds at their sides, their throats, cheeks, indeed their whole faces covered by hair, filling the air with foul smoke (but only on one side of the room), and exchanging crudities . . . and in this manner they drink coffee and discuss Titian and Pordenone . . ." Such was the impression of the place created by Felix Mendelssohn Bartholdy writing to his father in 1830.

Among these "awful people" were all the representatives, the famous and the not-so-famous of the 19th-century "école de Rome", ranging from the celebrated sculptors Bertel Thorvaldsen and Antonio Canova to the Nazarenes, a group of romantic artists who had emigrated from Vienna in 1809, and who were so named on account of their hair which they wore *alla nazarena*, and to the numerous anonymous art students from all the countries of Europe, who in some instances resided for years in the city.

Even in faraway Rome the German artists did not neglect to form themselves into an association. They called their group the "Colonna-Gesellschaft" (Colonna Association), having constituted themselves in about 1860 in the Caffè Colonna.

Between 1850 and 1870, the Caffè Michelangelo, situated in Florence's Palazzo Medici, was a typically Italian establishment. The daily gathering of painters, which soon overflowed into the back-room, prompted the proprietor to convert his tavern into a coffee-house. The more than twenty painters and sculptors who collected here, among them Giovanni Fattori, Telemaco Signorini and Adriano Cecioni, nearly all actively involved in the Risorgimento, had rejected romantic art but had yet to arrive at a naturalistic approach. They christened their movement "macchia", meaning spot. They not only painted their pictures in this style, they also defended their position in two art journals. Contemporary critics derided them as "Macchiaiuoli" or daubers, but like the French Impressionists after them, whose pictures were claimed to induce miscarriages, this nickname was later to become a mark of distinction, and the one with which they have gone down in the history of art.

AUSTRIA/HUNGARY/CZECHOSLOVAKIA   From about 1900 onwards, the main centres of activity of Austrian writers and artists in Vienna were the Café Griensteidl, the Café Central, the Café Herrenhof, the Café Museum, the Café Imperial and the Café Sperl.

Caffè Greco, Rome

"All the writers and artists who came to Rome made for the Greco. Casanova himself sat here in the company of Raphael Mengs and Winckelmann, Goldoni and Gogol came here, the composers Rossini, Berlioz, Liszt, Gounod, Richard Wagner and Felix Mendelssohn, the artists Canova, Thorwaldsen, Marées, Schwind, Feuerbach, Böcklin, Lenbach, and also Mickiewicz, Grillparzer and Gregorovius, Lord Byron and Shelley, Nathaniel Hawthorne and Mark Twain, Ampère and Hippolyte Taine, Hans Christian Andersen and Friedrich Nietzsche, Heinrich Mann and Thomas Mann, Edschmid, Wolfgang Koeppen and G. R. Hocke."
Hermann Kesten, Dichter im Café, Munich, 1959, p. 315.

Theory of the Café Central in Vienna

"The Café Central in Vienna is not in fact a coffee-house like any other, rather it is a whole outlook on life, and one whose most fundamental principle consists in ignoring the world . . . It is a place for people who have taken their decision to live and let live, but who lack the necessary strength of character to live up to it. It is a veritable refuge for people who have to kill time before time itself kills them. It is the trusted surrounding for those to whom trusted surroundings are anathema, a refuge for married couples and lovers from the horror of undisturbed intimacy, a haven for troubled souls who spend their waking hours there in search of themselves, or alternatively in flight from their true selves, burying their fugitive Id behind newspapers, tedious conversation and playing cards, and forcing their pursuer Id into the role of an onlooker compelled to keep silent . . . The Café Central is a provincial backwater in the womb of the big city, deadened by gossip, inquisitiveness and malicious tattle. I often think that the regular customers in this coffee-house must lead an existence similar to the fish in an aquarium, constantly circling each other, constantly busy in the pursuit of nothing, always full of expectation but also full of anxiety that something new could fall into the glass tank; playing the game of life in the deep sea on their sea bottom en miniature, and completely lost if, God forbid, the aquarium would be transformed in a banking-house."

Alfred Polgar, Die Mission des Luftballons. Skizzen und Erwägungen, *Berlin, 1975, p. 106 f.*

Without these coffee-house "cultural institutions", there would probably have been no Viennese contribution to the literature of the *fin de siècle*, no advance on the part of Austria to world literary status, and no Viennese Secession.

The Café Sperl, which opened in 1880, became the stronghold of painters, sculptors and graphic artists, who sat around the *Genietisch* (the table of geniuses) and made disparaging remarks about the historicist architecture of the Ringstrasse and the Makart studio. The requisite turnover for ensuring the proprietor's commercial survival was provided by the military, which from the rank of lieutenant upwards sat daily around the *Artillerietisch* (table of the artillery) and cast pitying glances across at the poor artists who sat at the "table of geniuses", where from about 1885 the "Hagen-Gesellschaft" (Hagen Society) and from about 1895 the "Siebenerclub" (the Club of the Seven) was actively engaged in creating what was later to go down in history as the so-called Viennese Secession.

The Café Griensteidl, opened in 1844, had already been the witness to not a few events of literary and political significance (particularly during the years 1848/1849), by the time in the 1890s when it provided a regular meeting place for two groups of customers who were later to win political and literary renown and glory. On the one side sat the Marxist "Privy councillor of the Revolution"[112], Viktor Adler, with his group of followers, while on the other side collected the literary group "Jung Wien" around Hermann Bahr, responsible for Viennese aestheticism. Only one unifying spirit prevailed in the "Griensteideleum", and this was an opposition to female emancipation. Female visitors were rarely if ever to be seen in the place. The bizarre juxtaposition of Austrian Marxists on the one hand and the "most tender blooms of decadence"—as Karl Kraus liked to call them—on the other, continued until the café's demolition, to be revived with renewed vigour in the Café Central, the successor of the "Griensteidl".

At least two dozen Viennese coffee-houses—out of a total of six hundred in 1900—can be said to be of significance as informal meeting places for the art and literary world. From 1900 the Café Imperial became a focal point for the followers of Karl Kraus. In addition to its architect Adolf Loos, the Café Museum was the haunt of his friend Georg Trakl. After 1910 one could find here Hermann Broch, Franz Blei, Alfred Polgar, Franz Werfel and Robert Musil. After the First World War the Café Central became the venue for the regular Monday meeting of the "Mocha Symposium" around Franz Blei and Erhard Buschbeck, although mocha was not the main drink of the group. The Café Herrenhof was declared the "latest" literary café by Anton Kuh, who, adept at the art of self-propaganda, derided the frequenters of the Café Central as being "mummified".

The romantic poet Sándor Petöfi set up residence in Budapest's Café Pilvax, from where he set out in 1849 to the battlefield as a Major in the liberation army, never to return.

The literary and political "Society of Ten" which Petöfi had established in the "Pilvax", not only regarded itself as a Jacobinic club during March 1848, it acted as one until the final defeat of the revolution (cf. p. 176 f.).

Apart from the "Pilvax", which until its demolition in 1912 remained a meeting place for writers and artists, there were several dozen coffee-houses in Budapest which have gone down in the annals of Hungarian art and literary history as important artists' rendezvous and which deserve mention here, although we will restrict ourselves to just a few examples. The best-known is the café-restaurant "New York" (today the "Hungaria") which opened in 1894, who's visitors' book, with due appropriateness for the imposing décor, is known as "The Great Missal", containing when not mistaken the name of every world celebrity to have trodden Hungarian soil. In fact the "living realm of true writers"[113] and artists of Hungarian origin would appear rather than the "New York", to have frequented the Café Balaton, the Café Vigadó or the Café Gresham.

From 1909 the painter Lajos Tihanyi was a habitué of the Café Balaton, surrounded by his circle of colleagues who made up the Nyolcak Group (Group of Eight).

The editorial board of the magazine *Nyugat* (West), founded in 1908, among them Endre Ady, would meet once a week in the Café Vigadó, although it has been claimed that these gatherings took place in the "New York". This journal was to become one of the most important literary organs for the young Hungarian intelligentsia, now looking to the influence of France and Germany in its quest for emancipation. During 1917 and 1918, Franz Molnár and Tibor Déry, two Hungarian writers who were subsequently to attain international renown, could be found in the Café Gresham. During the inter-war years an informal group was to meet regularly at the "Gresham", made up of artists, art experts and art dealers, which has gone down in Hungarian art history as the Gresham circle.

In Prague, the third centre of what was once the cultural domain of the Habsburg empire, there were four coffee-houses in existence in the first three decades of this century which were particularly popular among Czech and German writers. For their part, the more successful among the Germans tended to frequent the Café Continental, which formed the focal point of the German-Jewish intelligentsia in Prague. The poets who embodied "official" Prague literature in the years preceding the First World War, were those individuals who "would never be seen in a bi-lingual café, frequenting solely the German Café Continental or the German Casino. The prince of poets for these people was the long-haired gynaecologist Dr. Hugo Salus"[114]. Such was the situation as described by Egon Erwin Kisch, who in those days was more frequently to be found among the clientèle of the bi-lingual Café Central, in the company of the younger generation of poets, who ostantatiously rejected the national exclusivity of the leading artists' clique in the Café Continental. And it was the regulars who gathered here, whose number included Antonín Macek, Rainer Maria Rilke, Franz Kafka, Max Brod, Egon Erwin Kisch and others who began to bridge the gulf between the two. The ice had been broken initially in 1896 by the publication of the then unknown René Rilke, of an extraordinarily delicate declaration of love for the Czech Prague. The departure of the regulars from the Café Central to take up residence at the Café Arco was commented upon by Karl Kraus in his poem "The Arconauts":

> "Es *werfel*t und *brod*et
> Und *kafka*t und *kisch*t . . ."

This onomatopoeic play on the names of the chief protagonists of the Arco coffee circle, intended as a mildly ironic criticism, could well serve today as a schoolboy's aide memoire of the leading representatives of Prague's world-class literature.

GERMANY   "An apparently large number of new coffee-houses have set up business. There Germania's sons sit drinking their coffee, smoking cigars, making a clatter with the dominoes, and scanning the newspapers. Literature has found its salvation in the coffee-house and with it its exponents. There the army of collaborators and review writers ogle with the journals, each with his own . . ." Such is the description provided by

130　Artists' café. Drawing by Alfred Kubin, 1926.

the *Leipziger Tageblatt* in 1901, in its comment on the literary coffee-houses. In fact it was not that much of a novelty for the German literary world to have also taken up residence in the coffee-house. Such a phenomenon had been evident during the 19th century, mostly in the shape of private clubs and societies, the most famous of which was the Sunday society called "Tunnel über der Spree" (tunnel over the River Spree) which existed in Berlin between 1827 and 1898. That it was of all people a feuilletonist and theatre critic from distant Vienna who first established this Prussian writers' and artists' society, is one of those surprises which the cultural history of the coffee-house continues to throw up. Moritz Saphir first appeared in Berlin in 1825, organized the publication of three journals, founded this society, threw the received proprieties of *Biedermeier* Berlin into disarray with his mordant wit and sarcasm, and then completely disappeared from Prussia again in 1829. The members of the "Tunnel" continued to meet every Sunday for more than seventy years. Among their number were Franz Kugler, Adolph Menzel, Theodor Storm, Theodor Fontane, Paul Heyse, Theodor Hosemann and many others. For many of the years of the society's existence its convening place was the great hall of the Café Belvedere. Those who participated in the society's meetings spoke highly of them, and without doubt they must have played a by no means minor role in providing an opportunity for mutually-helpful criticism and for the Berlin literary scene as a whole. In his memoirs *Von Zwanzig bis Dreissig* (From twenty to thirty), Theodor Fontane, who had been a member since 1844 under the name of Lafontaine, proffered the view: "However much I must give the Tunnel its due, nevertheless one has to say that on many Sundays it was little more than a smoking and coffee salon, whereby while the waiter came and went something or other would be read aloud." Following his promotion to Professor of Poetry in Munich, Emanuel Geibel summed the society up as a "kindergarten for minor poets".

We know that there were regular gatherings of writers and publishers around 1825 in Leipzig's Café-Konditorei Wollenweber, from the descriptions of his "free hours in the confectionery" left to posterity by Karl Herlossohn. Of far greater significance, however, were the regular meetings of the so-called "Davidsbündler", centred around Robert Schumann, who from 1833 convened in the "Kaffeebaum", and who with the establishing and publishing of the *Neue Zeitschrift für Musik* laid the foundations for bourgeois music criticism in Germany.

In Munich there was a verse which went:

> "In the holy pond of Singapore
> There lies an old crocodile
> Of extremely sullen nature
> Chewing on a lotus leaf."

It was recited at the christening of the "Crocodile Society"—a literary association—which took place in 1856, and whose core was made up of individuals summoned personally to Munich by the Bavarian king, Maximilian II, who paid their keep. Between 1856–57 the "Crocodile" met in the Café Stadt München, followed by the Café Daburger, and from 1883 the Café Dall'armi. Among those who appeared at the regular sessions of the club were Professor of Literature and Lecturer Royal, Emanuel Geibel, the Professor of Legal History Felix Dahn (who had already been a member of the "Tunnel"), and Adolf F. Schack and Paul Heyse, who had similarly been summoned to Munich by the Bavarian king. This Munich poets' circle began to lose significance when the first Bohemians of a more naturalistic tendency, among them Frank Wedekind, took up their places in the Café Minerva. The awarding of the 1910 Nobel Prize for literature to the German poet Paul Heyse was really more of a gesture of acknowledgement for the century then gone, for the main protagonists of the twentieth century were now firmly ensconced in the Café Stefanie in Munich or the Café Luitpold, the Café des Westens or the Café Bauer in Berlin, or the Café Merkur in Leipzig.

The Café Luitpold (Ill. 89), which had ben opened in 1888, not only bore "with the most gracious permission" the name of the sovereign, it was also built in the same palatial Wittelsbach style, and like the Café Central of Vienna, attracted not only the aristocratic young bloods and *jeunesse dorée* but also the numerous members of the world of the arts. The "Luitpold" was directly associated with a major event in German art history, for in 1911 it witnessed the birth of the "Blue Rider" School of artists, founded by Wassily Kandinsky, Franz Marc and the art dealer Goltz, to which Alfred Kubin, August Macke, Paul Klee and Arnold Schönberg also belonged. By the outbreak of the First World War in 1914, the Expressionist protest movement set in motion by the "Blue Rider" School had become so much part of the established scene that it was already being rejected by the more left-wing Bohemian artists who frequented the Café Stefanie.

SPAIN/PORTUGAL   By the beginning of the 20th century, Barcelona already had turned into a modern industrial and commercial centre of Europe, which with its progressive bourgeois atmosphere had become the home of an impressive offshoot of the *école de Paris*. The Café Els Quatre Gats provided the meeting place for the Catalan painters who from here, in constant interplay with the styles and trends emerging from Paris, contributed to the creation of a socially critical and symbolic modernism. This group of painters has in fact gone down in the history of Spanish art as "Els Quatre Gats". It was here in 1897 that a sixteen-year-old prodigy by the name of Pablo Picasso presented his pictures to the world for the first time.

During the first two decades of the 20th century, the main gathering place for writers in Madrid was the Café del Pombo, where the various trends and tendencies and "isms" of world literature took on a specifically Spanish character. For many years there was a group of writers and artists gathered around Ramón Gómez de la Serna, the story of which formed the basis of his two-volume work *Pombo* written in 1918. And it was in this café that he created the Greguería literary paradox which from henceforth was to become an indispensable part of Spanish lyric writing. When Picasso made one of his appearances here, his visit was occasion for major celebrations.

During the 1920s and '30s, Madrid's Café de Gijón (Ill. 128), opened in 1916, became a cultural clearing house for the most varied elements of the Spanish tradition. A regular customer here was the philosophy professor Ortega y Gasset, as well as the young Federico García Lorca. As a high-school student the latter had taken the decision to embark on a literary career in the Café Alameda in Granada. In Madrid he was also to be found among the clientèle of the Café Comercial, the Café del Prado and the Café del Oriente, where in 1924 he was drawn by his friend Salvador Dalí (Ill. 131).

In Portugal, which like Spain also possesses a special coffee-house culture all its own, it is the Café A Brasileira (Ill. 86), opened in Lisbon in 1904, which the literary world has elevated to its chief rendezvous. The poet Fernando Pessoa became a regular customer here. On account of his excellent knowledge of English he was able to write bi-lingually, thereby performing a service of world proportions for Portuguese poetry.

131   Federico García Lorca in the Café del Oriente in Madrid. Indian ink drawing by Salvador Dalí, 1924.

THE UNITED STATES OF AMERICA   "In America there are no coffee-houses where one can sit for hours at a time, and if there were they would not be at all congenial, and if they were they would long have gone out of business."[115] This remarkable assertion is attributed by Alfred Polgar to an American publisher who is somewhat unenthusiastically dealing with the story of an Austrian emigrant in the 1930s. No doubt at the time there were indeed few homy coffee-houses in the specifically Austrian sense in America, but that is not to say that there were no literary cafés at all. It was simply that they were not *gemütlich*, whatever one was supposed to understand by this elusive word in the German speaking countries.

During the 1920s in New York, the Café Royal and the Waldorf Cafeteria were the most prominent venues for gatherings of writers and artists. And with immigrants arriving in their thousands in the country, an increasing number of coffee-houses were established in Greenwich Village, the traditional artists' quarter, which in appearance and service are little different from their European counterparts. To distinguish them from the cafeterias or coffee shops they were known as coffee cafés. The best-known were the Café Rienzi, the Peacock Café and the Café Limelight, whose clientèle was composed predominantly of emigrant writers and artists. These and other cafés dotted around Greenwich Village, which somewhat ironically acquired the name Java spots, have in the meantime become the haunt of American writers, publishers, actors and film-makers of every field.

"Epatez les bourgeois!"— Bohemians in the coffee-house

A gypsy café in Paris

"*Forgetful of the fact that a café is a public place, Monsieur Marcel had taken the liberty of setting up his easel on the premises, together with his paint box and the rest of his painting paraphernalia, and has carried his impropriety so far as to enable persons of both sexes in the room to pose for him, a situation which can have the direst consequences for the morals of the public . . .*"

Henry Murger, Bohème. Szenen aus dem Pariser Literaten- und Künstlerleben, *Leipzig (1882), p. 177.*

A considerable number of the artists, journalists and politically committed intellectuals we have mentioned, moved in Bohemian circles or could themselves be labelled as Bohemians. And on account of the fact that the coffee-house was one of the most important meeting places of the Bohemia, we shall devote a special section to this particular group, as we do remaining mindful of the shifting ground on which, on account of its diffuseness in international terms, the phenomenon is based.

The Bohemian life-style—a description which says so much and yet ultimately says nothing. It is a label which defines and paraphrases the sub-culture of intellectuals in the "industrialized or industrializing societies of the 19th and 20th centuries, which afford sufficient free play of individualism and tolerate symbolic aggression", for "socially marginal groups involved predominantly in literary, artistic and musical activities, or harbouring ambitions in such fields and adopting pronounced a-social or anti-bourgeois attitudes and modes of behaviour. Such groups include in their number authors and artists both major and minor, renowned and notorious or simply insignificant."[116] They range from those whose life-style is little different from that of gypsies or vagabonds, from forms such as the *grand bohème* and the *bohème galant* to the political or literary Bohemia and intellectual proletarians, and finally to the twilight world of the wrecked existence of the rootless. We shall follow the view that the Bohemian world is not a category of aesthetic criticism as such, but rather one of a more socio-historical character[117] augmented by an essentially socio-psychological element, and we will restrict ourselves to the pin-pointing of two characteristic features of this particular species of coffee-house customer. It consists of mutually attracting individualists who at first sight appear to lead their lives outside the ambit of bourgeois "normality" inasmuch as they are all distinguished by at least one characteristic at some time or other, that is to say they have no permanent domicile, and who in the truest sense of the word are without house or home, or who seek to rid themselves of the comfortable trappings of their bourgeois origins. Their overnight accommodation consists of hotels, lodging-houses and hostels, and their most frequent daytime haunts, apart from studios and taverns, specially selected coffee-houses which serve as the social framework for their self-styled anti-bourgeois outlook and life-style. Joseph Roth, the Austrian Bohemian par excellence, writing in 1929 describes the phenomenon with a clarity born of first-hand knowledge: "Even one hundred, fifty, or thirty years ago, 'bohème' was never anything other than an expression of the bourgeois mentality against which it fought and from which it had sought to escape. When a member of the middle classes rebelled, he became a Bohemian. The security and conviviality of an artists' pub and of a studio were nothing else than the relaxed comfort of the familiar surroundings of home. It was the libertinage of the summer-house."[118] Such was the candid criticism from the pen of Joseph Roth who was acquainted with the European Bohemia in all its guises, and who, as one of his friends wrote later, was at home in all the coffee-houses of the world, himself contributing to a considerable degree to its character and of whom it cannot in any way be said that he numbered among the fashionable weekend Bohemians, a criticism which could be levelled at not a few of his successful fellow-writers who from time to time would bask in the illustrious company and conviviality of their artist colleagues in the *cafés à la bohème.*

As we have already noted it was the three decades from about 1890 to 1914 which witnessed to increasing degree European art and literature taking up residence in the coffee-houses. The leading literary salons of the 19th century might have survived, and indeed continued to exist, but they no longer enjoyed the importance they had once possessed. With the exception of the important literary salons with a Bohemian touch and modernistic trends in the USA (such as the Bohemian Club in San Francisco) which possessed a marked club character, in Europe itself the urge to participate in the mainstream of public life became particularly apparent during these years. But what a contrast this movement presented to the periods in the past when the writers of England and France took up residence in the coffee-houses with the declared aim of contributing to the emergence of the new-found self-awareness of the middle classes. For now, the representatives of anti-bourgeois literature were setting up home in what had become establishments epitomizing bourgeois opulence and ostentation to propagate their counter-principles to the bourgeois ideal. Those affecting the Bohemian way of life were to be found not in the proletarian coffee snug, but far more in the most luxurious and elegant establishments in the most fashionable parts of the town. The more successful and dedicated among them were hardly to be distinguished from the privy councillor or bank director seated at the neighbouring table. Like these latter, they came here regularly, but only for a brief visit, not spending the whole day here. Generally they have an appointment or come to visit one of those "qui établissent leur domicile au café"[119].

Those who have yet to attain the ranks of the successful, "come not just once a day, but four, five or even six times, five times simply to have a look to see who is there, and a sixth time to sit down; indeed, in winter some of them virtually live there, and the installing of a large hotel had to be rented by the hour is merely a matter of time"[120], such was a description of life in the Café Merkur in Leipzig, which was the haunt of the Bohemia of Saxony, whose king during the 1920s was one Max Schwimmer. But Leipzig was not an international centre of the Bohemia, and the men and women flaunting their unconventional, anti-bourgeois way of life were for the most part "part-time"

Berlin, circa 1920

"In the 'Café des Westens', a rendezvous for the Bohème both talented and untalented, one could witness the most remarkable goings-on . . . Among them one could see the most conspicuous of them all: Else Lasker-Schüler . . . daughter of a respectable Rhineland family, had brought to her second marriage, to Herwarth Walden, a son from the first marriage. This couple, with their incredibly spoiled child, could be found from noon until late into the night in the 'Café des Westens' surrounded by the wild young budding artists . . . To the same extent that the couple was spiritually endowed, they were lacking when it came to more earthly matters. It seemed to me that the small family's sole source of nourishment was coffee, for which the decrepid head-waiter of the 'Café des Westens' granted them respite in payment or which was paid for by some kind-hearted guest."
Tilla Durieux, Eine Tür steht offen. Erinnerungen, Berlin, 1965, p. 107f.

132   Erich Mühsam, who took a leading part in the Munich "Räterepublik", shown in the Café Stefanie in the same city in 1909. In this year he was tried for anarchistic agitation. The figure standing at the left is probably Frank Wedekind. Drawing by Eduard Thöny, 1909. Ascona, Conte Rossini Collection.

133 Philistines in brain and appetite, customers in the Café des Westens in Berlin. Caricature by Karl Arnold in: *Simplicissimus*, No. 9, 1921.

134 Bohemian habitué of the Romanisches Café in Berlin. Caricature in: *Neue Revue*, No. 5/1931.

Bohemians who, having made their public appearance, would retire to their homes or their studios.

But things were very different in Paris, Vienna, Berlin, Munich, London. Here there were dozens of coffee-houses where the Bohemia was at home. They lived here, worked here, and suited the boundaries of art to their own ends; faithful to the motto "épatez les bourgeois", they would astonish or shock the other customers by their provocative and highly-imaginative unconventional behaviour. A scandal was caused by the entry of Charles Baudelaire to the Café Riche in Paris, dressed in a green wig, comparable to the one fifty years later which was created by the Italian writer Filippo Tommaso Marinetti when he sat down in the elegant Corso cafés in Rome with a glass hat on his head.

There were several cafés in Paris frequented by the Bohemia of the world, for the Germans it was the Café le Dôme, for the Scandinavians the Café de l'Ermitage and for the French themselves, most of the cafés in Montparnasse.

In Vienna the "Griensteidl" and the Café Central were the main gathering places of Bohemians, in Berlin (Ill. 133) it was the Café des Westens (where Else Lasker-Schüler was one of the most prominent guests), and in Munich the Café Stefanie (Ill. 132).

All the major cafés of this kind in the German-speaking countries were at one time or another dubbed "Café Grössenwahn" (roughly café megalomania), the "Griensteidl" as well as the Café des Westens, the Café Stefanie and even Leipzig's Café Central.

Unfortunately it is only possible to observe the scene in progress in these and other coffee-houses through the eyes of the Bohemian representatives themselves who in their memoirs, recalling the Storm and Stress period of their youth, frequently allow their recollections to become somewhat clouded: "I saw my friend Kisch for the first time before the First World War," writes Leonhard Frank, "when he moved into the Café des Westens . . . Our heated discussions on literature started forthwith. They continued every day until five in the morning, as we had to be back in the café without fail by four in the afternoon at the latest, and, as I can distinctly remember that we occasionally had some hours of sleep, I ask myself in vain when we actually can have had time to write our books. The First World War destroyed this idyll for ever . . ."[121]

These and similar memories (for instance the many wistfully nostalgic accounts of the Viennese cafés) surround the coffee-house, and in particular its Bohemian element in a golden haze of such intensity that one almost overlooks the fact that the heyday of the marriage of art, literature, art criticism and the café around the turn of the century was at the same time the low-point of artistic awareness in late bourgeois society.

The opposition of the international avant-garde to the stagnation of art and literature either in a naturalistic copying or eclectic conglomeration was vented after 1900 in aggressive manifestoes and appeals which were frequently drafted and debated in the Bohemian cafés. One of the most far-reaching in its consequences was the Futurist manifesto produced in Paris in 1909 by Filippo Tommaso Marinetti, who together with his followers dubbed himself "la caffeina dell' Europa" (caffeine of Europe).

The effect of the socio-political programme outlined by the Futurists was particularly marked in revolutionary Moscow among the artistic intelligentsia. From 1916 onwards artists' cafés proliferated in the city. The threat to received propriety was abroad in Russia, and took up residence in the coffee-house. Among others, the main focal points of the avant-garde were the Café Domino, the Café Pegasus Stall and the best-known of all, the Poets' Café where Vladimir Mayakovski gathered the Futurists around him "like Robin Hood and his band of robbers".

When one reads the recollections of the poets one gets the impression that these cafés were a constant hive of activity, every week new poetic instructions would be drafted and proclaimed here . . . only the drinking of coffee was missing for the simple reason that there wasn't any. Russia was starving!

Such an artists' café can be mentioned as typical of the Russian *stolovaya*, a simple room with chairs and tables, everything reduced to the bare necessities. The revolutionary artists occupied such premises, and if the landlord permitted the place was decorated. The small room of the Poets' Café was painted in bizarre fashion, as Ilya Ehrenburg later recalled in his memoirs: "The walls were embellished with grotesque paintings and no less grotesque inscriptions. 'I love to watch children dying . . .' these lines from an Mayakovski poem were emblazoned on the wall to shock the customers."[122]

The repudiation of Futurism and everything hitherto understood by the term art was the main objective of the representatives of the German Dadaist movement returning from exile in 1918, whose guiding principle was one of anti-art: "Vomited up from the slaughterhouse of the world war, we turned to art . . . We sought an elemental art which, so we believed, could redeem mankind from the frenzied insanity of these times . . . We wanted an anonymous and collective art."[123] The Dada Manifesto, published in 1918, formed the basis of the public scandals staged by the Dadaists in the early 1920s.

Artists' cafés decorated by artists

When one considers the clientèle seated at its tables, the coffee-house has a social function as an element in the culture of a society, and is at the same time a product of that same culture if we look at it in terms of its interior design and décor. As has already been noted, one could in one sense trace the whole history of bourgeois interior design through coffee-house architecture and design, while in another sense one could also demonstrate the long-established capacity of the coffee-house trade for adhering to the traditional and proven forms of everyday architecture and design of public catering establishments. Both aspects together provide a fascinating proposition.

We shall restrict ourselves here to some of the more notable and innovatory examples of artists' cafés designed by prominent interior designers, and which had a provocative effect on the parameters of the respective prevailing coffee-house physiognomy. In this respect we shall forbear at this point from a description of artists' cafés whose interior design has been the result of an improvised agglomeration of ideas. Suffice it only to say that from Jean Ramponaux (proprietor of the "Royal Drummer" *taverne à la mode* in Paris about 1670) to Jan Michalik (proprietor of the Lemberg confectionery in Cracow 1910) there have always been coffee-house proprietors who have permitted those artists among their circle of regular customers a free reign with the painting of the tables and walls of their premises.

The eclectic Egyptian style of decoration which became all the fashion in England after 1800 and in France following Napoleon's military campaign in the land of the pyramids, had had its origins some fifty years earlier in Italy. The fact that it was a coffee-house of all places which provided Giovanni Battista Piranesi with the opportunity to give concrete form to his trend-setting adaption of Roman, Etruscan and Egyptian styles has by now been all but forgotten. According to Italian sources, the situation one day in Rome in about 1765 must have been approximately as follows: As on any other normal day the artists, travelling salesmen and tourists had gathered at the Caffè Greco, most of them from England and Germany. It would appear that the Germans made such a commotion and probably there was so much rowdy behaviour on the part of both nations towards each other that the English rose from their seats and left the premises as one body, to take up their new headquarters in the Piazza di Spagna number 88, a few hundred meters further down the street. From this day on this establishment acquired the name Caffè degl'Inglesi. Whether Piranesi had been commissioned with the re-design of the premises already earlier or at this juncture, or somewhat later, is now no longer ascertainable, for this coffee-house existed for less than twenty years. But in view of the fact that Piranesi was already well-known among the English to a greater degree than any other Roman artist of the day—as an art and antique dealer he had been a corresponding member of the London-based Society of Antiquarians since 1757—it is highly conceivable that the proprietor commissioned the celebrated Piranesi in order that the English might have "their" coffee-house decorated by Rome's most renowned artist. It is even probable that the whole affair was intended as a deliberate provocation to the German habitués of the Caffè Greco, who—with Winckelmann in the forefront—adopted a completely different attitude to ancient art and culture. Unfortunately Piranesi's coffee-house has only come down to us in the form of two draft designs which he included in his *Diverse maniere* . . . published in the year 1769.

On paper, as etchings, the fantastic Egyptian designs for the chimney-piece look remarkably good, but one has to ask what would have been their effect on visitors to the coffee-house who would be compelled from every corner to cast their eyes on the formidable and imposing architectural spectacle. The customer sat in the midst of "magnificent façades, through the openings of which he was afforded a sweeping view over the desert and the banks of the Nile, and to streets with sphinxes and enormous statues, to temples, pillared halls and a near limitless number of pyramids. Stark and bleak, with no attention to scale the wonders of the world are lost between the legs of the caryatids . . . The almost meaningless architecture displays in its entirety the wealth of whole dynasties of obsessively ornamental rulers, and what should be an elegant coffee-house becomes nothing other than the vestibule of some proportionless sanctuary . . ."[124]

This kind of decoration was somewhat exaggerated. There were not many visitors who felt comfortable in this "Egyptian darkness", and we know from several guests that for them it was eerie.

But the concept and design of the Caffè degl'Inglesi appears as a mere trifle compared to the ambitious project thought up four decades later by the Italian café proprietor Pedrocchi in Padua, whose plan was to create the most beautiful coffee-house for artists and the *haute volée*, and who commissioned the best architects available for the purpose. As the financial sponsor of the idea, Pedrocchi thought of everything, and between 1816 and 1831 the Caffè Pedrocchi was erected in the centre of the town under the direction of Guiseppe Japelli, which upon its completion emerged as one of the first of the buildings for bourgeois representative purposes with a specifically coffee-house function to be built during the first half of the 19th century. After the building had been completed and the funds had dried up in the meantime, art historians looked upon it as one of the major examples of Italian Classicism, while the clientèle in 1842 regarded it as a conglomeration of the most divergent styles which—in the interior at least—gave due credit to the intention of the building's designers to present a history of interior decoration through the ages. Apart from the Gothic wing, which in 1837 acquired the delicate name "Il Pedrocchino", the exterior is Greek. In the same manner as those on the ground floor, the rooms on the first floor (billiard, reading and dining halls) reflect the whole gamut of earlier interior styles. Everything is represented from the Gothic suite to the Egyptian porter's lodge. The marble used in the building's construction was Roman, and genuinely so, for during the excavation of the foundations the builders came upon antique remains which were incorporated into the design. The Caffè Pedrocchi was intended to be the most beautiful of all coffee-houses, but ended up as one of the most eclectic examples of coffee-house architecture and interior design.

Towards the end of the 19th century, when the styles of *art nouveau*, *modernismo* and secession as an expression of the movement of general social reform which was in progress countered the bankruptcy of bourgeois ideas as mirrored by eclecticism with flowing lines in subtly divergent patterns, surrounded with an eccentric decorative allure, a coffee-house building was executed in Vienna which represented a radical break with everything which had gone before. Adolf Loos, an architect with several years of study in the United States behind him, in 1899 created a milestone in interior decoration in the Café Museum—though against the wishes of the proprietor—which was to set the tone for the functional style of the 20th century. The effect was extraordinary, the public was united in their disapproval and dubbed its anti-ornamental concept "Café Nihilism".

What in the case of the Café Museum had been to some extent a matter of chance, was now applied in Moscow's Café Pittoresque (1917) and in 1927 in the Café-restaurant Aubette in Strasbourg with all thoroughness as a conscious adoption of the evolving theories of the new realism and functionalism, which reflected the experience of the environment of the big city and industrial developments.

When in 1916 the "capitalist Fillipov", who owned nearly all the bakeries in Moscow, awarded the contract for the re-designing of a coffee-house to Georgi Yakulov, the latter summarized this unique opportunity as follows: "The second half of the 19th century has changed the face of the city, which has been embellished by electric lighting, new forms of transport and the development of industry . . . The Café Pittoresque had to reflect the aesthetic problems of the modern city and lay the foundations of the new style both in painting and in the other fields of the arts."[125]

At least a dozen artists participated in the design of the coffee-house, among them Vladimir Tatlin and Alexandr Rodchenko. In addition to twenty lamps the latter also drew up the design of the ceiling. The declared objective of the group of artists was that the Café Pittoresque (after 1917 it was named the "Red Cockerel", and somewhat later Café of the Revolutionary City) should be a living example of the synthesis of art, literature and theatre, but in the wake of subsequent political events this was not achieved. All that remains of these ambitious plans was the description of what was realized—and this was enough in itself:

"The building achieves a surprising effect through its dynamics. Bizarrely-shaped objects made of cardboard, veneer and fabric: lamps, rings, cones, reflecting material, fitted with light bulbs. The whole place was flooded in light, everything turned and pulsated, and it appeared as though the whole ensemble was in motion. Red and orange-yellow tones predominated, with contrast being provided by the cold colours. These remarkable objects hung from the ceiling, thrust out of the walls, and their boldness astonished the onlookers."[126]

What surprised visitors here in terms of the functional single-mindedness of the individual objects and the overall aesthetic impression thus created, was brought to its ulti-

Café Museum in Vienna, 1899

"With the Café Museum, it was not the intention of Loos to create anything original, but rather a Viennese café from the year 1830, a time when the obsession with style had still not arrived. Nevertheless the whole effect was revolutionary on account of its simplicity, and was christened 'Café Nihilismus' by its detractors . . . There was quite a struggle with the owner (who subsequently became one of his most enthusiastic supporters), who, in accordance with the fashion then prevailing, wanted to have the mahogany wood stained in green and violet. Loos resisted what he regarded as such a violation of the material."
Heinrich Kulka, Adolf Loos, Vienna, 1931, p. 27.

Commentary on the "new style" of the Aubette interior

"'What do you think of the newly-opened Aubette rooms?' One can say both very much and very little about it. Very much if one attempts to explain the new concepts of architectural form it expresses. Very little if one rejects this new architecture. Specialists, modern architects, say for example: The 'Dancing Caveau' designed by Hans Arp, and the upper Aubette rooms, designed and executed by Theo van Doesburg and Sophie Täuber-Arp, represent two completely different kinds of style. They epitomize the two characteristic design options of our age: the pre-morphistic and the elemental.

To the layman, for whom after all the rooms have been designed, the style might appear as follows: He observes the clear and simple effect of the arrangement, which admits only of right angles, quadrangular spaces, in short—a cubiform cell structure. So-called 'snug corners' typical of the old romantic style are not evident. The walls are devoid of every kind of superfluous decoration or ornamentation, lending emphasis to the modern materials deriving from and rendered necessary by the manner of construction, materials such as iron, reflecting glass, nickel, concrete. Further effect is provided by the choice of colour and the artificial light.

Colour and artificial light are the animating elements of these lounges, which are necessary for modern-day urban dwellers, subjected as they are to the noise of the traffic, the intrusive clamour of advertising and the all-pervading tumult of the big city."
"Neueste Nachrichten", 4 March, 1928. Quoted in:
De Stijl, Internationaal Maandblad . . ., Leiden, 87–89/1928, p. 38.

mate conclusion in the "Aubette" in 1927, creating a sensation among the citizens of Strasbourg who—although accustomed to political upheavals—were less used to such startling artistic innovation. The coffee-house customers experienced in questions of art knew the new style only from hearsay.

Hans Arp, a native of the city, had received the commission from the café's licencees in 1926 to re-design the premises, a commission which he carried out in collaboration with his wife Sophie Täuber-Arp and an old friend from his Dadaist days, Theo van Doesburg of Holland. The whole operation took two years to complete, involving the transformation of the existing rooms into a brasserie, a restaurant, a tea salon, the so-called Aubette Bar and the Bar Américain, a basement cabaret and a billiard room. The first floor incorporated a room for dancing and cabaret and two dining rooms. All the side-rooms and foyers were included in the final design. Each of the three were responsible for about one third of the commission: the bars and the tea salon were the work of Sophie Arp, the restaurant and brasserie were executed by Van Doesburg, while Arp himself used the dancing vault for the painting of his first major abstract frescoes. Van Doesburg decorated the dance hall with a diagonal construction which lent expression to his "neo-plastic purism": "If I was to be asked what did I intend with the composition of this room, I could only reply—to pose against the material room with its three dimensions an oblique, ethereal and picturesque room."[127]

Expressed another way this entailed a lack of secluded corners and intimate seating arrangements, no more "mendacious illusions of poetry and feeling" with subdued lighting and colour schemes—only straight lines, three colours and white neon lighting. The negative reaction on the part of the sponsors and the general public led Van Doesburg to conclude in a letter that "the time is not yet ripe for a 'fully-integrated' form of design . . . Because the proprietors allowed themselves to be swayed by public opinion (which naturally found it cold and uncongenial), everything was brought in which did not belong. The public cannot bring itself to leave its 'brown' world and obstinately refuses to accept the new 'white' world. The public wishes to live in dirt and so it should die in the dirt. The architect can give the public what it wants, the artist is concerned with transcending public taste and demands new conditions . . ."[127]

The proletarian coffee-house

So far in accounts of the cultural history of public catering and in particular the coffee-house, the existence of the proletarian coffee-house has largely gone unrecorded. Even the many histories concerned with the culture and life-style, the leisure habits of the working classes make no mention of the coffee parlour nor the café as a form of proletarian public life. The lack of any research on the subject is correspondingly great and hence it is only possible to undertake little more than an intermediate outline account. The contours of the proletarian coffee-house will only appear in vague form, in the truest sense of the word they have yet to be "discovered" by the historians and the sociologists.

The view of this type of coffee-house has traditionally been obscured by the prominence afforded the bourgeois café of the 19th century and the idyllic and romantic aura with which such establishments were surrounded, and no more so than in the frequent evocation of the poets' or artists' café, or the better class of café frequented by the upper middle classes from which, in general, the proletariat maintained a certain distance. A further, no less minor, reason would appear to be the exclusivity attached to the public house, such as pubs, ale-houses etc., as the only catering establishment serving the social needs of the proletariat, a view expressed by Karl Kautsky in 1891, and one which has lost little of its validity even down to the present day, though individual distinctions have to be made.

It will have already become apparent at several junctures that a continuous and direct line leads from the Arab and Turkish coffee parlours of the 16th and 17th centuries via the coffee taverns of England and France in the 17th and 18th centuries to the proletarian coffee rooms of the 19th and 20th centuries. Wolfgang Schivelbusch writes that, in contrast to the bourgeois salon, the coffee-house is "a thoroughly bourgeois, indeed near sub-bourgeois plebeian institution. It is the reconstituted successor to the tavern or the public house."[128] One must go one stage further here and assert that the coffee-house is not only the "reconstituted successor", rather it continues to exist as before as a tavern or a public house. The concept of the public coffee-house exists to cover such an establishment, which means to say it existed both in its original plebeian versions down the centuries as well as in petit bourgeois and proletarian form with the advent of bourgeois institutionalization. Leaving aside for the moment all differences of time and place, and taking into account the different historical situations prevailing in England at the end of the 17th century, in France in the 18th century, or in Austria and Germany during the 19th century, it nevertheless becomes readily apparent that—despite all variations of a mainly upper or lower middle-class nature—the coffee-house has remained, or repeatedly re-emerged in its own right, with the character which it always possessed, namely as a gathering place for members of the lower classes and strata. It would seem to be no exaggeration to say that after 1800 and down to the present day, every bourgeois coffee-house, regardless of when and where it has existed, has possessed

135 Normandy café. Illustration in: *Le Journal amusant*, Paris, 29 September, 1872.

its counterpart catering for the labouring population, in the form of the coffee parlour or coffee tavern. It would appear that among the clientèle of the elegant cafés situated around London's Piccadilly Circus around 1860, only Friedrich Engels, Gustave Doré and Charles Dickens were aware that there were also coffee-houses to be found in Whitechapel and Seven Deals (Ill. 145). Everyone visiting Berlin around the turn of the century spoke of the Café Bauer (Ill. 83), but who speaks of the Café Filzlaus, of which nothing remains than a tiny sketch from the pencil of Heinrich Zille? In Moscow and St. Petersburg during the revolutionary days of October 1917, dozens of small coffee parlours were filled with men wearing red arm bands and carrying rifles, warming themselves over a mug of *ersatz* coffee, while at the same time in the gaming rooms of the great cafés, bets were being made as to how long this new government would be able to retain power. In the Café de l'Europe in Vienna, "where the rest of the world rubbed shoulders with Viennese high society", there also appeared the first political emigrants from Germany after 1933 (among them Bertolt Brecht and Oskar Maria Graf), but at the same time as this, who was frequenting the Café Arbeiterheim?

The frequent assertion that as a traditionally exclusive institution, the café was rarely frequented by workers, proceeds from the implicit assumption that there were no other cafés apart from the exclusive coffee-houses. None of the approximately two thousand coffee-houses which existed in London around 1700 were exclusive any more than is the case with the majority of the one thousand two hundred cafés in Paris. Although certainly no-one has counted them, we can assume with considerable certainty that more than half the cafés in Paris or Amsterdam, in Rio de Janeiro or Mexico City, particularly

136   Nocturnal clientèle in the Café Nikola in Vienna, end of the 19th century. Woodcut from a drawing by G. Zafaurek in: *Illustrirte Zeitung*, Leipzig, 16 April, 1887.

137 "Out of work. In the coffee booth behind the piss-house", is the inscription on the back of this charcoal drawing by Alfred Ahner, 1925. Weimar, Ahner Collection.

those located in traditional working-class quarters, are frequented by workers—if not exclusively, than to a major degree. Naturally coffee will not be the only drink served in these places, but, as we have already noted, this was also never at any time the case with the bourgeois coffee-house.

If one takes a look at London around the year 1700, one could form the impression that the whole population was seated in the coffee-houses, but in fact it was only one half—although the other half would be seated not only in the ale and gin-houses but also in and around the coffee stalls, the name given to coffee shops catering for those earning their money through the sweat of their brow. They consisted of small wooden booths which stood in their hundreds in the streets of the city, where an indefinable coffee drink was served (bocket, saloop), which was so popular because it was cheap that it was also served in more refined establishments such as Reads's Coffee-House.

During the 18th and 19th centuries, travellers from countries north of the Alps, when visiting more southerly countries, in particular Italy and Portugal, noticed something extremely striking: that not only in the small towns, but even in every village the local inns would go under the name "caffè" or "café". German travellers in particular never ceased to be astonished by this feature, and made a special point of taking note of this amazing fact in their travelogues. Coffee-houses catering to the rural proletarian strata (or rather the menfolk) were completely unknown in the German states, although such places were not totally unheard of in France (Ill. 135) and England.

In the course of its evolution from a workers' movement to a mass movement, during the 19th century the emergent proletariat was to be found in public in the most varied localities. Next to the public house and the brandy shop it was primarily the coffee stalls which they took over completely for themselves, while at the same time making partial use of the bourgeois coffee-houses and catering establishments.

Sirmione, circa 1900

"With some effort I haul my relics back to the little town, in order to wish it a happy risorgimento (resurrection), seated in the Café Risorgimento in the shadow of the Skaliger castle. And as I sip the exquisite white Lugano wine, which the divine Dante had already relished so many years before, I ask myself how such a splendid establishment could bear a title so absurd as 'café'. It is as if the Sultan Bajazid had named the most fiery of his Arab steeds . . . old nag."

Hanns Barth, Osteria. Kulturgeschichtlicher Führer durch Italiens Schenken vom Gardasee bis Capri, *Stuttgart*, *²1911, p. 62.*

It was in particular the members of the service sector, such as porters and drivers who appear to have had their "own" coffee shops. In Vienna from 1800 onwards, the equivalent function served for the workers of London after 1700 by the coffee stall, was performed for the fourth estate by the "Tschecherl", "where connoisseurs from among the hoi polloi can buy a bowl of the drink and a roll for one *Kreuzer*"[129].

As was the case in Paris and in London, so in Vienna, too, there were coffee stalls for drivers and hauliers. So-called Fiaker cafés or cabbies' cafés were situated in imperial Vienna wherever the drivers had their ranks. The one on the Rabensteig was situated in two back-rooms of a pub, providing an extra source of income for the landlord. Similar kinds of coffee stalls for coachmen and drivers of every description (including dog-cart drivers) existed in Berlin from the middle of the 19th century. With due Berlin sarcasm they were dubbed *Kaffeeklappen*, because in contrast to breakfast parlours, liquor shops etc. one could drink cheap milky coffee and cocoa here.

During periods of unemployment, which occurred continuously from 1816 onwards as a consequence of economic crises, the "leisure" time of the proletarian unemployed was correspondingly increased, and in France they spent this free time in their inns, taverns, wine-houses and *petits cafés*. The revolutionary spirit which the French Revolution had drawn from the political coffee-houses was drawn by subsequent revolutions, which were mainly instigated by the Commune and the unemployed, from the "bulwarks" of the proletariat (Kautsky), of which the cafés formed a part. The "spirit" prevalent here was in no way different from the spirit prevailing in ordinary public houses. Only the name over the door and the entry in the town's commercial register betrayed the fact that it was a café which was being referred to. In the same way as the public house, the *petit café* was a "labour exchange" and gathering place for both those working and for the unemployed among the male population. Here one person would arrange a casual job for another, here a thin chicory drink would be served or sorrows drowned in brandy, however here, too, the "splendid sappers" were at work who instigated the unemployed workers' revolts.

For those less inclined to make direct reference to cafés for the unemployed, the application of the term becomes a matter of necessity when attention is focussed on the coffee-houses of the German industrial centres of Hamburg, Chemnitz or on the Ruhr during the "golden twenties", where mass unemployment prevailed on a hitherto unprecedented scale. "Out of work. In the coffee stall behind the piss-house. 1923"—this was the grimly laconic comment inscribed on the back of a drawing by Alfred Ahner who lived in the German town which gave its name to the Weimar Republic. Unemployed—to be out of work means not only the oft-documented vigil outside the labour exchange, it is also, as captured by Ahner's drawing, the resigned and despairing silence of the old and the watchful sullen expression of the young man in the coffee room (Ill. 137).

For the legendary Red Vienna, the "golden age" of the twenties was also overshadowed by a black background. Apart from the more social than socialist associations established by the Social-Democrats which met in the coffee-houses, as a consequence of the fact that the Austrian "labour movement evolved magnificently into a cultural movement"[130], cafés with a specifically working-class character were built. The Café Arbeiterheim which witnessed fierce fighting during the February uprising of 1934, will serve as an example here.

The partial utilization of the coffee-house as a meeting place and centre of organization of the international workers' movement was occurring here at the same time as the

138   In the Coffee Kitchen. Painting by
Michael Neder, *c.* 1863. Vienna, Historisches
Museum.

140 Caffè Greco. Painting by Renato Guttuso, 1976. Aachen, Ludwig Collection.
Alongside a thoroughly average international
tourist clientèle, Guttuso has portrayed or
"quoted" several modern artists, among them
at the left-hand table in the centre of the picture, Giorgio de Chirico (next to Chirico's self-
portrait from 1942), himself in the foreground
at the centre table (reading newspaper), Guil-
laume Appollinaire (with spectacles, from a
picture by Chirico) and André Gide. Seated
half-concealed at the back (smoking a cigar) is
Marcel Duchamp, the bust on a stand is a
celebrated work by Picasso. For an interpreta-
tion of this imaginary artists' circle cf. in the
bibliography Guttuso (79).

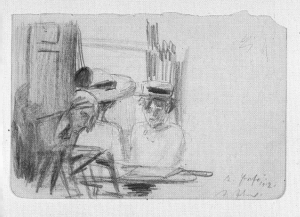

141 Sketches from various coffee-houses in Germany, 1912–1961. Pencil, charcoal, crayon by Alfred Ahner. Weimar, Ahner Collection.

142 Cafeteria. Painting by Isaac Soyer, 1930. Memphis, Tennessee. Brooks Museum of Art, gift of Mr. E. R. Brumley.

143 Hunger marchers outside the Café Republik. Painting by Hans Grundig, 1932. Dresden, Staatliche Kunstsammlungen, Gemäldegalerie Neue Meister.

144   Street coffee vendor in London. Wood engraving from an original by Gustave Doré in: *"London". A Pilgrimage by Gustave Doré and Blanchard Jerrold*, London, 1872.

145   Coffee-house in the London working-class district of Whitechapel. Wood engraving from an original by Gustave Doré in: *"London". A Pilgrimage by Gustave Doré and Blanchard Jerrold*, London, 1872.

146   Small café in a Greek provincial town.

147   Greek street café in Athens.

148   Café de la Paix in Audierne, Finistère. Photo by Paul Strand, 1950.

149   Three directly adjacent cafés in Ghent: Café de Ploeg, Café Borluut and Café Français, the latter with a sign advertising a room for hire in the left-hand window.

150   Café De Dokter in Amsterdam, known in accordance with national custom by its diminutive "'t dokterje".

151   Café Hoppe in Amsterdam, one of the oldest coffee-houses in Holland.

152 Inner courtyard of the Café Popolore in northern Melbourne.

153 Espresso bar in the Hotel Alcron in Prague.

154 Small café in Osaka.

155 Grand Café Excelsior in Nancy.

156   A small coffee-house in Amsterdam, which, with its combination of café, confectionery and restaurant represents the typical modern-day café.

bourgeoisie and the upper middle classes were setting about transforming the café into a place of exquisite elegance. As decreed by the ironies of history, some leaders of the labour movement, that is to say the "portion of the bourgeois ideologists who have raised themselves to the level of comprehending theoretically the historical movement as a whole", as it is put in the Communist Manifesto, sit figuratively speaking in the upper-class cafés, gradually working away at the pillars holding up the social edifice, while their predecessors engaged in similar work, such as Voltaire or Diderot, sat in the Café Procope which is now the haunt of workers. Between 1837 and 1841 the refined Café Stehely in Berlin played regular host to Karl Marx at the gatherings of the Doctors' Club. In the same café, during 1841/42 Friedrich Engels, Max Stirner and Mikhail Bakunin were daily to be seen at table. During the morning they would attend the university together to listen to Professor Werder's lectures in logic, and then they would spend the afternoon in discussion at the "Stehely". All three were thinkers possessed of a remorseless logic which each proceeded to elaborate in his own way: Engels made the acquaintance of Karl Marx, Stirner went on to write his notoriously celebrated book, *The Ego and His Own*, banned for two days, and during the whole of 1848, Bakunin hurried from barricade to barricade.

Marx, Engels, Bakunin and many others were to meet each other again in exile, where not a few emigrant societies and associations set up their headquarters in coffee-houses, or were later to do so (see p. 178 f.).

The utilization of the bourgeois coffee-house for several hours became clearly apparent from the mid-19th century, when institutionalized workers' associations of the most varied kind (ranging from thrift clubs to workers' educational associations to Social-Democratic Party groups) took up residence in the private back-rooms of coffee-houses. The significance of cafés of this kind in the development of the proletariat is probably no less than that attaching to long established locales set up by Social-Democratic organizations. A second form of "proletarian presence" in bourgeois coffee-houses is of a more informal kind. We have already noted elsewhere that the regular clientèle of one and the same coffee-house can be composed of different groups, depending on the time of day. But there are also not a few instances of which the following are two examples where a solid middle-class café becomes a proletarian café by night: At the end of the 19th century, the golden age of the Viennese coffee-house, some of which were open all through the day and night, the so-called *Draxler*, workers in mother-of-pearl regularly appeared at the Café Ritter during the middle of the night. They never came alone, but congregated in large groups, taking over the coffee-house for themselves for the rest of the night, filling the air with their loud voices, availing themselves for example of the age-old traditional right of the "Blue Monday", a day of rest. The *Draxler* remained in the café until the early hours of the morning over their coffee and liqueurs, whereupon rising and leaving the premises as one body they would hand the coffee-house back to its more conventional clientèle. A similar kind of nocturnal guests (to be clearly distinguished from the declassé proletarians who could also be counted among the customary nighthawks) regularly congregated during the night preceeding market days at the Café Nikola (Ill. 136) and Café Täuber. At around midnight peasant women from the outlying villages, market women and casual workers, would take up temporary residence, surrounded by their enormous quantities of baggage, huge baskets and wrapped-up bundles, in the coffee-houses, in order to await the arrival of dawn and the opening of the market stands. As this was a time when the normal citizens had long retired, their television programme titles, such as "Rock Café", "Literary Café" etc. These names are not meant to imply any gastronomic venue, it is rather a manifestation oft-repeated in the cultural history of the coffee-house, that specifically coffee-house terms are one of the best means of making a name in the entertainment field.

The coffee-house of today

In every major city around the world, gastronomic establishments with the description café have come into being, which, despite their immense variety, national characteristics and functional particularities, ultimately continue to offer what the coffee-house trade has offered since its inception, namely a blend of refreshment, games, entertainment and education. Coffee-café, café-coffee shop, cafeteria, café-bar, café-espresso, café-brasserie, café-theatre, theatre-café, jazz café, chanson café, mocha bar, coffee-house with dancing, café-confiserie, café-konditorei, literary café, press café, club café . . . are all terms which we can find over and over again, regardless of where we are, whether in Europe, America, Asia, Africa or Australia.

During the mid-1950s there was a marked increase of coffee-houses in London, decorated for the most part in Spanish, Italian or Mexican style. Tropical plants and caged birds were by no means unusual features. The American self-service cafeteria has by now become commonplace throughout Europe, the American coffee bar cum snack bar and the Italian espresso bar are all establishments which do not signify the end of the coffee-house as such, but rather are representative of further variations of type.

Even down to the present day the coffee-house has not lost its function as a place for the production and dissemination of the printed work. That even in the second half of the 20th century progressive journalists can sit in a coffee-house and use it for the production of their paper is demonstrated by the editorial board of the world-famous photo magazine *magnum*. During the mid-1950s the editors met "alternatively in a dozen different coffee-houses in Vienna, where the themes of the individual numbers were first thought up"[133]. The chief meeting place was the Café Hawelka, which achieved fame not least from the presence of these journalists and the results of their labours, for instance the publication of a photographic essay on the "Hawelka" in 1960.

The significance which can be attached to the activities of the press in coffee-houses even in our times can be gauged by the following example from Cairo with an educational aspect. In 1959/60 there were some three thousand coffee-houses in the city. A law was passed requiring the withdrawal of all coffee-house licences, and the issue of new licences only on condition that such establishments conformed to the requirement for the provision of "healthy and instructive" journals and books.

Right up to the present day, examples repeatedly come to light of the mutual attraction between the publishing houses and the bookselling trade and the coffee-house. In Paris alone there are some fifteen *cafés littéraires*, where publishers, writers and booksellers are regular customers. Among them are the Café aux Deux Magots, the Café Colisée, the Café la Coupole, and the Café de Flore. The esteem in which these coffee-houses are held by the French literary world can be gathered from the existence of the Deux Magots Prize for literature and the Cazes Prize, which are awarded in these cafés. In Amsterdam, a gathering place for writers and artists is the Café Hoppe (Ill. 151).

In the German-speaking countries a renewed association between literature and the coffee-house is also becoming apparent. Those who consider the staging of book premieres in cafés (for example in West Berlin's Café Einstein, in Leipzig's Künstlercafé

Paderborn 15, 40–42
Padua 15, 86, 176, 206
 – Caffè Pedrocchi 176, 206, 207; *121*
Pain, Andreas 105
Pakeman, D. 136
Paraguay 90
Paris 16, 17, 19, 35, 37, 38, 42, 46–48,
 92, 93, 96, 102, 104, 105, 126–128,
 136–138, 152, 156, 166, 170, 172,
 178, 179, 181–183, 185–187, 197,
 202, 204, 210, 212, 228, 229, 231; *65*
 – Café aux Deux Magots 182, 188, 230;
 123
 – Café Cazes 230
 – Café Chartres 174
 – Café Chrétien 174
 – Café Colisée 230
 – Café Convent 173
 – Café d'Apollon 154
 – Café de Flore 188, 230; *125*
 – Café de Foy 153, 172, 173
 – Café de la Nouvelle Athènes 187, 188
 – Café de la Paix 99, 170, 182; *126*
 – Café de la Régence 151, 172, 187
 – Café de la Terrasse 140
 – Café de l'Ermitage 188, 204
 – Café des Avengles 153
 – Café d'Orsay *119*
 – Café Guerbois 185, 187
 – Café Hottot 173
 – Café Italien (Café Corazza) 153,
 173, 174
 – Café la Coupole 230
 – Café La Palette *124*
 – Café le Dôme 182, 188, 204
 – Café Lemblin 180
 – Café Mahieu 182, 183
 – Café Mécanique 97
 – Café Méphisto 183
 – Café Militaire 102, 174; *90*
 – Café Molière 187
 – Café Mutualité 183
 – Café Procope 96, 104, 140, 172,
 187, 225
 – Café Riche 204
 – Café Select 181, 182
 – Café Tortoni 168, 187
 – Café Turc 187
 – Café Venuas 174
 – Café Voltaire 187, 188
 – Grand Café 169, 170
 – Royal Drummer 205
Parnall & Sons 55
Pascal 104
Paschius, George 12
Passini, Johann Nepomuk *109*
Passini, Ludwig *139*
Patriotic Association 133
peas 44
Pechstein, Max *110*
Pécs
 – Café Nádor 99

Pedro II 22
Pedrocchi 206
Pemperton 131
penny universities 130
Pepys, Samuel 186
permit for serving coffee 104–108,
 125, 155; *95*
Persia, Persians 9, 13, 170
Pessoa, Fernando 201
Peters, Franciscus 63
petit café 94, 212
Petit, Léonce *108*
Petöfy, Sándor 177, 198
pewter jug 85
Philadelphia 171
Philippines 20, 21
Picasso, Pablo 188, 201, 229; *140*
Pinkerton, John 136
Piranesi, Giovanni Battista 205, 206
Piron, Emil 169
Piscator, Erwin 183
Plekhanov, Georgi 180
Poland 166, 167, 176, 179, 205
Polgar, Alfred 185, 198, 202
political coffee-house 170–177, 212;
 120, 121
Pollak, Ernst 199
Polo, Marco 8
Pomet, Peter 17
Pompadour, Jeanne de 64
Pope, Alexander 186
porcelain bowl 9, 60
Portugal, Portuguese 18–22, 24, 53,
 102, 103, 201, 211
Prague 105, 137, 150, 182, 199; *153*
 – Café Arco 152, 199
 – Café Central 199
 – Café Continental 182, 199
 – Cafe Evropa 99; *88*
 – Café Slavia *87*
 – Café Stefan 199
 – Golden Snake 105
Presley, Elvis 230
press café 230
proletarian coffee-house 38, 86,
 208–212, 225–228; *145*
Prévot, René 185, 187
prohibition laws for coffee 52
proscription 39–42, 107
Prutz, Robert 176
public coffee hall(house) 209, 226, 227
Pückler-Muskau, Hermann Ludwig
 Heinrich von 89
Puerto Rico 21
Pufendorf, Johann August 134

Rabener, Gottlieb Wilhelm 133
Racine, Jean Baptiste 37
Ragusa (Dubrovnik) 14
Ramponaux, Jean 205
Rastenberg 105
Rauwolf, Leonhart 7, 8, 9, 86; *1*

reading room 137, 138, 140, 149, 207; *101*
reading society 140
Rebmann, Georg Friedrich 174, 175
Remarque, Erich Maria 183
Renoir, Auguste 188, 229
Repin, Ilya 229
Reuter, Fritz 47
revolving drum 54; *21*
Richey, Michael 133
Richter, Enoch 134
Rilke, Rainer Maria 199
Rimbaud, Arthur 188
Rio de Janeiro 20, 210
roasting pan (drum) 54, 63
roasting, roasted coffee 35, 42, 45, 49,
 54, 55; *21, 22*
Robespierre, Maximilian Marie Isidor 151
Robinson, Edward Forbes 55
Rock café 230
Rodchenko, Alexandr 207
Rome 8, 9, 96, 134, 154, 177, 197, 206
 – Caffè Antonini 152
 – Caffè Colonna 197
 – Caffè degl' Inglesi 206
 – Caffè delle belle Arte 177
 – Caffè Greco 185, 197, 205, 206;
 139, 140
 – Palazzo Ruspoli 96
Roque, Jean de la 11; *6*
Roque, Pierre de la 16
Rosée, Pasqua 104, 108
Rossini, Gioacchino 197
Rostock 17
Roth, Joseph 183, 203
Rottenhöfer, Johann 88
Rousseau, Jean-Jacques 134, 151, 172
Royal Society 130, 138, 186
Rubiner, Ludwig 181
Rugendas, Moritz *13*
Russia, Russians 9, 152, 176, 204, 205
Rutenberg, Arnold 176

Salerno 11
saloop 211
Salus, Hugo 199
Salzburg 105
 – Café Tomaselli 96, 106
sampling of coffee 34
Sanary-sur-Mer 183
San Francisco 203
Santos 34
Saphir, Moritz 200
Sartre, Jean-Paul 188; *125*
Savage, Richard 186
Schack, Adolf F. 200
Schickele, René 183
Schiller, Friedrich 43
Schiltberger, Hans 8
Schindler, Anton 58
Schivelbusch, Wolfgang 209
Schlegel, August Wilhelm 133
Schlegel, Friedrich 133

Schönberg, Arnold 156, 201
Schütz, Philipp Balthasar von *see* Faramund
Schumann, Robert 184, 200
Scotland, Scots 127
Schwender, Karl 166
Schwimmer, Max 203
Schwind, Moritz von 197
Seghers, Anna 183–185
serving and drinking vessels 38, 60–63
Sévigné, Marie de 37
Seydlitz, Friedrich Wilhelm von *53*
Shakespeare, William 186, 199
Shelley, Percy Bysshe 197
sherbet 104, 126
Sherley, Anthony 9
Sherwood *23*
Shrewsbury 93
Signorini, Telemaco 197
Simon Augustus of Lippe 40
Sirmione
   – Café Risorgimento 211
Skalde, Hermann 183
slaves (on coffee plantations) 21, 22
Sloane, Hans 130
smoking 93, 139, 170, 175; *70, 72, 74*
Società del Caffè 134
Society of Ten 198
Soyer, Isaac 229; *142*
Soyfer, Jura 168
Spain, Spaniards 18, 19, 21, 22; 53, 201
Spon, Jacob 63, 86; *4*
Sri Lanka 17, 19
St. Michielsgestel
   – Café Victoria 231
Staiger, Anton 106
Steele, Richard 131, 186
Stendhal 96, 185
Sternheim, Carl *110*
Steward, A. T. *19*
Stirner, Max 225
Stockholm 133
   – Altenecks Coffee-House 133
   – Grigsby's Coffee-House 133
storage of coffee 34
Storm, Theodor 51, 200
Strasbourg
   – Café-Restaurant Aubette 207
Strauss, Johann senior 156
Strindberg, August 188
Strixner, August *103*
Struys, Alexander 86
Sweden 40, 52, 133
Swift, Jonathan 130, 186, 187
Switzerland 48, 53, 106, 134, 136, 169,
   178, 179, 181–183
Syria, Syrians 10, *t*03, 105

Taimanov, Mark 151
Taine, Hippolyte 197
Talmeyr, Maurice 178
Tatlin, Vladimir 207
Täuber-Arp, Sophie 181, 207, 208

Taubert, Gustav *101*
taverne à la mode 93, 128, 205
Tavernier, Johann Baptist 22, 170
tea 46, 47, 51, 52, 85, 87, 104, 126,
   139, 151, 171, 226
taxation 39, 125, 165
Tentzel, Wilhelm Ernst 132
Teply, Karl 104
Teuteberg, Hans J. 46
Texeira, Pedro 7
The Hague 174
Theuerkauf, Gottlob *83*
Thöny, Eduard *132*
Thomasius, Christian 132
Thomassin, Simon 6
Thonet chair 100, 101; *65*
Thonet, Michael 100, 101
Thorvaldsen, Bertel 197
Tihanyi, Lajos 199
Toller, Ernst 183
Tommaseo, Niccolò *127*
Toulouse-Lautrec, Henri de 229
Trakl, Georg 198
Trebinje *70*
Trieste
   – Café San Marco 102
   – Café Tommaséo *127*
trottoir (pavement) café 228; *65*
Tucholke, Dieter *91*
Turcomania 37, 64; *55*
Turkey, Turks 8, 16, 17, 37, 56, 92,
   103–106, 176; *14*
Turkish coffee-house 92, 94, 152, 209;
   70
Twain, Mark 57, 85, 197
Tzara, Tristan 181

Uganda 90
Ukers, William Harrison 57, 93; *59*
Ulm
   – Spangenberg'sches Kaffeehaus 140
Urwin, William 186
USA 21, 35, 52, 54, 57, 98, 138, 171,
   172, 178, 179, 202, 203, 207, 226,
   230
Utrecht
   – Café van Ouds de Vriendschap 92

Valetti, Rosa 167
Valle, Pietro della 9, *152*
variety show (variété) 155, 166–169
Varnhagen von Ense, Karl August 140
Venezuela 21
Venice 8, 14, 15, 59, 93, 104, 105,
   134, 197
   – Caffè Florian 176
Verdi, Giuseppe 165
Verlaine, Paul 188
Verri, Alessandro 134
Verri, Pietro 134
Versailles *61*
Vian, Boris 188

Vienna 16, 37, 56, 60, 86, 96, 100,
   104, 105, 125, 126, 135, 155, 156,
   166, 168, 176, 182, 200, 204, 207,
   212, 228; *61*
   – Augustini Coffee-House 155
   – Café Arbeiterheim 210, 212
   – Café Arkade 168
   – Café Central 138, 151, 152, 185,
     197, 198, 201, 204
   – Café de l'Europe 210
   – Café Dobner 168
   – Café Döblingerhof 168
   – Café Eckl *112*
   – Café Gluck 137
   – Café Griensteidl 150, 197, 198,
     204
   – Café Hawelka 230, 231
   – Café Herrenhof 168, 197, 198
   – Café Imperial 197, 198
   – Café Jüngling 156
   – Café-Kiosk Schrangl *85*
   – Café Laferl 165
   – Café Louvre 140
   – Café Milani 95, 102
   – Café Museum 101, 197, 198, 207
   – Café Nikola 225; *136*
   – Café Prückel 168
   – Café Rebhuhn 176
   – Café Ritter 225
   – Café Schiller 140
   – Café Sperl 102, 197, 198
   – Café Täuber 225
   – Café Thonethof *64*
   – Colosseum 166
   – Daumsches Kaffeehaus 100
   – first Prater coffee-house 155, 156
   – Hugelmannsches Kaffeehaus 150
   – Kramersches Kaffeehaus 100
   – Silbernes Kaffeehaus (Neunersches
     Café) 96, 151, 176
   – Zweites Cortisches Café 156
Viennese café 96, 98, 100, 103, 105,
   156, 168, 207, 225, 230
Viertel, Berthold 182
village café 102, 103, 211, 226
Vogler, Johann Christian 153
Voltaire, François Marie Arouet 151,
   172, 187, 188, 225

Wagenmann and Böttger *24*
Wagner, Johann Jacob *102*
Wagner, Richard 197
Wahlberg, Alfred 188
Waiblinger, Friedrich Wilhelm 154
Walden, Herwarth 203
Ward, Edward 95
Washington, George 172; *41*
Wedekind, Frank 201; *132*
Wedekind, Georg Christian 175
Weill, Alain *108*
Weimar 106
   – Café Residenz (Resi) 201

Weinert, Erich 167
Weitling, Wilhelm 178, 227
Werfel, Franz 183, 198
West Indies Company 18, 19
Wetzlar 40
Whistler, James Abbot McNeill 187
Wiegand, Martin 155
Willich, August 179
Winckelmann, Johann Joachim 134,
  197, 206
wine 7, 11, 51, 91, 107, 108, 125,
  126, 139; *14*

Wolf, Friedrich 183
Wood, Anthony 103
Würzburg
  – Zum Hirschen 96
Wycherley, William 186

Yakulov, Georgi 207
Yemen 10, 11, 13, 17

Zachariä, Justus Friedrich Wilhelm 133
Zaire 90
Zandvoort

  – Bodega Kiosk 96
Zanko, Tamas 228
Zedler, Johann Heinrich 19
Zille, Heinrich 210
Zurich 48, 139, 181–183
  – Café Odeon 136, 181, 182; *105*
  – Café Saffran 152
  – Café Voltaire 181
  – Grand Café Zürcherhof *114*
Zwaardecroon, Henricus 19
Zweig, Arnold 183
Zweig, Stefan 137, 181